FAIRNESS AT WORK

Fairness at Work

*A Critical Analysis of the Employment
Relations Act 1999 and its Treatment of
"Collective Rights"*

by
TONIA NOVITZ
and
PAUL SKIDMORE

·HART·
PUBLISHING
OXFORD – PORTLAND OREGON
2001

Hart Publishing
Oxford and Portland, Oregon

Published in North America (US and Canada) by
Hart Publishing c/o
International Specialized Book Services
5804 NE Hassalo Street
Portland, Oregon
97213-3644
USA

Distributed in the Netherlands, Belgium and Luxembourg by
Intersentia, Churchillaan 108
B2900 Schoten
Antwerpen
Belgium

Hart Publishing is a specialist legal publisher based in Oxford, England.
To order further copies of this book or to request a list of other
publications please write to:

Hart Publishing, Salter's Boatyard,
Folly Bridge, Abingdon Road, Oxford OX1 4LB
Telephone: +44 (0)1865 245533 or Fax: +44 (0)1865 794882
e-mail: mail@hartpub.co.uk
WEBSITE: http//www.hartpub.co.uk

British Library Cataloguing in Publication Data
Data Available
ISBN 1–84113–083–4 (paperback)

Typeset by Hope Services (Abingdon) Ltd.
Printed and bound in Great Britain by
Biddles Ltd, www.biddles.co.uk

Preface

This book is the result of a larger collaborative research project, which considered the full range of policies which New Labour pursued under the title "Fairness at Work". These policies span so many diverse facets of British labour law that we realised it would be impossible to do justice to all these in one slim volume. For this reason, our book focuses on the treatment of collective rights under New Labour. We have endeavoured to state the law as at 1 August 2000.

We owe a considerable debt of gratitude to our former colleague at Bristol, Claire Kilpatrick. Her enthusiasm for this research project was instrumental in its genesis. Many of the arguments presented in this book stem from lengthy discussions between the three of us together. In numerous respects, we have benefited from her valuable comments on earlier drafts. For all errors and weaknesses, we, as authors, remain fully responsible.

The research and writing process has been assisted by periods of study leave for both authors, granted by the Department of Law at Bristol, for which we are grateful. We would also like to thank Benjamin Capps, Pat Hammond and Molly Thompson for their invaluable assistance in completing the manuscript. In addition, thanks are due to Andrew Sanders, Alexander Schantz and Phil Syrpis for all their support over the past year.

Finally, we also wish to acknowledge the generous support, patience and encouragement of our publisher, Richard Hart.

TONIA NOVITZ
PAUL SKIDMORE

Table of Contents

Table of Cases

EUROPEAN COURT OF HUMAN RIGHTS

ILO COMMITTEE ON FREEDOM OF ASSOCIATION

Table of Legislation

Statutory Instruments

Codes of Practice

INTERNATIONAL AND EUROPEAN SOURCES

European Community

Abbreviations

ACAS	Advisory Conciliation and Arbitration Service
ARD	Acquired Rights Directive
BCC	British Chambers of Commerce
BJIR	*British Journal of Industrial Relations*
BT	British Telecommunications
CA	Court of Appeal
CAC	Central Arbitration Committee
CBI	Confederation of British Industries
CCSU	Council of Civil Service Unions
CFA	Committee on Freedom of Association
CIR	Commission on Industrial Relations
CLJ	*Cambridge Law Journal*
CMLRev.	*Common Market Law Review*
CO	Certification Officer
CPAUIA	Commissioner for Protection Against Unlawful Industrial Action
CRD	Collective Redundancies Directive
CRTUM	Commissioner for the Rights of Trade Union Members
DDA	Disability Discrimination Act
DPA	Default Procedure Agreement
DTI	Department of Trade and Industry
EA	Employment Act
EAT	Employment Appeals Tribunal
EC	European Community
ECHR	European Convention on Human Rights
ECtHR	European Court of Human Rights
EIRR	*European Industrial Relations Review*
EJIR	*European Journal of Industrial Relations*
EPA	Employment Protection Act
EPCA	Employment Protection (Consolidation) Act
ERA	Employment Rights Act
ERDRA	Employment Rights (Dispute Resolution) Act
ERelA	Employment Relations Act
ET	Employment Tribunal
ETUI	European Trade Union Institute
EU	European Union
EWC	European Works Council
EWCD	European Works Councils Directive
FAW	*Fairness at Work* (Government White Paper)

FSB	Federation of Small Businesses
FWR	Fair Wages Resolution
GCHQ	Government Communication Headquarters
HC	House of Commons
HL	House of Lords
IAB	Industrial Arbitration Board
IJCLLIR	*International Journal of Comparative Labour Law and Industrial Relations*
ILC	International Labour Conference
ILJ	*Industrial Law Journal*
ILO	International Labour Organisation
IRA	Industrial Relations Act
IRJ	*Industrial Relations Journal*
JNB	Joint Negotiating Body
JLS	*Journal of Law and Society*
LQR	*Law Quarterly Review*
LS	*Legal Studies*
MLR	*Modern Law Review*
MNC	Multi-National Companies
NIRC	National Industrial Relations Court
NUM	National Union of Mineworkers
OJLS	*Oxford Journal of Legal Studies*
PLD	parental Leave Directive
POEU	post Office Engineers Union
QC	Queen's Counsel
RIA	Regulatory Impact Assessment
RRA	Race Relations Act
SDA	Sex Discrimination Act
SNB	Special Negotiating Body
TICER	Transnational Information and Consultation of Employees' Regulations
TUC	Trades Union Congress
TULRA	Trade Union and Labour Relations Act
TULRCA	Trade Union and Labour Relations (Consolidation) Act
TUPE	Transfer of Undertakings (Protection of Employment) Regulations
TURERA	Trade Union Reform and Employment Rights Act
TURM	Trade Union Recognition (Method of Collective Bargaining) Order
UKAPE	United Kingdom Association of Professional Engineers
WERS	Workplace Employment Relations Survey
WIRS	Workplace Industrial Relations Survey
WTD	Working Time Directive

1

Introduction

FROM THE GOVERNMENT White Paper, *Fairness at Work*,[1] it seemed that the enhanced protection of "collective rights" was central to New Labour's industrial relations settlement. In this core chapter of the White Paper, reforms were promised relating to diverse matters such as blacklisting, discrimination against trade union members, trade union recognition and industrial action. Moreover, the Blair Government sought to portray trade unions as suitable representatives of workers in the context of grievance and disciplinary procedures, appropriate recipients of information and consultation and potential contributors to a new "culture of labour relations". This culture was encapsulated in the term "partnership".

This book examines the rhetorical claims made in the White Paper (and later in Parliament) alongside the actual reforms contained in the Employment Relations Act (ERelA) 1999. Our aim is not to provide an exhaustive commentary on the statutory provisions nor to provide a comprehensive text on the protection of collective rights in Britain. Instead, we seek to identify how, in this sphere, New Labour has sought to distinguish and distance itself not only from the present opposition and from Conservative governments of 1979–97 but also from the Labour administrations of 1974–9.

The election of a Labour Government in 1997 promised to usher in a new style of social democratic politics described by Tony Blair as "the third way".[2] In this book we hope to identify what third way politics in the field of collective labour law look like, by examining critically the themes of the policy documents and legislative instruments adopted by New Labour. This analysis cannot be carried out in a vacuum, but is set in the institutional, legal, political and economic context of labour relations in the UK in the late 1990s. This requires us to take into account the legacy of existing labour law bequeathed by Labour and the Conservatives. The system-specific heritage of British labour law and industrial relations limits and constrains future developments.[3] We, like New Labour, therefore take this as our starting point. In addition, although the size and ambit of this book do not permit systematic comparative analysis with other national legal systems, we do acknowledge the increasing relevance of European and

---

[1] *Fairness at Work*, Cm 3968 (London: TSO, 1998), hereafter "*FAW*".
[2] T. Blair, *The Third Way: New Politics for the New Century* (London: Fabian Society, 1998). See also R. Undy, "Annual Review Article: New Labour's 'Industrial Relations Settlement': The Third Way?" [1999] 37 *BJIR* 315, 316–8.
[3] O. Kahn-Freund, *Labour Relations: Heritage and Adjustment* (Oxford: OUP, 1979).

international legal norms and their potential influence in shaping the Government's policies.

We are also well aware of the other dimensions of the *Fairness at Work* project. In this book we focus on the collective dimension. Our analysis reveals that in spite of the rhetoric the reality is one of minimal change to collective rights in British labour law. Armed with these findings, future commentators may well be correct to conclude that the reforms to "individual rights" and "family-friendly" policies are the more significant outcomes of the Employment Relations Act.

In this Introduction, we briefly examine the case for collective rights made in international organisations such as the International Labour Organisation (ILO) and the Council of Europe. We then consider why, despite the strength of these arguments, the New Labour Government has pursued a different agenda. We identify various factors, highlighted in *Fairness at Work*, which appear to have set the parameters for collective rights reforms. Finally, we consider the dimensions of "partnership", which New Labour has presented as its blueprint for industrial relations of the future.

A. THE CASE FOR "COLLECTIVE RIGHTS"

It is perhaps hard to believe that it is still necessary to state the case for "collective rights" in the context of labour law. The ILO regards as fundamental the right to form a trade union, which can engage in collective bargaining and organise industrial action.[4] These rights are also set out in the Council of Europe's Social Charter.[5] It is true that the European Union (EU) does not, as yet, make any explicit demands that Member States respect freedom of association, collective bargaining or the right to strike.[6] However, the mechanism of "social dialogue",[7] the potential for implementation of directives by collective

---

[4] See B. Gernigon, A. Odero and H. Guido, *Collective Bargaining: ILO Standards and the Principles of the Supervisory Bodies* (Geneva: International Labour Office, 2000); B. Gernigon, A. Odero and H. Guido, *ILO Principles Concerning the Right to Strike* (Geneva: International Labour Office, 1998).

[5] European Social Charter 1961, Arts. 5 and 6. See also N.A. Casey, *The Right to Organise and to Bargain Collectively: Protection within the European Social Charter* (Strasbourg: Council of Europe, 1996).

[6] It seems from Art. 137(6) EC that it is not likely to do so. However, initiatives to include social rights in an EU Charter of Fundamental Rights may lead to change in this sphere. See European Commission, *Affirming Fundamental Rights in the European Union: Time to Act* (Brussels: European Commission, 1999).

[7] Arts. 138 and 139 EC . See for useful discussion of the dynamics of social dialogue, T. Treu, "European Collective Bargaining Levels and Competences of the Social Partners" in P. Davies, A. Lyon-Caen, S. Sciarra and S. Simitis (eds.), *European Community Labour Law: Principles and Perspectives: Liber Amicorum Lord Wedderburn* (Oxford: Clarendon Press, 1996); A. Jacobs and A. Ojeda-Aviles, "The European Social Dialogue—Some Legal Issues" in ETUI, *A Legal Framework for European Industrial Relations* (Brussels: ETUI, 1999); and P. Syrpis, "Social Democracy and Judicial Review in the Community Legal Order" in C. Kilpatrick, T. Novitz and P. Skidmore (eds.), *The Future of Remedies in Europe* (Oxford: Hart, 2000).

agreement,[8] and the broad provision made for "workplace agreements" under the Working Time and Parental Leave Directives[9] indicate that it is expected that the EU Member States (who are all members of the ILO) will abide by their ILO obligations.[10]

The reasons for legal protection of collective rights are almost self-evident. Yet it is as well to be reminded of them, for, as was wryly observed in the Parliamentary debates, "discussing the principles behind trade unionism with the Conservative party is like trying to explain origami to a penguin".[11]

An enduring feature of the employment relationship is the relative subordination of the worker.[12] Those who own capital are usually privileged compared to those dependent upon working for a living. The financial ability to employ another usually denotes a degree of prosperity which, in turn, gives rise to "greater access to information, greater mobility, greater flexibility in the deployment of resources, control of the media, superior status and greater influence within society at large".[13] It is not only that an individual employer is likely to have greater bargaining power than the individual worker, but that the employer is often a corporation, the powers of which are all the more extensive. The manager who conducts the company's business is, of course, an individual, but it is unlikely that such a manager will empathise with the circumstances of the worker. The manager's personal success and career trajectory will be bound to the success of the employer and the manager's decisions will be backed by the power customarily exercised by cumulative capital.

The result is that an individual worker has little opportunity to bargain over terms and conditions of employment and may be vulnerable to arbitrary and unfair treatment. There is strong statistical evidence to the effect that workers outside collective bargaining structures have greater difficulty negotiating favourable terms and conditions of employment. They "are less favoured than those covered by collective bargaining in almost every sphere, including pay, job security, health and safety, grievance procedures and consultation".[14]

---

[8] See Case 143/83 *Commission* v. *Denmark* [1985] ECR 427, para. 8 and Case 235/84 *Commission* v. *Italy* [1986] ECR 2291, para. 20. See also as an example of express provision made for implementation by management and labour in the European Works Councils Dir., Art. 14: EC Dir. 94/45 [1994] OJ L254/64.

[9] EC Dir. 93/104 [1993] OJ L307/18, Art. 17 and Council Dir. 96/34 [1996] OJ L145/9, Annex, Cll. 2 and 3.

[10] This expectation is also evident from the Community Charter on the Fundamental Social Rights of Workers 1989, Arts. 11–14, now referred to in Art. 136 EC .

[11] HC Hansard, 9 Feb. 1999, col. 200, per Mr Johnson.

[12] Lord Wedderburn, "Labour Law and the Individual in Post-Industrial Societies" in Lord Wedderburn, M. Rood, A. Lyon-Caen, W. Däubler and P. van der Heijen, *Labour Law in the Post-Industrial Era* (Dartmouth: Aldershot, 1994), 44.

[13] B. Burkitt, "Excessive Trade Union Power or Contemporary Myth?" (1981) 12 *IRJ* 65 at 65.

[14] B. Hepple, "The Future of Labour Law" (1995) 24 *ILJ* 303 at 307. See also W. Brown, "The Contraction of Collective Bargaining in Britain" (1993) 31 *BJIR* 189; S. Dunn and D. Metcalf, "Trade Union Law Since 1979" in I. Beardwell (ed.), *Contemporary Industrial Relations: A Critical Analysis* (Oxford: OUP, 1996), 91; and J. Rubery, "The Low-Paid and the Unorganized" in P. Edwards (ed.), *Industrial Relations: Theory and Practice in Britain* (Oxford: Blackwell, 1995), 543.

As individual contracts of employment allow little scope for workers to influence the conditions under which they work, collective organisation and action appear to present a solution. On this basis, workers have formed trade unions. Through association, they have been able to co-ordinate their demands and assert their combined bargaining power. Where employers are unco-operative, workers have sought concessions by the use of industrial action, such as a strike, a "go-slow" or a "work-to-rule". This is not an ideal solution for the workforce, since the withdrawal of labour usually involves a loss of wages and risk to jobs.[15] Nevertheless, the threat of recourse to such action is often the sole bargaining tool which workers have in any given situation. It is for this reason that the right to strike is regarded by the ILO as "one of the essential means through which workers and their organizations may promote and defend their economic and social interests".[16]

If trade unions are to provide credible representation of workers in the context of disciplinary procedures, information and consultation procedures, collective bargaining and industrial action, they need to be independent of both employers and the state. This is why the principle of "trade union autonomy" or independence is so crucial to the collective interests of workers and is recognised as such within the ILO.[17] While the government may lay down legislative procedures designed to improve democratic participation within workers' organisations, these must not be such as would give any outside influence precedence, nor must they unduly stifle or disrupt ordinary trade union activities.[18] Moreover, as a member of the ILO, the UK is under a duty to promote collective bargaining.[19] The UK government also has an obligation to protect organisers of industrial action, as well as individual participants in such action.[20] The aim of all these obligations is to achieve a counter-balance for workers in terms of bargaining power and thereby promote fairness within the employment relationship.

---

[15] This will ultimately depend on the legal regime in force; only the diminution of wages is commonly accepted as a suitable sanction for industrial action. See A.T.J.M. Jacobs, "The Law of Strikes and Lock-Outs" in R. Blanpain and C. Engels, *Comparative Labour Law and Industrial Relations in Industrialized Market Economies* (Deventer: Kluwer, 1993) at 441–5.

[16] ILO, *Digest of Decisions of the Freedom of Association Committee of the Governing Body of the ILO (ILO Digest)* (4th edn., Geneva: International Labour Office, 1996) at para. 475.

[17] ILO Convention No. 87 on Freedom of Association and Protection of the Right to Organise 1948, Art. 3; see also *ILO Digest*, n.16 above at para. 417.

[18] See the summary of ILO jurisprudence on this point in T. Novitz, "Freedom of Association and 'Fairness at Work'—An Assessment of the Impact and Relevance of ILO Convention No. 87 on its Fiftieth Anniversary" (1998) 27 *ILJ* 169 at 177–8.

[19] ILO Convention No. 98 on the Right to Organise and Collective Bargaining 1949, Art. 4.

[20] *ILO Digest*, n.16 above, at paras. 475, 480 and 602. See also ILO, *General Survey of the Committee of Experts on Freedom of Association and Collective Bargaining* (Geneva: International Labour Office, 1994), paras. 147–51.

B. THE PRESSURES ON NEW LABOUR

There is little doubt that, on coming to power in 1997, the Labour Government was well aware of the above case for "collective rights" and the numerous statements made by ILO supervisory organs relating to UK breach of these rights.[21] The *Fairness at Work* White Paper acknowledged the tendency towards imbalance in bargaining power between the employer and the individual employee, admitting that "collective representation of individuals at work can be the best method of ensuring that employees are treated fairly".[22] In Parliament, Labour ministers criticised recent Conservative Governments for breaches of their international obligations relating to labour standards.[23] Nevertheless, as shall become evident in the main body of this book, New Labour has pursued its own agenda with regard to collective rights, picking up on international recommendations selectively and sparingly. We can only speculate on why this might be, but *Fairness at Work*, together with other sources, indicates that the reasons were three-fold.

First, "Old Labour" has been characterized as a movement defeated by strong trade unions and extensive industrial action. There was therefore considerable pressure on "New Labour" to avoid being tarred with the same brush. While in Opposition, Labour had begun to distance itself from its collectivist roots. The Party was already starting to repackage and utilise the populist language of "individual rights" and "choice", which had previously come to be associated with the "New Right".[24] In government, they were likely to seek to distinguish their policies from those of previous Labour administrations. This was reflected in Blair's strong statement that there would be "no going back".[25]

Secondly, global pressures towards flexible production and labour deployment have challenged traditional models of trade union organisation, collective bargaining and industrial action. The mass production firm provided opportunities for unions to organise around hierarchical job packages and pay-scales. By contrast, the "flexible firm" may require a devolution in decision-making, greater individual responsibility for devising and executing tasks and a merit system of rewards.[26] While some consider that the declines in membership and

---

[21] See e.g. K.D. Ewing, *Britain and the ILO* (2nd edn., London: Institute of Employment Rights, 1994); and B. Creighton, "The ILO and Protection of Freedom of Association in the United Kingdom" in K.D. Ewing, C. Gearty and B. Hepple (eds.), *Human Rights and Labour Law* (London: Mansell, 1994).

[22] *FAW*, para. 4.2.

[23] See HC Hansard, 10 June 1997, col. 930, per Mr Cook and HC Hansard, 13 July 1998, col. 73, per Mr McCartney.

[24] Labour Party, *Jobs and Social Justice: Labour's Response to the Green Paper on European Social Policy* (London: Labour Party, 1994) at 23.

[25] *FAW*, Foreword.

[26] See for a discussion of these challenges H. Collins, "Flexibility and Empowerment" in T. Wilthagen (ed.), *Advancing Theory in Labour Law and Industrial Relations in a Global Context* (Amsterdam: North-Holland, 1998), 117.

industrial strength of trade unions[27] are due to the legislative constraints placed on trade union governance, representation and industrial action by Conservative governments,[28] others consider that this may stem from new modes of production generated by global competitiveness and technological innovation. *Fairness at Work* suggests that unions should learn to play a new role within "a flexible and efficient labour market" which will foster the growth of British business.[29]

Finally, to avoid industrial unrest and maintain capital investment in the UK, New Labour needed to secure the co-operation of both unions and business. The Government had to respond to the most pressing claims of the union movement, if the Labour Party was to retain its traditional membership and base of support. However, the substantial and progressive decline of union membership meant that the TUC was weaker than it had been hitherto, while the employer lobby was stronger. New Labour was also well aware that, during the 1970s, employers had demonstrated their ability to undermine legislative initiatives which they regarded as unreasonable.[30] Much of *Fairness at Work* seeks to phrase the Government's proposals in a form palatable to business. Moreover, there is evidence to suggest that the relative strength of lobbying from these two sides of industry has heavily influenced the collective content of the Employment Relations Act 1999 and associated statutory instruments.

1.   "No going back"

In the Foreword to *Fairness at Work*, Tony Blair was adamant that there would be "no going back". "The days of strikes without ballots, mass picketing, closed shops and secondary action are over." It is hard to make the case for restoring the closed shop, following the decision on its legality given by the European Court of Human Rights in *Young, James and Webster* v. *UK*;[31] nor is it unreasonable to require some form of balloting to ensure democratic accountability in trade unions where strikes are called.[32] However, it is curious that, given

---

[27] Union density has fallen from a peak of 65% in 1980 to 36% in 1998. Coverage of collective bargaining has fallen from 70% of all employees in 1984 to 41% in 1998. See M. Cully, S. Woodland, A. O'Reilly and G. Dix, *Britain at Work: As Depicted by the 1998 Workplace Employee Relations Survey* (London and New York: Routledge, 1999) at 235–42. Union membership in 1997 stood at 7.94 million, the lowest figure since 1945. See *Labour Market Trends*, July 1998, (London: Central Statistical Office) at 353.

[28] See R. Welch, "The Behavioural Impact on Trade Unionists of the Trade Union Legislation of the 1980s: A Research Note" (1993) 24 *IRJ* 236.

[29] *FAW*, para. 2.10.

[30] See Chap. 4 at 67–72 for discussion of employer resistance to the compulsory recognition procedures contained in the EPA 1975.

[31] Judgment of 13 Aug. 1981 (A/44) [1981] IRLR 408. Approved by the Committee of Independent Experts (now the European Committee on Social Rights) responsible for assessing compliance with the European Social Charter in *Conclusions IX–1*, 79 and *Conclusions X–1*, 69.

[32] *ILO Digest*, n.16 above, at para. 425.

explicit criticism from the ILO as regards UK legislation on secondary action[33] and legitimate concerns over restrictions on picketing,[34] these facets of collective labour rights were not considered as suitable subjects for reform.

New Labour's position seems to be a reaction to a collective memory of industrial relations under the last Labour Government of 1974–9.[35] According to this constructed popular history, the last Labour administration presided over a system which failed to constrain the unreasonable behaviour of trade unions, who then became involved in widespread and damaging industrial action. This is in many respects a fallacious memory.

The laws regulating strikes as consolidated by Labour in the Trade Unions and Labour Relations Act 1974 essentially re-enacted the same compromise with the common law as had been achieved by the Trade Disputes Act 1906.[36] Given the autonomy of industrial relations as practised in the UK it had not been seen necessary to impose statutory procedural requirements on trade unions when calling a strike. The attempt by the Conservative Government of 1970–4 to put industrial relations into a statutory straightjacket (via the Industrial Relations Act 1971) was generally seen to have failed.[37] Thus with regard to the laws on strikes, there was nothing radical or innovative in the legislation of the last Labour Government.

Nevertheless, from 1979 onwards, the Conservatives claimed that Labour was to blame for a system which had allowed trade unions to become too powerful. The demonology of the "Winter of Discontent", a series of mainly public sector strikes in 1978–9, generated the popular belief that the government was no longer in control and that the unions were seeking to run the country. Similar arguments also emerged at the same time from the Court of Appeal which attempted to interpret the statutory immunities in a restrictive fashion in order to limit the scope of lawful industrial action.[38] Thus the Conservatives felt fully justified in progressively tightening the legal restrictions on taking strike action throughout the 1980s and early 1990s.[39] They also placed new constraints on the internal management of trade union affairs and introduced novel modes of scrutinising compliance with these rules.[40]

When a Labour Government was again elected to power, and began to embark on reform of UK labour laws, Conservative members were waiting to pounce, predicting that the new legislation would begin "a journey back to

---

[33] *Ibid.* at para. 283.

[34] See Novitz, n.18 above, at 187.

[35] J. O'Farrell, *Things Can Only Get Better* (London: Doubleday, 1998).

[36] TULRA 1974 ss. 13 and 14.

[37] See B. Weekes, M. Mellish, L. Dickens and J. Lloyd, *Industrial Relations and the Limits of Law* (Oxford: Blackwell, 1975).

[38] *Associated Newspapers Group* v. *Wade* [1979] IRLR 201 (CA); *Express Newspapers* v. *McShane* [1979] ICR 210 (CA); *Duport Steel* v. *Sirs* [1980] IRLR 112 (CA).

[39] See S. Dunn and D. Metcalf, "Trade Union Law Since 1979" in I. Beardwell, *Contemporary Industrial Relations* (Oxford: OUP, 1996). Also see below Chap. 5 at 132 *et seq.*

[40] See below Chap. 3.

e".[41] The response of the Labour Party has not been to challenge this flawed history. One Labour peer went so far as to concede that "there was a case for reform" in the 1970s and that "the role undertaken by trade unions during the winter of discontent was arrogant".[42] New Labour has sought to distance itself from this legacy, refusing to countenance any measures which would restore to British unions their previous entitlements to take industrial action.

2. A flexible and efficient labour market

In *Fairness at Work* the Government presented its normative definition of the labour market. The two key factors it identified for delivering efficiency and fairness were "flexibility" and "employability".[43] Whilst these concepts are often associated with a particular vision of individual labour law, they also shape New Labour's approach to collective labour law, by delimiting the role which trade unions can play.

The White Paper stated that "[f]lexibility means businesses being able to adapt quickly to changing demand, technology and competition. By enabling business success, flexibility promotes employment and prosperity".[44] Theoretical models suggest that there are two key axes along which this business adaptability can be developed: first, numerical flexibility whereby enterprises can vary the quantity of labour utilised in response to changes in the market; secondly, functional flexibility whereby labour is "multi-skilled" and hence capable of being moved quickly from task to task without needing new training.[45]

These dimensions to flexibility are well-established in British labour law. Enterprises have many opportunities to acquire just the right quantity of labour, given the priority given to managerial prerogative in British employment protection legislation.[46] With regard to functional flexibility, there is little standing in the way of employers who seek to achieve flexible re-skilling of their workforce,[47] but few positive initiatives have been taken to ensure that workers have access to training which promotes employability and labour mobility. Neither legislation nor the common law has imposed a duty on employers to maintain their workers' skills to enable them to keep abreast with the labour market, despite the imposition of a reciprocal obligation on employees to be adaptable.

[41] HC Hansard, 21 May 1998, col. 1106, per Mr Redwood.
[42] HL Hansard, 10 May 1999, col. 985, per Lord Clinton-Davis.
[43] *FAW*, para. 2.13.
[44] *Ibid*.
[45] See J. Atkinson, "Flexibility: Planning for an Uncertain Future" [1985] *Manpower Policy and Practice* Summer, 26.
[46] Now contained in the ERA 1996. See also H. Collins, *Justice in Dismissal* (Oxford: Clarendon Press, 1992).
[47] *Cresswell* v. *Board of Inland Revenue* [1984] IRLR 190 illustrates the common law's willingness to facilitate managerial prerogative by implying a duty of adaptability on employees, in this particular case to learn how to use a computerised operating system.

Flexibility was also an important tool in the reshaping of collective labour law by the Conservative governments of 1979–97. National collective bargaining was said to make it difficult for enterprises to vary the task and/or pay of a particular worker and was considered to create unemployment by pricing workers out of jobs. "Individual employees will increasingly want terms and conditions . . . which reflect their own skills, efforts, capacities and circumstances and which are not solely the outcome of some distant negotiation between employers and trade unions."[48]Measures taken by the Conservatives on this basis included the repeal in 1980 of Schedule 11 to the Employment Protection Act 1975 which permitted trade unions to apply to have collective terms and conditions "extended",[49] rescission of the Fair Wages Resolution in 1982, and final abolition of Wages Councils in 1993.[50] Emphasis was placed on individual employment rights as an alternative to collective protection and security.[51] Flexibility for the Conservatives also meant a general reduction in the regulatory constraints which labour legislation might place on business.[52]

This pre-existing policy emphasis on flexibility could not easily be ignored by New Labour. Accordingly, Blair sought to reassure British business that "[e]ven after the changes we propose, Britain will have the most lightly regulated labour market of any leading labour market in the world".[53] The Regulatory Impact Assessment (RIA) was later to assess the burdens and benefits of the Employment Relations Act 1999. These detailed costings sought to provide the economic evidence to back up Blair's claim.

The White Paper also observed that "Britain's labour market has seen large-scale structural changes" which were due to "global competitiveness" and "technological innovation".[54] The challenge was to devise a new flexible and efficient labour market which would meet the demands of the global economy and new modes of business organisation. The earlier Conservative response had been to deny that trade unions or collective bargaining could have any continuing relevance under these conditions.[55] Where *Fairness at Work* is distinguishable from Conservative policy statements on flexibility is in its view that trade unions can potentially play a useful role in facilitating workplace change and employability.

---

[48] *Employment for the 1990s*, Cm 540 (London: HMSO, 1988), para. 2.14, see also *ibid.*, para. 2.5.

[49] Employment Act 1980 s.20(3).

[50] P. Davies and M. Freedland, *Labour Legislation and Public Policy* (Oxford: Clarendon Press, 1993), 538–50.

[51] B. Ryan, "Unfinished Business? The Failure of Deregulation in Employment Law" (1996) 23 *JLS* 506.

[52] See e.g. *Lifting the Burden,* Cmnd 9751 (London: HMSO, 1985) and *Building Businesses . . . not Barriers*, Cmnd 9794 (London: HMSO, 1986).

[53] *FAW*, Foreword.

[54] *FAW*, para. 2.9.

[55] "Traditional patterns of industrial relations, based on collective bargaining and collective agreements, seem increasingly inappropriate and are in decline": *People, Jobs, Opportunity*, Cm 1810 (London: HMSO, 1992), para. 1.15.

The White Paper presents the argument that collective representation of workers is not necessarily obstructive. "It can facilitate negotiation on terms and conditions without preventing the recognition of good individual performance."[56] This seems to be an implicit message to trade unions that they can and should move away from their past focus on set wage hierarchies and embark on negotiations for more flexible job packages. Moreover, it is said that "representatives who are respected by other employees can help employers to explain the company's circumstances and the need for change".[57] It is not envisaged that trade unions will necessarily play this role, but they are to have the option to do so where they have convinced employers and employees of their "value".[58]

Secondly, *Fairness at Work* emphasised "employability". It states that the Government's aim is to ensure "that people are well prepared, trained and supported, both before they enter the labour market, and throughout their working lives".[59] This might seem ironic, for New Labour, since coming to office, has created no measures which impose comprehensive obligations on employers to provide or fund training either for unemployed workers or for their existing workforce.[60] The key exception to this is the new limited right for 16 and 17-year-old employees to paid time off for study and training to bring them up to a basic standard of education.[61] Employability for the unemployed has been developed through the "New Deal" and financed by central government.[62] Despite its acknowledgement that training is significantly under-prioritised by some employers (especially small and medium sized enterprises),[63] the Government has largely maintained the private-sector approach of its predecessor, relying on voluntary solutions. In this model employer-led organisations determine both local (Training and Enterprise Councils) and national (National Training Organisations) training agendas. However, there are indications that the Government does consider that trade unions can play a part in a training and "employability" strategy. The Education Green Paper envisages that, fulfilling "new" and "modern" roles, trade unions can enter into "partnerships" with employers with regard to time off for training, or employer contributions into

[56] *FAW*, para. 4.3.

[57] *Ibid.*

[58] See e.g. *FAW*, para. 4.11.

[59] *FAW*, para. 2.13. This is also a key plank of the EU's new employment policy. See J. Goetschy, "The European Employment Strategy: Genesis and Development" (1999) 5 *EJIR* 117; C. Barnard and S. Deakin, "A Year of Living Dangerously? EC Social Rights, Employment Policy and EMU" (1999) 30 *IRJ* 355, 355–61.

[60] Plans to impose a new training levy were dropped whilst in opposition: D. King and M. Wickham-Jones, "Training Without the State? New Labour and Labour Markets" (1998) 26 *Policy and Politics* 439. The powers of the Construction Industry Training Board and the Engineering Construction Industry Training Board to raise a levy from employers to fund training remain unaltered: Industrial Training Act 1982 s.11.

[61] ERA 1996 ss. 63A–63C.

[62] Summarised in *Opportunity for All: Tackling Poverty and Social Exclusion*, Cm 4445 (London: TSO, 1999), 84–8.

[63] *The Learning Age*, Cm 3790 (London: TSO, 1998) paras. 3.2 and 3.13–3.15.

Individual Learning Accounts.[64] *Fairness at Work* also invited views on whether its proposed compulsory recognition scheme should cover training.[65]

This preoccupation with flexibility and employability seems to be driving New Labour to explore new roles for trade unions. The Government's perception of the "value" of unions in the workplace does not seem to reside so much with the conventional case for collective bargaining outlined above,[66] but rather with their ability to contribute to a flexible and efficient labour market which has economic benefits for Britain.

3. Appeasing the employer and trade union lobby

By the early 1990s, the Labour Party had already begun to redefine its relationship with the trade union movement so as to create greater distance between the two.[67] This shift related not only to the myths about strikes in the 1970s, but also fears associated with the involvement of trade unions in the "Social Contract" with the last Labour Government. Davies and Freedland have criticised the crude view that the Social Contract was merely an arrangement whereby the TUC promised pay restraint in return for favourable labour law measures.[68] They have identified a broader and more radical programme of social and economic reform which the TUC sought to negotiate with the Labour Party whilst it was in opposition, of which labour law was only a component part. Furthermore they have questioned the label of "contract" which suggests that Labour was legislating at the behest of the TUC and saw no intrinsic merit in the measures enacted. Merely in terms of labour law outcomes one must also doubt whether the "Social Contract" deserves such a label. The validity of these criticisms nevertheless does not detract from the popular understanding that there were significant attempts on the political left in the 1970s to achieve consensus between Labour and the TUC in shaping economic and social policy. New Labour in the 1990s did not want to be cast in the same light. There was no chance of a new Social Contract with the trade union movement.

The long process of transforming the White Paper on *Fairness at Work* into law has been achieved along alternative lines.[69] Throughout this period, New Labour has attempted to show that it listens to the representations both of

---

[64] *Ibid.*, para. 3.10.

[65] *FAW*, para. 4.18.

[66] See above at 2–4.

[67] J. McIlroy, "The Enduring Alliance? Trade Unions and the Making of New Labour, 1994–1997" (1998) 34 *BJIR* 537, 540–6.

[68] Davies and Freedland, n.50 above, at 354–66.

[69] For a full list of commencement dates, see the Annex below at 181. At the time of writing not all provisions have been brought into force with more technically and politically difficult measures delayed. Those delayed include the new right to be accompanied in disciplinary and grievance hearings (ERelA 1999 ss. 10–15) and amendments to industrial action balloting and notice requirements (ERelA 1999 s. 4 and Sched. 3). There is still to be consultation later in 2000 on regs. to prohibit blacklisting, to be made under ERelA 1999 s. 3.

business and of trade unions. However, given the need to demonstrate that there will be "no going back", consultation and consensus-building has been presented in a form which both looks and is very different from the era of the Social Contract. Nor has there been any tripartite ILO-style meeting of government representatives together with representatives of both employers and workers organisations.[70] On the question of union recognition, the TUC and CBI were asked in a manner reminiscent of EU-level "social dialogue"[71] to see if they could reach agreement. In the event, the TUC/CBI discussions predominantly led to the parties merely recording their differences.[72]

Unsurprisingly, in the course of this process, it emerged that the interests of business resided largely in maintaining the *status quo* on collective rights, to the extent that this would be possible under a new Labour Government.[73] Where the TUC sought reform, the CBI sought to block or qualify the measures taken by the Government so as to limit their impact on business. New Labour was in a position where it could not readily please both sides of industry, with the result that many of the elaborate accommodations were reached, not on the basis of principle, but rather political expediency. The reforms made by the Employment Relations Act did not so much reflect the case for collective rights recognised within the ILO and Council of Europe, as the relative strength of the two key factions of lobbyists. Observers noted that the employer lobby tended to be the more successful.[74]

Consultation by government in the design of labour law is nothing new,[75] but the Government did go to extreme lengths to respond to lobbyists, even during parliamentary debates on the Employment Relations Bill. The Bill was so frequently subject to government amendment, in order to take into consideration demands of interest groups, that it was at times extremely difficult to follow the legislative process.[76] This parliamentary powerlessness has been heightened by the frequent use of enabling provisions,[77] permitting the Minister to make regulations, which must be accepted or rejected by the House of Commons *en bloc*. Whilst previous governments have used ministerial Codes of Practice as a way

---

[70] See generally on the principle of tripartite consultation, ILO, *Tripartite Consultation at the National Level on Economic and Social Policy*, ILC 83rd Session (Geneva: International Labour Office, 1996).

[71] See above this chap., n.7.

[72] The "Joint Statement" was briefly mentioned in *FAW*, para. 4.14. See for a fuller discussion of its content below Chap. 4 at 72–4.

[73] Undy, n.2 above, at 322.

[74] *Ibid.*

[75] Arguably the *Royal Commission on Trade Unions and Employers' Associations 1965–68*, Cmnd 3623 (London: HMSO, 1968) (Donovan Commission Report) was an attempt to obtain expert views on the need for legislative reform. A more recent and direct example is the 1994 Green Paper on the tribunal system, *Reforming Employment Rights Disputes: Options for Reform* Cm 2707 (London: HMSO, 1994).

[76] See, e.g., comments made in HC Hansard, 31 March 1999, col. 1200.

[77] See ERelA 1999 ss.3, 17, 19, 23 and 38, ERA 1996 new ss. 71–79. Similarly powers to amend the union recognition provisions can be found in TULRCA 1992, Sched. A1 paras. 7(6), 29(5), 121(6) and 166.

of making "soft law",[78] these powers reserved to Ministers by the Employment Relations Act go further, in that they allow the Minister to respond in an *ad hoc* fashion to the political demands of the moment.

C. THE "SOLUTION" PRESENTED BY "PARTNERSHIP": ITS DIMENSIONS

The divergent pressures, identified above, made legislating on industrial relations an unenviable task. The solution adopted by New Labour ultimately centred around the rhetoric of "partnership". This view of "fairness at work" takes pride of place at the very beginning of the Foreword to the White Paper and has subsequently shaped the content of the Employment Relations Act 1999. "Partnership" is evidently a "portmanteau term which can hold a rich diversity of ideological baggage".[79] Cynics may observe that this was why it was so well-suited to the Government's purposes. This was a means by which New Labour could attract popular support from across the political spectrum. "Who could possibly be against partnership?"[80]

Use of this term is a relatively recent political phenomenon. Unlike "flexibility", "partnership" is not a policy feature obviously inherited from previous governments. Nevertheless, since 1997 a very wide range of New Labour proposals for institutional co-operation have been labelled "partnerships".[81] We are concerned chiefly with the use of this label in the context of labour law. More optimistic accounts read this partnership as a new pluralist approach to industrial relations, in contrast to the anti-trade union human resource management and employee involvement discourses of the 1980s. For example, the TUC, anxious to dispel the image of trade unions as the "enemies within", advocated social partnership as the "cornerstone of its renewal strategy for the 1990s".[82] However it is equally possible to find unitarist accounts of partnership where trade unions are airbrushed out of existence.[83]

---

[78] Codes have been issued on picketing and industrial action balloting under the authority of TULRCA 1992 s.203. A new code on access to workers during recognition and derecognition ballots came into force on 6 June 2000.

[79] N. Thompson, "Supply-side Socialism: The Political Economy of New Labour" (1996) 216 *New Left Review* 38.

[80] J. Knell, *Partnership at Work* (London: DTI, 1999), 5. See also P. Ackers and J. Payne, "British Trade Unions and Social Partnership: Rhetoric, Reality and Strategy" (1998) 9 *International Journal of Human Resource Management* 529; Lord Wedderburn, "Collective Bargaining or Legal Enactment: the 1999 Act and Union Recognition" (2000) 29 *ILJ* 1, 23–6.

[81] See e.g. recent policy documents: *Building Partnerships for Prosperity*, Cm 3814 (London: TSO, 1997), *A New Contract for Welfare: Partnership in Pensions*, Cm 4179 (London: TSO, 1999), *Building Real Partnership: Compact Between Government and the Voluntary and Community Sector in Northern Ireland*, Cm 4167 (London: TSO, 1999), *A New Partnership for Care in Old Age*, Cm 3563 (London: TSO, 1997), *Developing Partnerships in Mental Health*, Cm 3555 (London: TSO, 1997).

[82] Ackers and Payne, n.80 above, at 536. See also TUC, *Partners for Progress: Next Steps for the New Unionism* (London: Trades Union Congress, 1997); and "Monks Tells Directors Partnership is the Key", TUC Press Release, 19 Apr. 2000.

[83] See for an overview of these diverse approaches Knell, n.80 above, at 5–15.

New Labour's interest in partnership appears to flow from its flirtation with ideas of "stakeholding". Tony Blair initially appeared attracted to the idea floated mainly by Will Hutton that enterprises should recognise the interests of various "stakeholders", who would include not only shareholders and consumers but also workers. The aim was to develop and encourage a new, more responsible corporate ethos, indirectly raising questions about ownership and control of the enterprise. This promised a voice for workers, but New Labour was vague about how this might be articulated. The label of "stakeholding" was however quickly dropped. It may be that New Labour thought that such policies would appear to revive 1970s notions of industrial democracy,[84] contrary to its desire to "break with the past".

In the 1997 New Labour election manifesto, the concept of "partnership at work", although discussed in the context of improving the conditions for business, nevertheless continued to keep alive (in a weaker form) debate about ownership and control of the enterprise. "We are keen to encourage a variety of forms of partnership and enterprise, spreading ownership and encouraging more employees to become owners through Employee Share Ownership Plans and co-operatives."[85]

This understanding of "partnership" did not feature in the 1998 White Paper and New Labour policy as presented in parliamentary debates on the Employment Relations Bill. Instead, its present dimensions can be dissected and explained in terms of five key features. Firstly, the "partnership" which New Labour seeks to encourage within the employment relationship is not one which necessarily involves trade unions. The partners are the individual employer and the individual worker. Secondly, New Labour is concerned not so much by the welfare of the collective as the autonomy or "choice" of the individual. The constraints placed on workers' choices, arising from the imbalance in bargaining power within the employment relationship, are only partially acknowledged. This emphasis on individual "choice" can be linked to the third "voluntary" dimension of partnership. The Government wishes to avoid harsh legal strictures, preferring to provide opportunities whereby agreements can be achieved voluntarily. Its aim is to create a new "culture" of co-operative and consensual workplace relations. Underlying the Government's agenda is the fourth facet of "partnership", namely the expectation that an employer and worker have sufficient interests in common for their dealings to be non-conflictual. Through mutual respect their interests can be aligned in a manner which boosts the profitability of the employer's business. New Labour seeks to achieve this alignment through the medium of "rights and responsibilities". This is the fifth feature of "partnership" whereby individuals are entitled to "minimum standards" of

---

[84] R. Levitas, *The Inclusive Society* (London: Macmillan, 1998), 115–8. The subsequent divergence between Hutton and New Labour is obvious from W. Hutton, "New Keynesianism and New Labour" (1999) 70 *Political Quarterly* 97.

[85] Labour Party, *New Labour: Because Britain Deserves Better* (London: Labour Party, 1997), 17.

treatment. The trade-off for such rights seems to be added responsibilities which constrict the actions of trade unions.

1. Who are the partners?

The "partnership" which the Government envisages is a mutually supportive relationship established between the individual employer and the individual worker. Tony Blair neatly summed up the government paradigm: "it is based on the rights of the individual, whether exercised on their own or with others".[86] This is the lens through which New Labour views collective rights: as the sum total of a bundle of rights belonging to individuals. The Government refuses to acknowledge that a trade union need not only seek to protect existing individual workers, but may wish to represent the interests of retired and future workers or the legitimate concerns of workers in general as a class.

Provision is made for the protection of individual trade unionists,[87] but the Government does not see unions as essential to the employment relationship. It is accepted that relations between management and labour can be mediated through a "wide range of representational mechanisms".[88] Even where trade unions are to be involved voluntarily or through a statutory recognition procedure, it is envisaged that this will be at only an enterprise level.[89] The "partnership" philosophy does not contemplate national or sectoral management–union relations,[90] reflecting a continuing trend away from multi-employer bargaining.[91] Nor is this a theory which seeks to implement ILO tripartite decision-making involving management, labour and government in roundtable discussions.[92] The Conservative opposition is given no opportunity to claim that New Labour is returning to a "Social Contract" scenario or restoring inflexible industry-wide collective bargaining.

2. The centrality of individual "choice"

It is individual choice which New Labour seeks to protect. For example, individual workers will have the "choice" to decide whether or not to join a trade

---

[86] *FAW*, Foreword.

[87] See below Chap. 2 and K.D. Ewing, "Freedom of Association and the Employment Relations Act 1999" (1999) 28 *ILJ* 283.

[88] *FAW*, para. 4.6.

[89] See *FAW*, Annex I, para. (i).

[90] Contrast the TUC rhetoric: TUC, *Partners for Progress: Next Steps for the New Unionism* (London: TUC, 1997).

[91] This was a development favoured by the Donovan Commission Report, n.75 above, at paras. 67–68. For analysis of its repercussions, see Brown, n.14 above, at 195–8; and Cully *et al.*, n.27 above, at 106. See below Chap. 4 at 81.

[92] See above this chap., n.70.

union[93] and whether or not to opt out of coverage by a collective agreement.[94] This can be linked to the emphasis which Conservative governments placed on individual as opposed to collective rights.[95] New Labour does not appear to accept that "freedom of contract" can be a fiction in the context of an employment relationship. There is certainly no express acknowledgement of Kahn-Freund's observation that "to restrain a person's freedom of contract may be necessary to protect his freedom, that is to protect him against oppression which he may otherwise be constrained to impose on himself through an act of his legally free and social unfree will".[96]

In the name of consumer or employment protection, the legislator often restricts an individual's contractual freedom, denying the "choice" to opt out of statutory rules. The "choice" to contract out of unfair dismissal,[97] or discrimination law[98] protection is withheld from workers for good reason. It would be a logical extension to apply this philosophy also to collective agreements, preventing individuals from contracting out of norms which have been agreed for their collective benefit. Instead, New Labour reforms presume that with regard to collectively agreed norms (unlike statutory ones) individuals are the best judges of their own individual interests[99] and therefore allows collective agreements to be undermined. Despite the White Paper's assertion that "individual contracts of employment are not always agreements between equal partners",[100] New Labour's policies do not reflect the necessary consequences of this statement. Instead, the flexibility this option presents is seen as beneficial to workers and business alike.

3. The "voluntary" aspect of partnership

Just as the "choices" of individual workers are given priority, so too New Labour emphasises the importance of voluntary agreements between employers and worker representatives, such as trade unions.[101] Partnership should be instantiated through a "cultural shift" which will lead to "more positive relationships between employers and employees *than the letter of the law can ever*

[93] *FAW*, para. 4.8. The symmetrical provisions of TULRCA which place an equally high value on trade union non-membership as membership remain. See in particular TULRCA 1992 ss. 137, 144, 145, 146 and 152.

[94] *FAW*, Annex 1, para. (viii): "[u]nder the existing law an employer and employee can agree different terms if they wish. Since the current law allows flexibility and works well, the Government sees no reason to change it."

[95] Ryan, n.51 above.

[96] O. Kahn-Freund, *Labour and the Law* (2nd edn., London: Stevens & Sons, 1977), 14.

[97] ERA 1996 s.203(1), subject to the possibility of compromise agreements (s.203(3)) or collective dismissal procedures (s.110).

[98] Sex Discrimination Act 1975 s.77(3), Race Relations Act 1976 s.72(3), Disability Discrimination Act 1995 s.9(1).

[99] *FAW*, para. 4.20.

[100] *FAW*, para. 4.2.

[101] *FAW*, para. 4.18.

achieve".[102] *Fairness at Work* purports to establish only the framework within which such agreements can be reached. It is not assumed that law itself is capable of effecting widespread institutional and organisational change; it is merely that "a change in law can reflect a new culture, can enhance its understanding and support its development".[103] This approach to law-making in the field of labour relations can be contrasted with that of recent Conservative governments which viewed law (and yet more law) as necessary to combat industrial relations "problems".[104] It can also be contrasted with the more prescriptive legislative measures taken by the last Labour Government.[105]

Yet while "partnership" between employers and workers is described as essentially "voluntary", this is a far cry from the days of British *collective laissez-faire*.[106] New Labour is interventionist in terms of the procedural framework it establishes by which these so-called "voluntary" agreements are to be reached. For example, while the compulsory statutory recognition procedure provides opportunities for the parties to resolve their differences, they are most likely to do so in response to the various deterrents associated with this process.[107] In addition, the Government is prepared to provide financial support for the creation of arrangements whereby consensual workplace relations can be developed. The "Partnership Fund" was conceived as one way in which to "spread good practice from the best organisations to the rest" and thereby achieve cultural change.[108]

4. Partnership as a non-conflictual relationship

The Government emphasises the "common interests" of management and labour in this "partnership", indicating that, through "trust and mutual involvement, instilling a sense of belonging and involvement", businesses will be helped to grow.[109] This is a deliberate antidote to accusations that New Labour policies will initiate a "return to strife".[110] The fact that a large number of workers do not identify with or share the values of their organisation is overlooked.[111]

---

[102] *FAW*, para. 1.8 (emphasis added)

[103] *FAW*, Foreword.

[104] P. Fosh, H. Morris, R. Martin, P. Smith and R. Undy, "Politics, Pragmatism and Ideology: the 'Wellsprings' of Conservative Union Legislation (1979–1992)" (1993) 22 *ILJ* 1, 19–20.

[105] E.g., compulsory trade union recognition which could ultimately lead to an award of terms and conditions of employment. See EPA 1975 s. 16, discussed below Chap. 4 at 67–72.

[106] See O. Kahn-Freund, "Legal Framework" in A. Flanders and H. Clegg (eds.), *The System of Industrial Relations in Britain* (Oxford: Basil Blackwell, 1954).

[107] Namely that it is onerous, time-consuming, unproductive and costly. See below Chap. 4.

[108] *FAW*, para. 2.7. See also ERelA 1999 s. 30 and Chap. 6 below at 168–9.

[109] HC Hansard, 26 July 1999, col. 48, per Mr McCartney.

[110] See above at 7–8.

[111] In the 1998 WERS Survey, only 51% said that they shared many of the values of their organisation and only 56% that they felt pride in telling people who they work for. M. Cully, A. O'Reilly, N. Millward, J. Fortii, S. Woodland, G. Dix and A. Bryson, *The 1998 Workplace Employee Relations Survey: First Findings* (Coventry: Industrial Relations Research Unit, University of Warwick, 1999), 18–19. See also Cully *et al.*, above n.27, at 185–9.

To the extent that trade unions are able to mediate between the partners to the employment relationship, they are to play an essentially co-operative role which will prove their "value" to both the employer and the workers they seek to represent.[112] This approach builds on the information and consultation requirements established under EC directives on collective redundancies, transfers of undertakings and European Works Councils. For example, when the employer seeks to restructure or make redundancies as may be necessary within the "flexible firm", unions are expected to operate as a useful tool of management, helping employers "to explain the company's circumstances and the need for change".[113] Less attention is paid to the more confrontational strategy of collective bargaining with recourse to industrial action, despite the fact that these are rights recognised by the ILO.

5. Rights and responsibilities

Much of New Labour's policymaking is infused with the rhetoric of "rights and responsibilities" which seeks to provide a moral underpinning for government action.[114] *Fairness at Work* is no exception. Tony Blair states that "it matches rights with responsibilities".[115] A basic core of individual rights is conferred on workers, including rights associated with freedom of association. By respecting the minimum rights of the individual worker, it is anticipated that the employer can achieve "enhanced employee commitment to the organisation, working towards shared goals—in the words of management consultants, 'alignment' ".[116]

However, access to new statutory rights can be made conditional on a worker's conduct. For example, as we shall see, a worker's right not to be subjected to detriment or dismissal on account of campaigning for (or against) union recognition exists only to the extent that the act or omission in question is not "unreasonable".[117] Moreover, the legislative framework in the Employment Relations Act is also designed to place pressure on trade unions to behave responsibly, in return for rights for their members. This is evident in

---

[112] *FAW*, para. 4.11.

[113] *FAW*, para. 4.3.

[114] See Blair, n.2 above, 12. In his Budget speech on 21 Mar. 2000, Gordon Brown commented that, "[t]he relationship we are forging between rights and responsibilities is firmly rooted in both economic opportunity and individual responsibility". Later, he added that "[a] strong civic society is built not by rights alone but by rights and responsibilities and by the shared pursuit of the common good—which every year enlists the energies and realises the idealism of more than 22 million British citizens". For an approving liberal socialist view, see S. White, "Rights and Responsibilities: A Social Democratic Perspective" (1999) 70 *Political Quarterly* 166.

[115] *FAW*, Foreword.

[116] HL Hansard, 10 May 1999, col. 969, per Lord Simon.

[117] TULRCA 1992, Sched. A1, paras. 156(3) and 161(3). Note how other rights "not to be subjected to a detriment" are not all limited in the same way: e.g., a worker does not have to act "reasonably" when refusing to sign a workforce agreement with regard to working time: ERA 1996 s.45A(1)(c).

relation to regulation of trade union governance,[118] the compulsory recognition procedure[119] and protection of striking employees from dismissal.[120] New Labour has been careful to ensure that there is little scope for accusations that the trade unions are unduly powerful or uncontrollable. Again, in this sense, there is to be no return to the policies of the last Labour administration.

The one crucial concession to TUC demands for genuine "collective rights" was the commitment to establish a compulsory recognition procedure, given in Labour's 1997 General Election manifesto. Indeed, this very general and imprecise undertaking provided the basis on which New Labour attracted and maintained union support.[121] A statutory recognition procedure had been introduced in 1975 under a Labour administration and had not been successful.[122] This was therefore a significant exception to the general reluctance of New Labour to return to the "mistakes of the past". In *Fairness at Work*, this policy initiative was defended, not in terms of Labour's electoral promises, but by reference to the protection of the individual rights and choices of workers.[123] It was evident that a trade union's statutory entitlement to represent workers would depend on the tallying of the preferences of individual workers through so-called "democratic" procedures.[124] Moreover, employers were told that if this is what workers desire, respecting their wishes would be good for business.[125] The problem was that, even when justified on these terms, compulsory recognition was difficult to reconcile with the other dimensions of "partnership". Statutory recognition of representative trade unions and compulsory collective bargaining could not guarantee an "alignment" of interests, but might instead provide workers with the means to confront and effectively oppose managerial decisions. This appears to have been appreciated by the Government which gradually whittled down the procedure for statutory recognition until it took a form which was acceptable to employers. Emphasis was placed on dialogue as opposed to co-decision-making and on individual choice as opposed to collective bargaining. Furthermore, New Labour's refusal to make extensive changes to the laws restricting strikes means that even those trade unions which achieve recognition will find that, in the face of unco-operative management, they are able to achieve very little.

---

[118] See below Chap. 3.

[119] See below Chap. 4.

[120] See below Chap. 5 at 133–6.

[121] B. Towers, "'. . . the most lightly regulated labour market . . .' The UK's Third Statutory Recognition Procedure" (1999) 30 *IRJ* 82 at 93.

[122] See EPA 1975 ss. 11–16.

[123] See the justification made for collective rights from an individual perspective: *FAW* at paras. 2.6 and 4.2.

[124] *FAW*, paras. 4.11–4.12. See HL Hansard, 7 June 1999, col. 1196, and HL Hansard, 10 May 1999, col. 1009.

[125] HC Standing Committee E, 16 Mar. 1999, at col. 349.

D. THE APPLICATION OF THESE PRINCIPLES IN THE EMPLOYMENT RELATIONS ACT 1999

The remainder of this book examines how the rhetoric of "partnership"has been translated into the concrete reforms contained in the Employment Relations Act 1999. We argue that, despite the sheer volume of legislative provisions relating to collective rights, remarkably little has been done which is likely to improve collective bargaining. New Labour have not implemented wholesale the reforms recommended by the ILO. Instead, directed by fears associated with Britain's industrial history, the demands of the "flexible and efficient labour market" and the employer and union lobby, New Labour has navigated a new passage between the perceived failings of "Old Labour" and the controversial Conservative policies of the 1980s and 1990s.

Chapter 2 examines many of the reforms described as "collective rights" in *Fairness at Work*, which are in actuality devoted to the protection of the *individual rights* of workers. These include the right to be accompanied by a trade union representative in disciplinary and grievance proceedings, protection of the individual from blacklisting, protection of union members from discrimination and provision made for striking employees to claim unfair dismissal. They are apparently regarded as contributing to the minimal foundation of individual rights which is necessary for the achievement of "partnership" within the employment relationship. While we welcome these measures, we also seek to identify their limitations. These reforms do not necessarily promote collective bargaining or support combined action in trade unions. Indeed, even the extent to which they actually succeed in promoting the welfare of individual workers is in many respects questionable.

Chapter 3 discusses the extent to which New Labour is interested in reforms relating to trade union autonomy. It emerges that, while the Government has recognised the fundamental importance of trade union independence, it is unwilling to make substantial changes to the statutory regime regulating trade union governance enacted by the Conservatives. The Employment Relations Act does seek to rationalise the mechanisms for scrutiny of union compliance with these requirements. However, the reasons given for these limited changes are merely that the current law places unacceptable "burdens on business" or involves unnecessary costs. New Labour appears to be reluctant to adopt policies which would enable trade unions to become more autonomous and thereby more effective in the collective representation of workers' interests. Their emphasis is on collective *responsibility* as opposed to collective rights.

The content of the statutory recognition procedure is outlined in Chapter 4. We begin by considering the historical and political context within which this measure is introduced, which in our view explains the form it has taken in Schedule A1, inserted into TULRCA 1992 by the Employment Relations Act. From close examination of the criteria for requests and applications, the delays inherent in the procedure, the numerical thresholds necessary to establish workplace support, the format of the ballot, and the limited consequences for collective bargaining procedures which follow from statutory recognition, we have concluded that the statutory mechanism provided for compulsory recognition is largely ineffectual. The Government's concerns with the promotion of individual rights, individual choice and voluntary agreement consistently undermine its efficacy.

In Chapter 5, we find that reforms made to protections of strikers from dismissal, as well as the changes made to balloting and notice requirements, will not greatly enhance the ability of a trade union to call industrial action. Instead, they confer significant responsibilities on trade unions which may be more restrictive than was previously the case. It seems that the non-conflictual relationship of "partnership" does not readily encompass a comprehensive right to strike.

Instead, New Labour appears most enthusiastic about developing alternative roles for trade unions within the workplace whereby they can contribute to a collaborative "partnership". The union recognised for purposes of collective bargaining is presented with the opportunity to play a part in information and consultation procedures as regards such matters as training, collective redundancies and transfers of undertakings. The opportunity to "accompany" workers in grievance and disciplinary proceedings also offers trade unions a facilitative and constructive role in the workplace. In addition, trade unions are able to seek financial assistance for particular co-operative projects from the "Partnership Fund". It is however important to observe that the entitlement to information and consultation remains an individual right, as does the right to be accompanied. The ultimate ability to enforce these rights rests with the individual worker and not the trade union, despite the difficulties which this may entail. Moreover, in the absence of a trade union, the information and consultation procedures can still operate, the right to be accompanied can still be exercised and grants from the Partnership Fund can still be made. Trade unions are not essential to these processes; instead, if the union wishes to be included, it must persuade the "partners" to the employment relationship that it has a valuable contribution to make. Traditionally, unions have been expected to defend workers' interests, if need be in opposition to the desires of employers. New Labour policies offer British unions a more passive and co-operative role. We conclude, in the light of the case for collective rights outlined above,[126] that the welfare of British workers is unlikely to be enhanced by the New Labour model of "fairness at work" centred on "partnership".

---

[126] Above this chap. at 2–4.

2

Individual Rights to Freedom of Association

A. INTRODUCTION

N EW LABOUR IS not opposed to trade unions. *Fairness at Work* upheld the right of every individual to join a trade union and indicated that unions can play a useful function in servicing the needs of individual trade union members. "Trade unions can be a force for fair treatment."[1] They provide a cheap mechanism (cheaper than lawyers or personnel departments) for helping to settle workplace disputes. Furthermore trade unions offer a ready-made conduit for employers who are required to inform or consult their workforces. Trade unions can be harnessed by management as they seek to build up a partnership with their workforce. For New Labour, it may therefore be helpful, but is by no means essential, that individuals join trade unions. According to the Government, the strategy that trade unions should adopt in order to attract membership and fulfil these functions is one of demonstrating "value".[2] This consumerist approach advocated by New Labour stresses the role of trade unions as providers of services to the employer as much as the individual employee; and pays little attention to the collective dimension of trade union membership.

Unlike the Government we believe that an important factor in maintaining trade union attractiveness to workers is their ability to harness and show collective strength. Empirical evidence confirms that collective reasons continue to have a significant influence on an individual's decision to join a trade union.[3] We argue in this book that New Labour is hesitant to accept the centrality of this premise in its development of labour law policy. Its vision of the collective strength of trade unions immediately conjures up the nightmares of the 1970s.[4] We suggest that the Government is trapped in a history which makes it virtually impossible for it to introduce legal changes which improve the position of trade unions as collective organisations *per se*. It has on the other hand been more

---

[1] *FAW*, para. 4.7.

[2] *FAW*, para. 4.11.

[3] See evidence e.g. in B. Burchell, D. Day, M. Hudson, D. Ladipo, R. Mankelow, J. Nolan, H. Reed, I. Wichert and F. Wilkinson, *Job Insecurity and Work Intensification* (York: Joseph Rowntree Foundation, 1999), 34–6; J. Waddington and C. Whitson, "Why Do People Join Unions in a Period of Membership Decline?" (1997) 35 *BJIR* 515, 520.

[4] See above Chap. 1, "no going back" at 6–8.

willing to create rights for individual trade union members which do not necessarily increase trade union strength. If as a result of its policies management is
better disposed towards trade unions, New Labour will be quite content. It will,
if it so wishes, be able to argue that it has in this way provided support for trade
unions (albeit indirectly and subtly) as management attitudes are known to be
significant in affecting union presence and density.[5] We remain to be convinced
by this approach. We doubt that New Labour's measures provide adequate support for trade unions. A trade union presence which is inherently dependent on
management attitude and goodwill is likely to remain weak and ineffective. In
this chapter we seek to explore the scope and content of those measures discussed by the White Paper under the heading of collective rights, but which are
essentially rights for individual workers. We will demonstrate that the new provisions which aim to improve the legal position of individual trade union members do so in a way which falls some way short of reinforcing the position of
trade unions as collective organisations. We now turn to the individual measures: the right to be accompanied in grievance and disciplinary hearings, provisions to prohibit blacklisting, further steps to limit discrimination against
trade union members, protection for individual workers in the recognition
process, unfair dismissal protection for striking employees, in order to substan-
tiate our thesis.

B. THE RIGHT TO BE ACCOMPANIED IN DISCIPLINARY AND GRIEVANCE HEARINGS

Grievance and disciplinary proceedings are important mechanisms available in
many enterprises to manage employee relations. The 1998 Workplace
Employment Relations Survey (WERS) of establishments with 25 or more
employees showed that 92 per cent had such disciplinary procedures, with a similar number (91 per cent) having formal grievance procedures in addition.[6] In
small firms these procedures are far less common.[7] Where they do exist, workers' trust and confidence in these procedures are undoubtedly improved if the
workers are permitted to be accompanied by another person to provide moral
support or help them present their case. This is in line with principles of natural
justice, and furthermore conforms to the ACAS Code of Practice.[8] Data suggests

---

[5] M. Cully, S. Woodland, A. O'Reilly and G. Dix, *Britain at Work* (London: Routledge, 1999),
85–90.
[6] *Ibid.*, 76–8. These figures are slightly up on those reported by WIRS 1990: N. Millward,
M. Stevens, D. Smart and W. Hawes, *Workplace Industrial Relations in Transition: the
ED/ESRC/PSI/ACAS Survey* (Aldershot: Dartmouth, 1992), 187–91. This suggests that these procedures are well established within British industrial relations.
[7] J. Earnshaw, J. Goodman, R. Harrison and M. Marchington, *Industrial Tribunals, Workplace
Disciplinary Procedures and Employment Practice*, Employment Relations Research Series No.2
URN 98/564 (London: DTI, 1998), 35.
[8] ACAS Code of Practice (No. 1): Disciplinary Practice and Procedures in Employment (1997). A
new version of this Code was laid before Parliament in June 2000.

that employers in general recognise this proposition. Only in 4 per cent of workplaces are employees denied the possibility of being accompanied at all in disciplinary proceedings.[9] Existing practice however varies considerably as to who may accompany the worker. Some workplaces permit the employee only to bring along her immediate manager or supervisor, whereas in around 40 per cent there is the freedom to be accompanied by any other person of the employee's own choosing.[10] In workplaces where there is no union membership or no recognition of trade unions, the procedures are far less likely to permit the accompanying person to be a trade union official.[11]

The Employment Relations Act 1999 builds on current practice by putting the right to be accompanied in disciplinary and grievance proceedings on a statutory footing.[12] The benefit of these provisions for many workers will lie in the fact that they will henceforth have the option of bringing along a suitably qualified trade union representative as their accompanying person.

1. The content of the right

The right as it has been enacted is unspectacular and permits an individual when taking a grievance or attending a disciplinary hearing to be accompanied either by a fellow worker (employed by the same employer), a paid official of the trade union, or a trade union official who has been trained or gained experience in disciplinary hearings.[13] The Act defines closely the nature of disciplinary and grievance hearings.[14] A grievance for these purposes relates only to the "performance of a duty" by an employer in relation to a worker. The new ACAS Code of Practice on Disciplinary and Grievance Procedures suggests that this means that a claim for a pay rise is not a grievance within the meaning of the statute, because the employer is under no contractual or statutory duty to offer a pay rise.[15] If this is correct then it seems that grievance proceedings relate to observance of *existing* terms and conditions, but generally do not include claims for *improved* terms, unless the employer is under a duty (statutory or contractual) to provide them.

Where the accompanying person cannot make the time of the meeting laid down by the employer, the worker can postpone the meeting to a reasonable alternative time within five working days of that proposed by the employer.[16] At the meeting the accompanying person may address the hearing and confer with the individual worker, but she has no legal right to act as the worker's

---

[9] Cully *et al.*, n.5 above, 97–8.
[10] *Ibid.*
[11] *Ibid.*
[12] ERelA 1999 ss.10–15, as had been proposed in *FAW*, para. 4.29.
[13] ERelA 1999 s.10(3).
[14] ERelA 1999 s.13(4) and (5) respectively.
[15] ACAS Code of Practice, para. 55, laid before Parliament 7 June 2000.
[16] ERelA 1999 s.10(4) and (5).

advocate.[17] If the accompanying person is a fellow worker, the employer must permit her reasonable time off[18] and she is given the same protection as if she were being given time off to carry out trade union duties.[19]

Should the employer ignore the worker's request to be accompanied the sanction is limited. The worker can present a claim to an employment tribunal and, if it is well founded, the maximum award is two weeks' pay.[20] There are additional flanking measures. The worker has the right not be subjected to a detriment or dismissed for invoking or attempting to invoke the right to be accompanied.[21] As ever, the difficulty with the flanking provisions is that of showing the causative link between attempting to exercise the right and the employer's retaliatory act, subjecting the worker to a detriment, or in the most serious cases dismissing her. In addition, in common with other employment law provisions, any attempt to contract out of these provisions will be void.[22] In line with the Government's commitment towards universalising employment rights, the personal coverage of these provisions is cast very widely, including homeworkers and agency workers.[23]

2. Support for trade unions?

The new right is important because it acknowledges the existence and role of trade unions even where they are not recognised by the employer. Traditionally trade unions in the UK have gained access to the workplace via recognition. Where they were not recognised, they had no legal rights. This new right ensures that individual trade union members[24] do have the right to call upon a trade union official in the context of individual dispute resolution. It is uncertain whether it can be said that the Government has gone as far as providing a right to "representation", as argued for by Hendy.[25] The accompanying person does not have the legal right to answer questions on the worker's behalf,[26] although

---

[17]   ERelA 1999 s.10(2).

[18]   ERelA 1999 s.10(6).

[19]   ERelA 1999 s.10(7). For an evaluation of the analogous right to time off for trade union duties see S. Deakin and G. Morris, *Labour Law* (2nd edn., London: Butterworths, 1998), 747–54.

[20]   There are rules against double recovery. No award will be made on a complaint under ERelA 1999 s.11 if a supplementary award is made under ERA 1996 s.127A when calculating unfair dismissal compensation.

[21]   ERelA 1999 s.12.

[22]   ERelA 1999 s.14.

[23]   ERelA 1999 s.13.

[24]   The right is open to all workers, but it is unlikely that someone who is not a trade union member will call upon the union's services. It is equally unlikely that a trade union will be willing to assist someone who is not a member of any trade union. In emergencies it may well help fellow trade unionists who are members of a different union.

[25]   J. Hendy, *Every Worker Shall Have the Right to be Represented at Work by a Trade Union* (London: Institute of Employment Rights, 1998).

[26]   ERelA 1999 s.10(2)(b).

she can address the hearing and confer with the worker.[27] Clearly some sort of advisory and advocacy role is envisaged for the accompanying person, but it seems that she is not quite a representative. Despite this qualification, it can be said that the new right is a useful, if modest, element of protection for the individual union member.

It is less clear how useful the right will be for trade unions collectively. The measure certainly gives trade unions an opportunity to demonstrate their utility to workers in the context of individual dispute resolution. Many unions may well see it as a recruitment opportunity. Conservative opposition members went as far as to fear that it would provide a "back-door" route especially for non-recognised trade unions to obtain influence in the enterprise.[28] This is probably over-optimistic in the context of statutory recognition. The membership thresholds for the statutory procedure seem too high[29] for these new provisions to have any significant impact.

Experience with other measures which have provided non-recognised trade unions with a way into the workplace is not particularly encouraging.[30] For example, research on the operation of the 1995 Regulations[31] which require employers to consult in certain redundancy situations with elected representatives as an alternative to recognised trade unions does not indicate that unions have been successful at exploiting this situation.[32] It is just conceivable, though, that the new provisions might possibly influence claims for voluntary recognition. If enough individual trade union members do make use of their statutory right, it will bring management into contact now and again with trade union officials. This may be sufficient to persuade management that trade unions are a useful managerial tool, and for such reasons worth recognising. Nevertheless this possibility is remote and it must be concluded that these provisions offer weak support for trade unions as collective organisations. Their focus is on individual workers.[33]

3. Improving workplace relations?

Whilst the right to be accompanied does include a nod in the direction of trade unions and improves the position of individual trade unionists, this is probably not the underlying rationale for its introduction. More plausible is that the

---

[27] ERelA 1999 s.10(2)(b) and (c).

[28] E.g., HL Hansard, 16 June 1999, cols. 333–4.

[29] See below Chap. 4.

[30] See discussion in P. James and D. Walters, "Non-Union Rights of Involvement: the Case of Health and Safety At Work" (1997) 26 *ILJ* 35, 47.

[31] Collective Redundancies and Transfer of Undertakings (Protection of Employment) (Amendment) Regs. 1995. SI 1995/2587.

[32] M. Hall and P. Edwards, "Reforming the Statutory Consultation Procedure" (1999) 28 *ILJ* 299, 317.

[33] See further below Chap. 6 at 167–8.

Government wanted to nudge employers towards operating better disciplinary and grievance procedures. It knew that the overwhelming majority of larger workplaces had these procedures and wanted to encourage their better functioning, avoiding abuse of workers' rights. Its starting point was not to impose mandatory disciplinary and grievance procedures.[34] This is perhaps a little surprising given its argument in the White Paper that individuals "should be able if need be to defend or advance their interests at work effectively".[35] Similar language condemning "bad" employers has generally been used within the context of *Fairness at Work* to justify statutory rights.[36] However the Government's belief in voluntary choices with regard to the management of workplace relations appeared to hold it back.[37]

The position it has adopted is one which defers to managerial prerogative. If the employer unilaterally decides to have disciplinary or grievance procedures, then statutory consequences follow.[38] Such an approach may yet be overtaken by judicial developments. In *Goold* v. *McConnell* a term was implied requiring an employer to provide an opportunity for grievances to be aired.[39] It also may be possible to argue similarly that it is a breach of the term of mutual trust and confidence not to allow employees a fair hearing.[40] Nevertheless for the purposes of the Employment Relations Act the Government went forward on the basis that disciplinary and grievance procedures are voluntary. Only where the procedures exist must worker rights be respected.[41]

Evidence suggests that employers have nothing to lose by this. They benefit from having genuine procedures (whether formal or informal) for handling disciplinary and grievance matters. Their chances of successfully defending unfair dismissal actions relating to the employee's conduct are significantly improved where they follow their own disciplinary procedures.[42] Disciplinary procedures are a useful tool of managerial prerogative[43] and are an effective mechanism for diffusing tension and preventing disputes from getting out of hand. Grievance procedures are probably on the whole less important to employers. They appear

---

[34] Although there are good arguments in favour of this: Lord Wedderburn, HL Hansard, 16 June 1999, col. 329. Statute already provides a weak encouragement: ERA 1996 s.3.

[35] *FAW*, para. 4.28.

[36] See e.g. the discussion of waiver clauses in *FAW*, para. 3.13.

[37] See above Chap. 1.

[38] This is analogous to the traditional public policy compromise with regard to union recognition, which defers to employer choice.

[39] [1995] IRLR 516 (EAT).

[40] See generally D. Brodie, "The New Contract of Employment?" (1998) 27 *ILJ* 79, especially 92–6. On incorporating notions of natural justice into the employment contract see H. Collins, "Market Power, Bureaucratic Power and the Contract of Employment" (1986) 15 *ILJ* 1.

[41] Even those employers with religious objections to trade unions will be required to respect the right of an individual to involve a trade union official. Opposition amendments to create religious exceptions were unsuccessful: HC Standing Committee E, 25 Feb. 1999, cols. 163–166 and HL Hansard, 8 July 1999, col. 1090.

[42] Earnshaw *et al.*, n.7 above, 42.

[43] S. Anderman, "Unfair Dismissal and Redundancy" in R. Lewis (ed.), *Labour Law in Britain* (Oxford: Blackwell, 1986).

to be little used. Cully *et al.* speculate that this may result from workers' lack of confidence in the procedures, although management representatives in the WERS Survey tended to suggest that the culture of their workplaces made formal grievance procedures unnecessary.[44]

The Government predicts that the benefits of the measure will include greater fairness for individuals. Although it will impose costs on those employers who do not currently permit a fellow worker to accompany an individual in disciplinary and grievance hearings, these costs may be outweighed if the measure leads to a fall in employment tribunal applications.[45] Steps in this direction had already been taken in the Employment Rights (Dispute Resolution) Act 1998 (ERDRA) which aimed to increase the use of internal dispute resolution mechanisms in order to save costs for employers and the state.[46] Whether the 1999 reform measure does improve fairness and contribute to saving costs will depend ultimately on the extent to which workers make use of it. This in turn hinges on whether they know about their right. Whilst trade unions are likely to inform their own members about this new service that they can offer and mention it in their recruitment literature, it is more doubtful whether news of it will reach the ever growing number of non-unionised workplaces.[47] Good employers are likely to invite workers to bring along an accompanying person or to inform them of their statutory right to do so. Whether others will is more doubtful. The new ACAS Code of Practice tucks away rather discreetly the suggestion that employers should inform workers of their statutory right to be accompanied.[48] With so little attention paid to enforcement and the weak sanctions for non-compliance with the new right,[49] it can legitimately be asked what impact this will have on practice in British workplaces.

C. PROTECTION FROM BLACKLISTING

Discrimination against trade union members takes many forms. One strategy used by anti-union employers has been to avoid recruiting individuals who have a history of trade union membership or activism. For the first time in 1990 legislative steps were taken to prevent this, with the enactment of provisions which

---

[44] Cully *et al.*, n.5 above, 77–8.

[45] The RIA estimated an increased cost burden on employers of £2.3m. annually. For every 500 fewer tribunal cases avoided the corresponding saving to employers would be in the order of £1m.: *Employment Relations Bill 1999 Regulatory Impact Assessment* (London: DTI), Annex, 25.

[46] ERDRA 1998 s.13, inserting ERA 1996 s.127A. The background to this provision is discussed in *Resolving Employment Rights Disputes: Options for Reform*, Cm 2707 (London: HMSO, 1994), paras. 4.19–4.26.

[47] Cully *et al.*, n.5 above, 86–7 report from the 1998 WERS Survey that in 47% of workplaces with 25 or more workers there was not a single trade union member.

[48] With respect to disciplinary procedures: Draft ACAS Code of Practice on Disciplinary and Grievance Procedures (laid before Parliament, 7 June 2000), para. 14. Earnshaw *et al.*, n.7 above, 40 note how employers are prone to read selectively the ACAS code.

[49] Above this chap. at 26.

make it unlawful for employers or employment agencies to discriminate in recruitment on grounds of trade union membership.[50] However the practice of "blacklisting" trade union members, that is the compilation and circulation of lists of trade union members, was not specifically outlawed by this legislation.[51] This lack of protection for trade unionists is perhaps not surprising, given that the original proposal prior to the introduction of the 1990 measures aimed to tackle the pre-entry closed shop and the position of non-unionists only.[52] It was only later that the then Conservative Government relented and introduced provisions which were even-handed in their treatment of trade union members and non-members. The Employment Relations Act 1999 seeks in a limited fashion to move away from this parallel treatment of trade union members and non-members[53] by introducing new measures to prevent the blacklisting of trade unionists.[54] It creates a power for the Secretary of State to make regulations which prohibit the compilation, sale, use or supply of lists which contain details of trade union members and their activities put together with a view to employers using them for the purpose of discrimination.

1. Weaknesses of the blacklisting provisions

The new provisions in respect of blacklisting aim to tackle from a different angle the fact that many employers do not wish to hire trade union activists whom they perceive to be "troublemakers". Existing measures fail to tackle this. Discrimination at the hiring stage is unlawful on account of an individual's trade union membership (or non-membership) only.[55] It does not offer any protection on account of previous union activities. In contrast it is automatically unfair to dismiss an employee on account of both union membership and union activities[56] when carried out "at an appropriate time".[57]

It is therefore particularly with regard to previous trade union activities that a problem arises. To avoid this individuals have resorted to self-help strategies by covering up details of their previous activities. Where this has been subsequently discovered, the courts have offered limited protection, as *Fitzpatrick*[58]

---

[50] See TULRCA 1992 ss.137–143; R. Townshend-Smith, "Refusal of Employment on Grounds of Trade Union Membership or Non-membership: the Employment Act 1990" (1992) 21 *ILJ* 102.

[51] See K.D. Ewing, "Freedom of Association and the Employment Relations Act 1999" (1999) 28 *ILJ* 283, who notes that blacklisting may have been unlawful at common law as conspiracy to injure.

[52] Townshend-Smith, n.50 above, n. 1.

[53] As might be expected this limited departure from a principle of symmetry was attacked by the Conservative opposition: HL Hansard, 16 June 1999, cols. 293–294, per Baroness Miller. She argued (apparently unaware of the Conservative legislation on secondary industrial action) that "blacking" of employers by trade unions ought similarly to be regulated.

[54] ERelA 1999 s.3.

[55] TULRCA 1992 s.137(1).

[56] TULRCA 1992 s.152(1).

[57] TULRCA 1992 s.152(2), which has been interpreted to cover only the present employment: *Beyer* v. *Birmingham City Council* [1977] IRLR 211 (EAT).

[58] *Fitzpatrick* v. *British Railways Board* [1991] IRLR 37 (CA).

shows. In this case, the applicant was dismissed on grounds of deceit when it came to light that she had deliberately suppressed details of her previous trade union activities. The industrial tribunal rejected on the facts dismissal on grounds of deceit and went on to consider whether or not it was a dismissal on grounds of trade union activities. It held that her dismissal fell outside the scope of the statutory protection. Allowing the employee's appeal, the Court of Appeal placed a new interpretation on section 152 of TULRCA 1992. It considered why an employer would want to dismiss an individual on account of her previous trade union activities. It decided that this arose out of a rational fear that these would be repeated in the present employment. Such a dismissal was in effect a dismissal on account of trade union activities in which the applicant proposed to take part, which is automatically unfair. Thus judicial extension of the statutory protection was achieved. However it must be remembered that this interpretation assists individuals only where employers are not successful in persuading the tribunal that the dismissal was for deceit or some other potentially fair reason.

The blacklisting provisions fail to make significant improvements in this area. The Secretary of State's power is limited. Regulations can be issued making it unlawful for employers to take recruitment decisions based on blacklists.[59] Where, however, an employer has obtained information about an individual's previous activities from other sources, which are not "lists",[60] or which have not been compiled for a discriminatory purpose the blacklisting provisions do not bite. It remains *prima facie* lawful not to hire an individual because in her previous employment she has acted as a shop steward, for example, helping others to raise grievances or in bringing an equal pay claim. Any success of the blacklisting measures is likely to flow from the prohibition on the compilation of lists and on targeting the compilers.[61] In the longer term these measures are likely to be overtaken by the provisions of the Data Protection Act 1998 which will regulate not only the processing of information about an individual's trade union membership and activities, but also other aspects of her private life.[62]

2. Strengthening freedom of association?

One of the Government's stated aims in introducing the blacklisting provisions was to improve freedom of association. The Minister noted that the UK had been found to be in breach of ILO Convention No. 98 on freedom of association

[59] Proving that the refusal to hire was on the basis of a blacklist will be extremely difficult.

[60] Defined ERelA 1999 s.3(5).

[61] Although the practical utility of even targeting compilers must be doubted when it appears that it will continue to be possible to circulate lists of "troublemakers" as long as they do not identify them as trade union members.

[62] This implements the Data Protection Dir. 95/46 [1995] OJ L281/31 which will be fully in force by 2007. It contains particularly strict rules with regard to the processing of "sensitive personal data". See Data Protection Act 1998 ss. 2, 4(3) and Sched. 3.

for its lack of protection for trade unionists.[63] He commented further, "[t]he clause underpins the fundamental rights of workers to belong to a trade union— a fundamental democratic right".[64] Whilst it is regrettable that New Labour is selective in its recognition of ILO standards; this is one concession to international labour standards which can be welcomed. One practical step the Government could take in concretising this commitment when drawing up the regulations would be explicitly to include participation in official strike action as an "activity of a trade union". This would help prevent the future victimisation of strikers. However given the Government's reluctance to acknowledge the legitimacy of strikes, it is perhaps too much to be hoped for.[65]

The ethos of the framework provisions sees freedom of association within an individual paradigm. There is no obvious realisation that blacklisting is a wrong committed against a trade union as a collective entity, or that it injures other workers who may be thus dissuaded from trade union membership or activities. The provisions focus on the harm suffered by the individual who has been blacklisted. The role of trade unions appears to have been limited to the possibility that they may be allowed to bring actions on a behalf of individuals who have been affected.[66]

It must be concluded that the blacklisting provisions are a relatively weak step towards strengthening freedom of association. Greater protection against discrimination on account of previous trade union activities at the hiring stage would be a useful parallel measure to improve the chances of the blacklisting measures having any impact. This is not the only possible route. Judicial development is also conceivable, as in Germany, where case law has developed a "right to lie" at the hiring stage to protect fundamental rights of workers. This may then be relied upon to defeat employer claims of deceit.[67] It offers a practical recognition that it is highly difficult to prove anti-union bias of an employer in an individual case. Whether British judges are prepared to take similar steps to protect freedom of association is much more doubtful.

D. PROTECTION FOR TRADE UNION MEMBERS AGAINST DISCRIMINATION

In addition to discrimination against trade unionists which may occur at the recruitment stage, some employers have over the years discriminated against trade unionists by harassing them in the workplace, providing them with disadvantageous terms and conditions of employment and in certain situations by

---

[63] HC Standing Committee E, 18 Mar. 1999, col. 459, per Mr Wills.
[64] *Ibid.*
[65] See below this chap. at 39–43 for new provisions on unfair dismissal of striking employees, and below Chap. 5 on industrial action.
[66] ERelA 1999 s.3(3)(d).
[67] See W. Däubler, *Das Arbeitsrecht 2* (5th edn., Reinbek: Rowohlt, 1995), 101–2.

dismissing them.[68] Since 1971 legislation has given employees a statutory right of action against their employer where they suffer action short of dismissal and dismissal on grounds of trade union membership,[69] but it has been shown to be limited in its application and effect.

It is fundamentally wrong to assume that the contours of this regime, as inherited by New Labour, flow simply from the desire to encourage and stimulate trade unionism. Whilst the legislative provisions of the "Social Contract" era relating to trade union membership could be characterised as supporting the development of independent trade unions,[70] a clear policy reversal took place under the Conservatives. They joyfully greeted the decision of the European Court of Human Rights in *Young, James and Webster* v. *UK*[71] on the scope of the closed shop as providing an opportunity to undermine the support for trade unionism offered by individual labour law. The right not to suffer action short of dismissal or not to be unfairly dismissed on grounds of membership of an independent trade union or for participating in its activities at an appropriate time was not however repealed. The strategy taken by the Conservatives was to treat the "right" *not* to join any or a particular trade union as equally deserving of protection.[72] It therefore appeared, paradoxically, to be strengthening the protection given to trade unionists, when it introduced the possibility of punitive awards of compensation for dismissal on grounds of trade union membership.[73] This was, however, simply a benign side-effect of its policy to destroy the closed shop.

The effectiveness of these legislative provisions in protecting trade unions came particularly to be tested in the 1990s, in the wake of employer derecognition of trade unions. Derecognition strategies ranged from the complete withdrawal of collective bargaining to the provision of inducements to sign "personal" contracts. As will be explained in more detail below, the House of Lords refused to acknowledge that such tactics constituted discrimination against trade union members. An omission to provide the same benefits to those who would not sign individual contracts, but wished still to be subject to collective negotiated terms and conditions, was not to be regarded as a discriminatory act precluded by the legislation. Indeed, as long as a worker could retain bare trade union membership, the fact that a worker was actively discouraged from engaging in collective bargaining was to be considered irrelevant. There was no recognition that membership of a trade union stems from a desire to engage in collective bargaining.

[68] E.g. in *O'Kelly* v. *Trusthouse Forte* [1983] IRLR 169 (CA) the waiting staff claimed that their dismissal was on grounds of their trade union membership. Their action failed on the preliminary issue that they were not "employees".

[69] The principal rights are now contained in TULRCA 1992 ss. 146 and 152. For a detailed account of their development see B. Simpson, "Freedom of Association and the Right to Organise: The Failure of An Individual Rights Strategy" (1995) 24 *ILJ* 235, 235–6.

[70] See EPCA 1978 ss. 23 and 58.

[71] [1981] IRLR 408 (ECtHR).

[72] EA 1982 s.3.

[73] EA 1982 s.5 introduced the special award, now repealed by ERelA 1999 s.33.

In *Fairness at Work*, it was observed that the existing law "currently allows for some discrimination against those involved in trade union activities".[74] Two sets of measures were introduced. First, amendments were made to the existing anti-discrimination provisions.[75] Secondly, a new power was introduced to allow the Secretary of State to make regulations to prevent individuals suffering a detriment when refusing to enter into an employment contract whose terms differ from those contained in an applicable collective agreement.[76] Despite the White Paper's symbolic affirmation of the interrelationship of individual and collective rights, it must be questioned, as will be seen below, how far these measures enacted do recognise the need to protect the collective dimension of trade union membership[77] and the implications that this has for collective bargaining in the light of the new trade union recognition provisions.[78]

1. The *Wilson/Palmer* litigation

To understand how gaps in the law protecting trade union members emerged, it is necessary to go back to litigation of the early 1990s. In *Wilson/Palmer*[79] the employees (trade union members) challenged their employer's practice of offering "sweetners" to employees who agreed to give up collective bargaining in favour of a "personal" contract (where the employer laid down the terms). The Court of Appeal upheld the initial tribunal finding that this conduct by the employer did constitute "action short of dismissal",[80] taken against employees on account of their trade union membership. Dillon LJ refused to accept the employer's argument that a distinction could be drawn between trade union membership and participation in collective bargaining, which he regarded as a vital service provided by trade unions.

The Conservative Government at the time reacted quickly to this Court of Appeal decision which it thought undermined its policy of encouraging employers to offer individual contracts. Viscount Ullswater introduced at the last minute an amendment to the Trade Union Reform and Employment Rights Bill 1993. This hastily introduced provision ("the Ullswater amendment"[81]) provided that where an employer wished to "further a change in his relationship with all or any class of his employees", a complaint of action short of dismissal would be excluded, unless "the action was such as no reasonable employer would take". This measure was designed to neutralise the effect of the

---

[74] *FAW*, para. 4.25.
[75] ERelA 1999 s.2 and Sched. 2.
[76] ERelA 1999 s.17.
[77] See Simpson, n.69 above, especially at 250.
[78] See below Chap. 4 on trade union recognition at 107.
[79] *Associated Newspapers* v. *Wilson* and *Associated British Ports* v. *Palmer* [1993] IRLR 336 (CA) and [1995] IRLR 258 (HL).
[80] Contrary to TULRCA 1992 s.146.
[81] Adding a new TULRCA 1992 s.148(3).

Wilson/Palmer judgment in the Court of Appeal, redefining what constituted discrimination against trade union members.

However these contorted provisions ultimately proved to be unnecessary when the House of Lords reversed the Court of Appeal's decision. The Lords, by a majority, held that the refusal of a pay rise to those employees who did not wish to give up their collectively bargained terms and conditions was an omission which did not fall within the statutory language of "action short of dismissal". Additionally they held unanimously, reflecting the lack of public policy support for trade unionism, that collective bargaining was not an essential feature of union membership. They offered an individualised view of trade unionism. A union unable to bargain on behalf of its members could still offer other important and valuable services.[82]

Thus the *Wilson/Palmer* saga left several large holes in the legal protection against trade union discrimination. First, legal protection against discrimination applied only where the employer took positive steps against the employee, secondly employers could discriminate by selectively offering inducements to employees willing to participate in the dismantling of collective bargaining arrangements. These defects meant that the UK was in breach of Article 1 of ILO Convention No. 98, which prohibits discrimination on grounds of trade union membership.[83] This view was later confirmed by recommendations made by the ILO Committee of Experts.[84] The Employment Relations Act 1999 has taken limited steps to remedy this breach.

2. Acts versus omissions

The acts/omissions issue has been addressed by replacing the phrase "action short of dismissal" with "subjecting an individual to a detriment" where this includes a "deliberate failure to act".[85] This has brought the law on discrimination on grounds of union membership or activities in line with protection offered in the Employment Rights Act 1996 for matters such as seeking to enforce the minimum wage or acting as an employee representative.[86] In these cases individuals are also protected against being "subjected to a detriment" which in each situation includes a "deliberate failure to act".

---

[82] [1995] IRLR 258 at 264, per Lord Bridge.

[83] As found by the Committee on Freedom of Association: Case No. 1730 (UK) *294th Report of the ILO Committee on Freedom of Association* (1994) para. 162 at para. 202. They noted "significant problems of compatibility with the principles of freedom of association".

[84] *Report of the Committee of Experts* (1996) ILC, 83rd Session, 224–5; referred to again in *Report of the Committee of Experts* (1998) ILC, 86th Session, 265.

[85] TULRCA 1992 s.146, as amended.

[86] ERA 1996 ss. 44–49.

3. Incentives to contract out of collective bargaining

The Government has refused to make a clear link between collective bargaining and trade union membership: "the right to belong to a trade union is separate from any rights to collective bargaining . . . The existing law makes that distinction and we wish to preserve it."[87] The "Ullswater amendment" has not even been repealed. The Minister argued (re-writing history) that to do so would "reintroduce uncertainty".[88]

New Labour's protection of collective bargaining is somewhat half-hearted. No substantive provisions have been introduced by the Employment Relations Act 1999, merely a power to bring in regulations at some unspecified time in the future.[89] These will permit the Minister to prohibit employers from subjecting any worker (not only trade union members) to a detriment for refusing to enter into a contract the terms of which do not include those collectively agreed. Not only do these provisions appear to break the link between trade union membership and collective bargaining, but they are also subject to a qualification which Wedderburn has described as "an own goal in extra time".[90] An Opposition amendment[91] was permitted to undermine any protective purpose of the new provisions, rendering them virtually useless from the outset.

The "Miller amendment"[92] deems that an employer does not subject a worker to a detriment by offering to pay higher wages or other benefits with a monetary value in return for giving up collective bargaining rights. The only limitations on this principle are that the contract which provides for higher pay must allow the worker to retain her union membership, and that the higher rates of pay "reasonably relate" to services provided by her under the contract.[93] This permits bribes or inducements to continue to be lawful.

The Government was cornered by this amendment, in particular because of statements made in the White Paper with regard to the effect of collectively agreed terms and conditions. There it noted that "[u]nder the existing law an employer and employee can agree different terms if they wish. Since the current law allows flexibility and works well, the Government sees no reason to change it".[94] This is

[87] HL Hansard, 7 June 1999, col. 1286, per Lord McIntosh.

[88] In response to an amendment by Lord Wedderburn to repeal TULRCA 1992 s.148(3): HL Hansard, 7 June 1999, col. 1286.

[89] ERelA 1999 s.17. Ministers explained that there had been "complications" in drafting a substantive clause which the Government was unable to deal with in the time available before the Bill completed its Parliamentary stages: HL Hansard, 26 July 1999, col. 1364.

[90] Lord Wedderburn, "Collective Bargaining or Legal Enactment: The 1999 Act and Union Recognition" (2000) 29 *ILJ* 1, 19.

[91] The Labour Party with its Commons majority could have sought to overturn this defeat inflicted on it in the Lords but chose to accept the principle of the amendment; subject to deletion of one para.

[92] Now ERelA 1999 s.17(4).

[93] ERelA 1999 s.17(4).

[94] *FAW*, Annex I, 42. Similarly, *FAW*, para. 4.20 says "[a]s under existing law, individual employees will continue to have the right, should they wish, to agree terms with their employer".

a view which fails to valorise the normative aspect of collective bargaining. It does not treat a collective agreement as an instrument which provides minimum guarantees, but sees it simply as one of several methods of setting the terms in an employment contract.

Stephen Byers MP persisted with this view in seeking to explain why the Government was prepared to accept the principle of the opposition amendment. On the one hand, "employers should remain free to offer more pay or to improve benefits to employees; even though there may be a collective agreement in place". On the other, individuals should not be penalised "because they choose to belong to a trade union, and to be part of a collective agreement".[95] He did not see these positions as contradictory. As McCarthy points out, this view fails to take into account existing practice in British collective bargaining. He argues that individual derogation is not practised in the overwhelming majority of enterprises where collective agreements apply. In such enterprises individualised terms, where they exist, generally apply to those matters *not* regulated by the collective agreement.[96] It is contrary to the British practice to have collectively agreed and individualised terms relating to the same matters operating in parallel in the same enterprise. Thus employers who are offering alternative "individualised" terms, are, contrary to the position of Stephen Byers, challenging the position of collective bargaining.

The legislative "solution" which New Labour has reached does not inspire great confidence for the future of collective bargaining, and the statutory union recognition procedure must be seen in this light.[97] Whilst the rights of trade union members *qua* individuals are to be protected, this does not extend to collective bargaining.[98] This has in effect been enshrined in legislation through the "Miller amendment". New Labour appears to have accepted the view of the courts, prioritising individual over collective rights.[99] If any regulations are adopted under these provisions, and at the time of writing the Government has not indicated an intention to bring forward such regulations, it is unlikely that they will depart from this position. Whether this will be accepted internationally as guaranteeing freedom of association in the UK is doubtful.[100]

---

[95] HC Hansard, 21 July 1999, col. 1270, per Mr Byers.

[96] Lord McCarthy, *Fairness At Work and Trade Union Recognition: Past Comparisons and Future Problems* (London: Institute of Employment Rights, 1999), 42.

[97] See further below Chap. 4 at 107.

[98] The recognition procedure makes this clear. Statutory recognition depends on an aggregate of individual preferences. See above Chap. 1 and in detail below Chap. 4.

[99] As in *Wilson/Palmer*, n.79 above, and *Powley* v. *ACAS* [1977] IRLR 190 at 195, where Browne-Wilkinson J described the statutory procedure for promoting collective bargaining under the EPA 1975 as the "compulsory acquisition of an individual's right to regulate his working life"; a right which is "not to be lost . . . except in strict accordance with the statutory procedure".

[100] Following the enactment of the Employment Relations Act 1999 the ILO Committee of Experts has again called upon the Government to review the operation of TULRCA 1992 s.148(3), noting that "such a provision could be considered as tantamount to condoning anti-union discrimination, and the provisions of the Employment Relations Act do not redress this situation": (2000) *Report of the ILO Committee of Experts* ILC, 88th Session.

E. PROTECTION FOR WORKERS IN THE RECOGNITION PROCESS

The limits of New Labour's individual protection model can be further illustrated by consideration of its legislative settlement with regard to union recognition which leaves trade union members vulnerable. In *Fairness at Work*, the Government made the commitment that employees campaigning for or against recognition would be protected.[101] Under Schedule A1 of TULRCA 1992, a worker has the right not to be subjected to any detriment by any act, or any failure to act, by his employer if the act or failure takes place because that worker has taken certain action indicating his support or desire to secure trade union recognition.[102]

There are three problems associated with these "flanking" measures which seek to support the recognition process. First, the scope of the protection appears to be inadequate to prevent anti-union employers creating a chilling atmosphere at work. There is no clear indication that it extends, as it should, to preliminary recruitment activities by trade unionists necessary to reach the 10 per cent membership threshold required for the CAC even to consider a recognition claim. If a worker engaged in such recruitment activities is subjected to threats or dismissed by her employer, then her legal protection as created by the Act depends upon the courts' construction of whether her acts were "with view to obtaining recognition of a union". The risk is that the recruitment activities will be interpreted as too remote from the recognition process to qualify for this protection.

Secondly, unlike in other instances where workers are protected against detriment or dismissal by their employer, the right in this instance has been hedged with the qualification that the worker's conduct must not be "unreasonable". This is an improvement on an earlier version of the Bill, which stated that if workers had breached their employment contract they could not claim protection,[103] but it nevertheless may substantially limit the extent of protection provided, depending on the courts' interpretation of this provision. There are no guidelines on what constitutes "unreasonable" behaviour, nor any indication whether this could also apply to activities undertaken outside working hours, for example, holding demonstrations, leafleting fellow workers, etc.[104] The

---

[101] *FAW*, para. 4.19.

[102] These are set out in TULRCA 1992 Sched. A1 para. 156(2) and para. 161(2).

[103] See HL Hansard, 7 June 1999, cols. 1262 and 1265–1267; HL Hansard, 8 July 1999, col. 1072; HC Hansard, 26 July 1999, cols. 37–38.

[104] Given existing case law on unfair dismissal, it cannot be assumed that employers will not argue that behaviour outside working hours is "unreasonable", especially if the employer sees its economic interests as threatened by trade union presence. Employees (not workers) may well be better off using the existing protections of TULRCA 1992 ss.146 and 152 which make it clear that trade union activities outside working hours are protected.

Code of Practice issued by the Secretary of State with regard to balloting arrangements does not offer any guidance on this matter.[105]

Given these shortcomings with the new provisions, employees may prefer to rely on their existing protection against detriment and dismissal on grounds of their trade union membership and activities.[106] However those provisions share a further problem in common with those introduced in Schedule A1. They rely upon proof of causality in each individual case. This is the third structural weakness. As a result they fail to offer protection against collective acts of victimisation perpetrated by employers. This can be illustrated by the experience of the dismissed employees in *Therm A Stor* v. *Atkins*.[107] In that case, the employer responded to a trade union's request for recognition by dismissing 20 employees. The statutory protection against dismissal on grounds of trade union membership proved to be of no avail. Whilst the Court of Appeal accepted that the reason for the dismissal was the request for trade union recognition, it considered that the employees had not been dismissed by reason of their individual membership or activities. They were dismissed by reason of the trade union's actions, not of anything they "had personally done or proposed to do".[108] Although the Court expressed sympathy for the plight of the employees, it was loathe to apply the "mischief rule" to ensure their protection.

These limitations on the individual protection model illustrate New Labour's apparent reluctance to strengthen collective rights and the position of trade unions through the statutory recognition procedure. The "flanking" rights for individuals provide at best only the minimum of support.

F. RIGHTS OF STRIKING EMPLOYEES TO PROTECTION FROM UNFAIR DISMISSAL

For reasons of what Ewing describes as the "Donovan catechism"[109] (the desire to avoid courts deciding on the merits of industrial disputes) unfair dismissal law in Britain has since its inception in principle excluded from its scope employees dismissed in the course of industrial action.[110] However worthy this aim of keeping the merits of industrial disputes away from courts, it has never justified this strange result that striking employees forfeit unfair dismissal protection. Other solutions are conceivable, for example, making dismissals in the course of industrial action automatically unfair. However the settlement of the 1970s set up the position which permitted tribunals jurisdiction to consider unfair dismissal complaints of striking employees only where it was shown that

---

[105] *Code of Practice: Access to Workers During Recognition and Derecognition Ballots.* It has a very limited ambit: para. 8.

[106] TULRCA 1992 ss.146 and 152.

[107] [1983] IRLR 78 (CA).

[108] *Ibid.* at 80, per Donaldson MR.

[109] Ewing, n.51 above, 291.

[110] The exact wording of this exclusion varied under the different formulations of the 1970s legislation.

the employer had selectively dismissed or re-engaged employees taking part in industrial action.[111] This provision was aimed at restricting the ability of employers to pick off individual strikers and make an example of them. Various qualifications to this principle were added by the Conservatives as part of their anti-trade union and anti-strike crusade, deliberately making the position of employees who engaged in industrial action even more vulnerable.

New Labour acknowledged that this position was in breach of the UK's international law obligations.[112] The Employment Relations Act 1999 therefore introduced a new and limited right for striking employees not to be dismissed.[113] It takes as its starting point the regime as bequeathed by the Conservatives and carves out of it a small niche of protection for certain employees.[114] To appreciate its scope and implications we must first understand the contours of the industrial action landscape in 1997.

1. Participation in industrial action after the Tory years

The Conservatives made two sets of changes to the basic compromise between strikes and the law on unfair dismissal which had been crafted in the 1970s. First, they made it much easier for employers selectively to dismiss or re-engage employees without running the risk that the industrial tribunal would have jurisdiction to hear any complaints of unfair dismissal. This was achieved through two measures. For the purposes of determining whether the dismissal of a striking employee was selective, the pool of relevant employees was redefined. Only those employees still taking part in the industrial action at the date of the complainant's dismissal were considered.[115] This meant that an employer faced with a strike which was dragging on could invite the employees to return to work on a particular date. All those who failed to turn up for work because they were still on strike could then be sacked without the employer having to worry about any potential unfair dismissal claims. In addition, a three-month limit was imposed on the rule against selective re-engagement.[116] As a result employers who wished to re-engage selectively had only to wait three months from the date of an employee's dismissal before they could re-hire with impunity. This set of measures made it much easier for employers to use a strike as an opportunity to shed some labour cheaply or to get rid of employees perceived to be "troublemakers" without being bothered by an unfair dismissal claim.

---

[111] For the law immediately prior to the Conservative amendments, see EPCA 1978 s.62.

[112] HC Standing Committee E, 9 Mar. 1999, col. 288.

[113] ERelA 1999 s.16 and Sched. 5.

[114] The protection is only for "employees" despite New Labour's enthusiasm to extend other individual employment rights, for example the right to be accompanied, to "workers".

[115] EA 1982 s.9(3).

[116] EA 1982 s.9(2).

The second set of measures arose out of the Conservatives' concern that their measures to curb strikes were not working properly. Their legislative changes of the early 1980s made it more difficult and onerous for trade unions to call strikes. Union leaders were therefore in some circumstances unwilling or unable to call strike action without running the risk of crippling tort actions or penalties for contempt of court. Union members nevertheless on occasion took (successful) strike action which did not have support from union leaders.[117] The Government decided in 1989 that further action was necessary in order to discourage this.[118] Employees who engaged in unofficial strike action were to have no legal protection against dismissal. Not only were they to be regarded at common law to have breached (or possibly to have given notice to terminate) their contracts, but were also to be denied the merest possibility of an unfair dismissal claim. As a result the paper-thin unfair dismissal protection which applied to industrial action dismissals was redefined to apply to official industrial action only.[119]

In principle New Labour does not resile from this position. It accepts that striking employees engaged in unofficial action should have no unfair dismissal protection.[120] In *Fairness at Work* it was, however, said to be illogical that where the employer sacked some, but not all, striking employees the tribunal could have jurisdiction, whereas if all employees were sacked there was no jurisdiction.[121] Nevertheless, the Government was content to leave in place the provisions relating to selective dismissal and re-engagement of employees who participate in official industrial action. Its key contribution was to create a third category of striking employees who can receive additional protection from unfair dismissal, albeit subject to many detailed and difficult conditions.

2. Circumscribed New Labour protection

New Labour has created a right with many limitations.[122] Where all the elements are satisfied, the dismissal is automatically unfair.[123] There are three main qualifications. First, it applies only where the industrial action is

---

[117] See in general P. Davies and M. Freedland, *Labour Legislation and Public Policy* (Oxford: Clarendon, 1993) 511–19; B. Simpson, "The Summer of Discontent and the Law" (1989) 18 *ILJ* 234.

[118] *Unofficial Action and the Law*, Cm 821 (London: HMSO, 1989).

[119] EA 1990 s.9.

[120] TULRCA 1992 s.237.

[121] *FAW*, para. 4.22, repeated by Ministers, e.g., Ian McCartney in HC Standing Committee E, 9 Mar. 1999, col. 325.

[122] TULRCA 1992 s.238A. No qualification period or upper age limit applies to this right: TULRCA 1992 s.239(1). The wording on the strike ballot paper has been amended accordingly: TULRCA 1992 s.229(4). The new right departs somewhat from the proposal made in *Fairness at Work*, paras. 4.21–4.23, which neither explicitly proposed that dismissals of striking workers should be treated as *automatically* unfair, nor mentioned an arbitrary eight week threshold.

[123] If an employee's claim under TULRCA 1992 s.238A fails, then her remaining entitlement to unfair dismissal protection requires her, subject to normal qualification rules, to persuade the tribunal that it has jurisdiction to hear her case under TULRCA 1992 s.238.

"protected".[124] This is a narrower category than "official".[125] For industrial action to be "protected", the trade union must not only have called or endorsed the action in question but must have complied with all the balloting and notice requirements so that it falls within the scope of the statutory immunity.[126] Secondly, and probably the most difficult aspect of the new right is that it applies only where it can be shown *that the reason* for dismissal was participation in protected industrial action.[127] In practice this causality is likely to be very difficult to show with the burden of proof *de facto* falling upon the employee.[128] Well-advised employers are likely to have good arguments up their sleeves to deny the causality between a dismissal and the employee's participation in industrial action. For example, it is not clear that even if these provisions had been in place they would have presented much of a threat to Rupert Murdoch in his dispute with the print unions in the 1980s. News International would have doubtless argued that its employees were sacked for refusing to adapt to new technology or for economic reasons. Thirdly, where the dismissal takes place more than eight weeks after the employee began to take industrial action (and the employee had not returned to work within those first eight weeks), the fairness of the dismissal will depend upon whether the employer took reasonable procedural steps to resolve the dispute.[129] In determining this question the tribunal is not to have regard to the substantive merits of the dispute,[130] but to consider the steps taken *both by the employer and the trade union* to bring the dispute to an end, such as negotiation, conciliation and mediation.[131] For employers the effect of this eight-week time limit means that, as long as they take reasonable steps to end the dispute, they know that once it has expired they will be able to dismiss all the employees[132] and hire an alternative workforce.

3. Implications for partnership

It is questionable how far these new provisions strengthen freedom of association. Contrary to opposition fears,[133] they do not make lawful industrial action

---

[124] TULRCA 1992 s.238A(1).

[125] Industrial action can be deemed to be official for the purposes of unfair dismissal protection. This depends upon the operation of TULRCA 1992 s.237(2)–(4) read together with TULRCA 1992 ss.20(2)–(4) and 21.

[126] TULRCA 1992 s.219.

[127] TULRCA 1992 s.238A(2)(a).

[128] See *Smith* v. *Hayle Town Council* [1978] IRLR 413 (CA). An amendment by Lord Wedderburn to reverse the burden of proof was rejected: HL Hansard. 16 June 1999. cols. 351–354.

[129] TULRCA 1992 s.238A(5) and (6).

[130] TULRCA 1992 s.238A(7).

[131] TULRCA 1992 s.238A(6). Even provisions of non-binding, unenforceable collective agreements are deemed relevant.

[132] TULRCA 1992 s.238 continues to apply, restricting the ability of employers to dismiss selectively.

[133] E.g., Tim Boswell MP argued the Government was going too far and sought to invoke the spectre of the 1970s, suggesting it was a return to the days when the shop steward "red Robbo ran British Leyland into almost terminal decline": HC Standing Committee E, 9 Mar. 1999, col. 293.

much easier.[134] Rather they increase the pressure on trade unions not to jeopardise the jobs of their members. This demands that they both ballot their members and notify employers correctly in order to ensure that the action is "protected". Furthermore the new measures require trade unions to consider carefully whether they are justified in resorting to industrial action in the light of existing collective agreements and employer attempts to settle the dispute by alternative means. If, in the view of a tribunal, they misjudge this situation, then in any dispute which lasts more than eight weeks their members may well feel let down when their claims for unfair dismissal are rejected. It can be argued that this is an example of "rights and responsibilities" at play.[135] Limited employee rights are heavily dependent on trade union responsibility. Paradoxically this ostensible increase in employee rights may encourage trade unions to become more rather than less cautious in their dealings with employers.

This limited scope of New Labour's intervention with regard to striking employees can perhaps best be explained in the context of its partnership model of employee relations. Given its desire to replace conflict with partnership, strikes are seen as somewhat anachronistic and not a legitimate measure to be used in the conduct of industrial relations. They are evidence that partnership has not fully taken hold of an enterprise, that workers wish to demonstrate their collective solidarity and their disagreement with management. This is contrary to the New Labour ethic and is too reminiscent of 1970s industrial relations. The Government continues to accept the common law position which categorises the strike as a fundamental breach of contract, whereby the employer can treat the contract as repudiated. Therefore it has taken only the smallest of steps to improve the position of striking employees in line with its international obligations. As a result employees continue to remain vulnerable when taking industrial action.[136] The very slim protection offered by the unfair dismissal remedy is in practice limited to the payment of compensation. In the context of strike dismissals, the chances of obtaining re-instatement or re-engagement are likely to be extremely low,[137] with employers arguing that it is not practical to take the employee back, because the strike has ruined any notion of mutual trust and confidence. Even under New Labour, a strike has no legitimate home within the legal order.

G. CONCLUSION

The remainder of this book will focus on the measures taken in the Employment Relations Act 1999 which directly relate to the collective rights of workers. As a

---

[134] The minor relaxations of Conservative laws in this respect are discussed below: see Chap. 5.

[135] See above Chap. 1 at 18–19.

[136] Emphasised by J. Elgar and B. Simpson, "The Impact of the Law on Industrial Disputes of the 1980s" in D. Metcalf and S. Milner (eds.), *New Perspectives on Industrial Disputes* (London: Routledge, 1993), 106.

[137] These remedies are subject to procedural restrictions whilst the strike is still underway: TULRCA 1992 s.239(4).

preliminary to this exercise, this chapter has considered the extent to which New Labour has provided support for collective rights through a model of individual protection.

The conclusion we have come to is disappointing. New Labour is *prima facie* well disposed to individual rights. The White Paper's chapter on "collective rights" begins with this very sentiment: "individual rights provide the essential underpinning of effective working relationships".[138] This may appear to suggest that trade unions will be supported and reinforced by strong rights for their members. This is not the case. Whatever the scope of New Labour's attraction to individual rights may be in other respects, with regard to its support for freedom of association it remains essentially cautious, if not ambivalent.

Its most innovative measure, the right to be accompanied in grievance and disciplinary proceedings, gives no preference to trade union modes of representation. Thankfully it acknowledges the existence of trade unions, but it treats them as no more important than any other channel for assisting individual workers. The onus is firmly placed on trade unions to develop their attractiveness to workers, such that individuals will as a matter of course want to rely upon union assistance. The framework provisions on blacklisting offer even less support to trade unions as collective organisations. Whilst they reduce the potential negative consequences of trade union membership, they do nothing however to make trade union membership more attractive.

The measures on discrimination against trade union members fail to take into account the collective dimension to freedom of association, to the extent that this encompasses collective bargaining. The mess of ERelA 1999 section 17 unmasks the Government's true position. Individual "choice" to opt out of collective bargaining has been preserved, at whatever cost to trade unions as collective organisations. This lack of support for collective organisation is also clear from the new protection against unfair dismissal for striking employees. When taken together with the Government's other reforms to the law on industrial action (discussed in Chapter 5) it seems that the strike has not been enhanced as an acceptable measure to be taken (or be threatened) in the scope of industrial disputes. The new provisions correct what was seen as an "anomaly" from the point of view of the individual employee involved in industrial action. They are a long way removed from creating a legal framework in which workers can develop a counterweight to the economic power of employers.[139]

Whilst the limited nature of the Government's measures can to a certain extent be explained by their desire to ensure that there is "no going back" to the industrial relations of the 1970s and their assessment of the contemporary labour market, it does raise profound questions about their vision of labour law in Britain. From the White Paper it is clear that "partnership" between employers and workers is the basis on which the Government hopes workplace rela-

---

[138] *FAW*, para. 4.1.
[139] See above Chap. 1, the case for collective rights, at 2–4.

tions in the future will be structured. The evidence from the individual rights measures relating to freedom of association creates no strong signal that trade unions are expected to play a leading role in developing this "partnership". There has been no paradigm shift in the legal position of trade union members. What future this leaves for trade unions as collective organisations will be explored in the chapters which follow.

3

Trade Union Autonomy

A. INTRODUCTION

T HE WHITE PAPER on *Fairness at Work* indicated that New Labour regards trade unions as potentially useful intermediaries in the "partnership" between employer and worker. To be effective intermediaries, trade unions are expected to be responsive to the interests and needs of their members. This requires the preservation of trade union independence from control by anyone other than these members. It is therefore not surprising that the Employment Relations Act 1999 continues the established practice of conferring additional entitlements on "independent" trade unions. What is of greater interest is the failure to repeal the extensive controls on trade union governance imposed by Conservative Governments between 1979 and 1997.

The legacy of Conservative "step by step" industrial relations policy[1] can be found in TULRCA 1992, which places detailed restrictions on the financial management of trade unions, requires that various decisions be taken by the trade union membership according to formal balloting procedures, and seeks to protect the interests of the individual worker over and above the collectivity. The constraints that such measures place on the efficacy of trade union governance do not appear to concern New Labour to any great extent. *Fairness at Work* speaks of the importance of avoiding "bureaucracy and unnecessary burdens on business",[2] but is not so wary of bureaucratic constraints on the operation of trade unions. Instead, the Government has endorsed the employment legislation of the 1980s and 1990s which was aimed at increasing individual choice and "democratic accountability" in trade unions.[3] New Labour will not protect "poorly run trade unions".[4] While the Employment Relations Act makes certain alterations to provisions in TULRCA 1992 which regulate trade union activity, these are not as substantial as the trade union movement might have hoped.[5] Moreover, those reforms which have been made are justified in terms of the

---

[1] R. Taylor, *The Trade Union Question in British Politics: Government and Unions since 1945* (Oxford: Blackwell, 1993), 269.

[2] *FAW*, para. 1.13.

[3] The White Paper went so far as to say that these measures "helped to improve employment relations": see *FAW*, para. 2.15.

[4] *FAW*, para. 4.31.

[5] See B. Crow and J. Hendy, *Reclaim Our Rights: Repeal the Anti-Union Laws* (London: Reclaim Our Rights Campaign, 1999), 12–13, and *Employment Rights: Building on Fairness at Work* (London: Institute of Employment Rights, 2000), 13–14, paras. 10.7–10.8. Both of these publications were sponsored by numerous trade unions.

importance of reducing costs and inconvenience to business, as opposed to any desire to enhance trade union autonomy.[6]

The 1999 Act does reform the mechanisms through which "democratic" rights of members may be enforced against a trade union. The office of the Commissioner for the Rights of Trade Union Members (CRTUM) has been abolished, as has its counterpart, the Commissioner for the Protection Against Unlawful Industrial Action (CPAUIA).[7] In their place, a new role has been given to the Certification Officer,[8] providing an alternative to intervention by the courts. While these measures may have some benefits for trade union autonomy, it is evident that the major motivation for these legislative changes was the saving of costs to the state. By and large, legislative controls on trade union governance are retained, albeit in a slightly different form, so as to ensure that trade unions act responsibly.

B. INDEPENDENCE OF TRADE UNIONS UNDER INTERNATIONAL AND DOMESTIC LAW

The effective collective representation of workers' interests relies upon the independence of trade unions from the state and employers. This is a principle recognised internationally.

Article 3(1) of ILO Convention No. 87 provides that workers' organisations "shall have the right to draw up their constitutions and rules, to elect their representatives in full freedom, to organize their administration and activities and to formulate their programmes". Under Article 3(2) public authorities are to "refrain from any interference which would restrict this right or impede the lawful exercise thereof".[9] Article 5 of the Council of Europe's European Social Charter requires that Contracting Parties undertake that national law shall not be such as to impair, or be applied so as to impair, the freedom of workers to form organisations for the protection of their economic and social interests.[10] Similar provision for trade union autonomy is made under Article 11 of the European Community Charter of the Fundamental Social Rights of Workers 1989.

The importance of trade union independence is also recognised expressly in domestic legislation. Under TULRCA 1992, an "independent trade union" means a trade union which:

---

[6] See below this Chap. at 53–4 and 56–8.

[7] ERelA 1999 s. 28. The role of CPAUIA was bound up with enforcement of TULRCA 1992 s.235A, but as we shall see below this chap. at 57, the latter provision survives.

[8] ERelA 1999 s. 29.

[9] See for further elaboration on these principles ILO, *Digest of Decisions and Principles of the Freedom of Association Committee of the Governing Body of the ILO (ILO Digest)* (4th edn., Geneva: International Labour Office, 1996), chs. 5–8.

[10] See, for further elaboration on these principles within the Council of Europe, L. Samuel, *Fundamental Social Rights: Case Law of the European Social Charter* (Strasbourg: Council of Europe Publishing, 1997).

(a) is not under the domination or control of an employer or group of employers or of one or more employers' associations, and

(b) is not liable to interference by an employer or any such group or association (arising out of the provision of financial or material support or by any other means whatsoever) tending towards such control.[11]

An application for a certificate of independence can be made by the trade union to the Certification Officer (CO). The CO will take a variety of factors into account in making the decision whether to issue such a certificate. These include the union's financial arrangements and other means of support, the history of the union's development, the union's membership base, the union's organisation and structure and its collective bargaining record.[12]

In 1993, the EAT upheld a decision of the CO not to grant a certificate of independence to the Staff Association at Government Communication Headquarters (GCHQ), where the Government had refused to allow workers to be members of the Council of Civil Service Unions (CCSU) or any other union.[13] Shortly after the 1997 election, the right to trade union membership was restored to workers at GCHQ, indicating that the Blair Government was more inclined than its predecessor to recognise how crucial trade union independence is to freedom of association.[14]

When a trade union receives a certificate of independence, certain entitlements are conferred both on the organisation and its members. These include protection from discrimination by an employer,[15] rights to information for purposes of collective bargaining where the trade union is recognised by the employer,[16] and rights to time off for trade union officials.[17] Labour has recently added to these entitlements. In the event of collective redundancy or the transfer of an undertaking, new regulations require that recognised independent trade unions have priority as regards rights to information and consultation.[18] The new Schedule A1 to TULRCA 1992 makes an application for statutory recognition contingent on trade union independence,[19] and special provision is made for derecognition where a recognised union is not independent.[20]

---

[11] TULRCA 1992 s. 5.

[12] *Blue Circle Staff Association* v. CO [1977] IRLR 20 (EAT); and *Squibb UK Staff Association* v. CO [1979] IRLR 75 (CA). For a more detailed discussion of the CO's application of these tests see C. Barrow, *Industrial Relations Law* (London: Cavendish Press, 1997), 36–9; and N. Humphreys, *Trade Union Law* (London: Blackstone, 1999), 29–34.

[13] *GCHQ* v. CO [1993] IRLR 260 (EAT).

[14] This was achieved just two weeks after gaining office and consolidated by a legally binding agreement on 3 Oct. 1997. See for the ILO's satisfaction at this outcome, (1999) *Report of the ILO Committee of Experts on the Application of Conventions and Recommendations* ILC, 87th Session, 289.

[15] TULRCA 1992 ss. 146 and 152.

[16] TULRCA 1992 s. 181.

[17] TULRCA 1992 ss. 168 and 170.

[18] Collective Redundancies and Transfer of Undertakings (Protection of Employment) (Amendment) Regs. 1999, SI 1999/1925.

[19] TULRCA 1992, Sched. A1 para. 6.

[20] TULRCA 1992, Sched. A1 Part VI.

C. DEMOCRATIC PROCEDURES WITHIN TRADE UNIONS

While trade union independence has been regarded as the hallmark of success-ful industrial relations, it has not always been considered sufficient to secure effective trade union representation of members' interests. It has been argued that trade unions must not only be independent, but also "democratic", reflect-ing the choices of their individual members.

Arguably, union democracy can be achieved through "trade union rules", which establish the basic constitution of the workers' organisation and the man-ner in which decisions are taken within the organisation. At common law, democratic control "is based on two principles—the right of courts to interpret the rule book—(the 'contract' between the member and his union)—and natural justice".[21] It was on the basis of noncompliance with trade union rules that courts acted to restrain NUM support for industrial action during the miners' strike.[22] However, from time to time, arguments have been made for more strin-gent legislative controls to ensure that unions remain representative and accountable.

1. Historical background

As early as 1871, statutory requirements as to the subject matter of trade union rules were imposed.[23] In 1968, the Donovan Commission recommended that trade union rules be subject to further controls.[24] External regulation was resisted by the TUC, which instead formulated recommendations for trade union rules, which it expected its members to observe. This attempt at self-reg-ulation has been described as "disappointing",[25] but was no more so than the experiment of regulation through registration under the Industrial Relations Act 1971.[26] The fuel for further regulation was trade union activism in the late 1970s.[27] Union leaders were accused of being "out of touch" with their mem-

---

[21] R. Kidner, "The Individual and the Collective Interest in Trade Union Law" (1976) 5 *ILJ* 90.

[22] *Taylor* v. *NUM (Derbyshire)* [1984] IRLR 440. See also K.D. Ewing, "The Strike, Courts and Rule Books" (1985) 14 *ILJ* 160.

[23] This legislation required that there be rules on the subject of: the union's objectives; members' rights to benefits; forfeitures and fines; appointment and removal of trustees, a treasurer, other offi-cers and a management committee; audit of accounts and provision for inspection of the books of account and the membership list. See Lord Wedderburn, *Labour Law and Freedom: Further Essays in Labour Law* (London: Lawrence and Wishart, 1995), 196.

[24] *Royal Commission on Trade Union and Employers' Associations 1965–1968 (Donovan Commission Report)*, Cmnd 3623 (London: HMSO, 1968), chap. XI; see also P. Elias and K. Ewing, *Trade Union Democracy, Members' Rights and the Law* (London: Mansell, 1987), 279–80.

[25] Elias and Ewing, n.24 above, 280–5.

[26] Wedderburn, n.23 above, 196–7. See also below Chap. 4 at 65–7.

[27] See for a much more detailed discussion of these causal factors P. Davies and M. Freedland, *Labour Legislation and Public Policy* (Oxford: Clarendon Press, 1993), 443.

bership. Trade unions were to be "given back" to rank and file members. Democracy was to be restored to trade union governance by legislative means.[28]

The series of statutory reforms which followed relied on a particular conception of democracy. In 1979, Kahn-Freund had observed how the decentralised representation of trade union members through the British shop steward provided democratic participation:

> The fact remains that direct democracy is much stronger in the living constitution of the British trade unions than in the British constitution . . .[29]

He recognised both the benefits and the potential dangers associated with this form of democracy.[30] Conservative governments from 1980 onwards were concerned less with direct representation on the shop floor and more with majority voting through special balloting procedures and protection of the rights of the individual. Theirs was a dual-faceted but limited model of democratic participation.

From 1980–93, successive Conservative governments enacted a series of industrial relations statutes which progressively imposed greater restrictions on trade union administration.[31] Detailed requirements for secret balloting were introduced in respect of industrial action,[32] the election of trade union executives[33] and management of political funds.[34] The individual interests of workers were protected by such measures as restricting the scope for disciplinary measures taken by unions against their members,[35] giving workers the right to join the union of their choice,[36] instituting a three-yearly re-authorisation for the "check off" system for deduction of trade union dues[37] and abolition of the closed shop.[38] In 1996, John Major's Government stated its intention to add to these restrictions on administration of trade union affairs.[39]

---

[28] *Trade Union Immunities*, Cmnd 8128 (London: HMSO, 1981), para. 245; *Democracy in Trade Unions*, Cmnd 8778 (London: HMSO, 1983), para. 1; S. Fredman, "The New Rights: Labour Law and Ideology in the Thatcher Years" (1992) 12 *OJLS* 24 at 25.

[29] O. Kahn-Freund, *Labour Relations: Heritage and Adjustment* (Oxford: OUP, 1979), 17.

[30] *Ibid.*, at 26.

[31] See the Employment Act 1980, the Employment Act 1982, the Trade Union Act 1984, the Employment Act 1988, the Employment Act 1989, the Employment Act 1990 and the Trade Union Reform and Employment Rights Act 1993.

[32] TULRCA 1992, ss. 226–235C.

[33] TULRCA 1992 ss. 46–59.

[34] The Trade Union Act 1984, Part III, elaborated on the Trade Union Act 1913, requiring that unions periodically ballot their members. The 1984 Act redefined and thereby expanded the application of the term "political objects" and limited the potential sources of trade union funding. The modern provisions are to be found in TULRCA 1992, Part I, Chap. VI, Application of Funds for Political Objects. See Elias and Ewing, n.24 above, at 170–3.

[35] TULRCA 1992 ss. 64–68A.

[36] TULRCA 1992 ss. 174–177, which had severe implications for the application of the TUC "Bridlington Principles"; see B. Simpson, "Individualism versus Collectivism: An Evaluation of Section 14 of the Trade Union Reform and Employment Rights Act 1993" (1993) 22 *ILJ* 181.

[37] TULRCA 1992 s. 68 (now partially repealed by SI 1998/1529).

[38] The pre-entry closed shop is prohibited by TULRCA 1992 s. 137 and the post-entry by TULRCA 1992 s. 152 and s. 146.

[39] *Industrial Action and Trade Unions*, Cm 3470 (London: HMSO, 1996), 10–12 and 17–19.

2. International labour standards

These legislative reforms were subjected to scrutiny within the ILO and Council of Europe. State regulation of trade union administration is acceptable to the ILO where legislation is aimed at "ensuring respect for democratic rules within the trade union movement" or is directed at the prevention of fraud.[40] In 1989, the ILO Committee of Experts found that British legislation regulating election of trade union officials, strike ballots and political expenditure did not constitute a violation of freedom of association under Article 3 of Convention No. 87.[41] An identical view was taken within the Council of Europe, under the European Social Charter.[42] These supervisory bodies did, however, express concern at the limitations placed on the capacity of trade unions to discipline their members for failure to take lawful industrial action.[43] What the Conservatives failed to appreciate was that there are boundaries to the acceptable range of statutory intervention, however well-motivated such intervention may be.

While accepting the utility of an overall framework promoting democratic procedures, supervisory bodies within the ILO and Council of Europe are wary of detailed regulation which limits the efficacy of trade union activities. In 1995 the ILO Committee of Experts noted its concern that, since its last substantive examination of the application of Convention No. 87, the UK Government had "adopted yet more detailed regulations concerning the internal functioning of workers' organizations".[44] The Committee warned that "the continuing regulation of workers' organizations may reach a point where the cumulative effect of such regulation, by virtue of its detail, complexity and extent, nevertheless constitutes an interference in the rights of such organizations under Article 3 of the Convention".[45] The Committee of Independent Experts, scrutinising compliance with the European Social Charter, also expressed their alarm at the three-yearly authorisation requirement for the "check off" system and at the fact that trade unions are no longer allowed to choose their own members.[46] Both Council of Europe and ILO supervisory organs have reiterated their concerns

---

[40] *ILO Digest*, n.9 above, paras. 425 and 441–4; *ILO General Survey of the Committee of Experts on Freedom of Association and Collective Bargaining* (Geneva: International Labour Office, 1994), para. 135.

[41] (1989) *Report of the Committee of Experts on the Application of Conventions and Recommendations*, ILC, 76th Session, 235–44. See K. Ewing, *Britain and the ILO* (2nd edn., London: Institute of Employment Rights, 1994), 38–43.

[42] (1989) *Conclusions X–1* (UK), 68.

[43] (1989) *Report of the ILO Committee of Experts on the Application of Conventions and Recommendations*, ILC, 76th Session, 235–44 and (1993) *Conclusions XII–1* (UK), 115.

[44] (1995) *Report of the ILO Committee of Experts on the Application of Conventions and Recommendations,* ILC, 82nd Session, 200.

[45] *Ibid.*, 200–1; see for further confirmation of this view, (1997) *Report of the ILO Committee of Experts on the Application of Conventions and Recommendations*, ILC, 85th Session, 204.

[46] (1998) *Conclusions XIV–1* (UK), 796–7.

relating to legislation which restricts trade unions' ability to discipline their members.[47]

This criticism from international sources can be understood by taking a broader view of the concept of trade union "democracy". Conservative Governments from 1980 onwards relied on a narrow conception of democracy, based on protection of individual rights and majority voting through elaborate, formal procedures.[48] However, if one endorses the view that "democracy means participation", trade unions can be seen as an important vehicle through which working people can participate in decision-making both within the enterprise in which they are employed and within society at large.[49] Any detailed, formal, technical rules imposed on a trade union by an external public authority, which create unwarranted bureaucracy and paperwork, impede trade unions' ability to serve this function and should be subject to suspicion. "The functional needs of the union and of its members do not necessarily fit *a priori* political concepts".[50] Protection of individual minority rights is essential to democratic governance of a nation state and trade unions must of course respond to the concerns of workers who, for reasons of race, ethnicity, gender and sexuality, fall outside the conventional stereotype of the old trade union member.[51] Nevertheless, the restrictions which Conservatives sought to impose went further, as they were designed to allow individual independent choices to undermine the collective solidarity and thereby the very bargaining power of the majority.[52]

3. The refusal to return to self-regulation

Fairness at Work did not signal a retreat from the undiscriminating application of "democratic" constraints on trade union governance. Instead, it advocated the moderation of their effect in two instances. First, the White Paper regarded as "damaging" the requirement introduced by Conservatives that employees re-authorise deductions from their pay for trade union subscriptions every three years.[53] Secondly, the law and Code of Practice on industrial action ballots and notice were said to be "unnecessarily complex and rigid" and in need of

---

[47] (1999) *Report of the ILO Committee of Experts on the Application of Conventions and Recommendations*, ILC, 87th Session, 290–1; and (1998) *Conclusions XIV–1* (UK), 796–7.[48] See Fredman, n.28 above, and M. Forde, "Citizenship and Democracy in Industrial Relations: An Agenda for the 1990s?" (1992) 55 *MLR* 241.

[49] B. Hepple, 'The Role of Trade Unions in a Democratic Society' (1990) 11 *ILJ (South Africa)* 645 at 646; and Forde, n.48 above, at 252. See also above Chap. 1 at 2–4.

[50] Wedderburn, n.23 above, at 181.

[51] See A. Morris, "Workers First, Women Second? Trade Unions and the Equality Agenda" in A. Morris and T. O'Donnell (eds.), *Feminist Perspectives on Employment Law* (London: Cavendish, 1999).

[52] Indeed, this may undermine "democracy". See H. Clegg, *The Changing System of Industrial Relations in Great Britain* (Oxford: Basil Blackwell, 1979), 210.

[53] *FAW*, para. 4.9.

reform.[54] However, the justification given for reform of these provisions was not the limitations they place on trade unions, but rather that they constituted a "burden on business", were "damaging to business efficacy" and were "not popular with employers".[55] New Labour took care to phrase its proposals for reform in language which employers could appreciate. There was little sympathy for the principle of self-regulation by trade unions.

In 1998, the check-off provisions were changed by Order under the Deregulation and Contracting Out Act 1994.[56] Schedule 3 to the ERelA 1999 reforms balloting and notice requirements.[57] It is apparent that New Labour will do nothing more.

The powerful rhetoric of "democracy" and "individual rights", used to justify Conservative regulation of trade unions, seems to have had its impact on New Labour's legislative strategies in the field of industrial relations; hence the language used in defence of the balloting mechanism utilised in the statutory recognition procedure.[58] Balloting requirements for election of the trade union executive and political funds, set out in TULRCA 1992, will stay in place and there is to be no return to the closed shop.[59] The refusal of the Government to consider these particular reforms is not objectionable under international law.[60] However, the failure to alter the law relating to disciplinary action by trade unions is disappointing, as is the decision not to restore the rights of trade unions to choose their own members. Moreover, controversy still surrounds the sheer wealth of detailed requirements with which trade union governance must comply.[61] This provides an interesting contrast with the Government's willingness to take steps to ensure compliance with ILO standards on blacklisting.[62] The key distinction may be that the latter was related to protection of vulnerable individuals, whereas the reforms recommended by the ILO relating to trade union autonomy could potentially enhance collective bargaining power, conjuring up the negative images associated with British industrial relations of the 1970s.[63]

---

[54] *FAW*, para. 4.26.

[55] *FAW*, para. 4.9; and *FAW*, para. 4.26.

[56] SI 1998/1529.

[57] See below Chap. 5 at 141–7.

[58] This is an observation made in part by K. Syrett, " 'Immunity', 'Privilege' and 'Right': British Trade Unions and the Language of Labour Law Reform" (1998) 25 *JLS* 388 at 390–1. This seems to hold true, given statements in HL Hansard, 7 June 1999, col. 1196 and HL Hansard, 10 May 1999, col. 1009. See below Chap. 4 at 88–9.

[59] *FAW*, para. 4.8.

[60] See above Chap. 1 at 6 and this chap. at 52–3.

[61] T. Novitz, "Freedom of Association and 'Fairness at Work'—An Assessment of the Impact and Relevance of ILO Convention No. 87 on its Fiftieth Anniversary" (1998) 27 *ILJ* 169 at 179.

[62] See above Chap. 2 at 31–2.

[63] See above Chap. 1 at 6–8.

D. SCRUTINY OF TRADE UNION GOVERNANCE

Conservative legislation did not only endow individual trade union members with certain "democratic rights", but encouraged them to take action for their protection.[64] The ordinary courts have shown themselves willing to uphold complaints from members challenging the legitimacy of their union's actions, in reliance either on statutory constraints[65] or common law obligations.[66] In addition, Conservative governments established special Commissioners to assist in the enforcement of statutory rights against trade unions. There was potential for a New Labour Government to remove these mechanisms for scrutiny of trade union governance. Cosmetically, it seems that progress has been made here in so far as these Commissioners have been abolished, but the enhanced powers of the Certification Officer are such as to ensure that internal management of trade unions does not escape external control. The changes made by Labour appear to be attributable to cost considerations, not protection of trade union autonomy.

1. CRTUM, CPAUIA and the Certification Officer

The Employment Act 1988 established a new Commissioner for the Rights of Trade Union Members (CRTUM) to assist in the enforcement of statutory controls on trade union administration.[67] CRTUM[68] was empowered to pay legal costs or obtain legal advice for members bringing cases against their trade unions or their union officials for breach of certain statutory duties. This support for legal action against trade unions was anomalous, given that legal aid was not available for legal representation before industrial tribunals, for example in unfair dismissal claims.[69] Shortly after CRTUM was created, the ILO Committee of Experts expressed concern that the Commissioner might operate in a manner inconsistent with the spirit of Convention No. 87.[70] The devotion of state funds and a public official to support complaints against trade unions

---

[64] *Trade Unions and their Members*, Cm 95 (London: HMSO, 1987), para. 95.

[65] See e.g. *NALGO* v. *Killorn and Simm* [1990] IRLR 464 (EAT).

[66] E.g. *Ecclestone* v. *National Union of Journalists* [1999] IRLR 166, in which the High Court held that a union has a duty at common law to act "rationally, fairly and in accordance with good employment practice" in setting the required qualifications for a post and setting up a short list of candidates. Criteria had to be laid down in advance and objectively applied.

[67] Employment Act 1988 ss. 19–21.

[68] Which also came to be known colloquially as "CROTUM", reflecting its unpopularity in certain quarters.

[69] D. Morris, "The Commissioner for the Rights of Trade Union Members—A Framework for the Future?" (1993) 22 *ILJ* 104 at 115–7.

[70] (1989) *Report of the ILO Committee of Experts on the Application of Conventions and Recommendations*, ILC, 76th Session, 235–44. See also K.D. Ewing, *Britain and the ILO* (2nd edn., London: Institute of Employment Rights, 1994), 38–43.

indicated a desire to constrain rather than promote freedom of association. However, no notice was taken of these concerns and the Commissioner's powers were extended by the Employment Act 1990 to encompass assistance for complaints relating to breaches of a trade union rule book.[71] This was followed by the creation of a another new post, a Commissioner for Protection Against Unlawful Industrial Action (CPAUIA), in the Trade Union Reform and Employment Rights Act (TURERA) 1993.[72] The creation of this body was designed to supplement the right given to private citizens to bring proceedings to stop industrial action induced by an unlawful act.[73] CRTUM and CPAUIA were part-time posts, held simultaneously by the same official.[74]

The Certification Officer (CO) was a post created by the Employment Protection Act (EPA) 1975, but the CO carries out functions which preceded the EPA.[75] The CO is "formally independent" of both the Government and ACAS.[76] The CO's functions, which also expanded with increasing controls on trade union management,[77] have come to include the hearing of complaints over ballots for elections of union officials,[78] breaches of rules relating to balloting for political funds,[79] merger of trade unions[80] and failure of a union to compile and maintain a register of members' names and addresses.[81] Following TURERA 1993, the CO was given the additional power to act on complaints by individual union members as regards union financial malpractice.[82] In response to such complaints, the CO can provide decisions and grant declarations.[83]

2. The rationale for reform

The White Paper made the case for the abolition of CRTUM and CPAUIA, but not on the basis that these offices potentially jeopardise protection of freedom of association. Instead, the reason given was their inefficiency in carrying out their given tasks. "CRTUM has assisted only nine applicants each year on aver-

---

[71] EA 1990 s. 10.

[72] See TURERA 1993 s. 22 which inserted ss. 235A–C into TULRCA 1992.

[73] TULRCA 1992 s. 235A.

[74] Mrs Gill Rowlands was appointed as the first CRTUM in Dec. 1988. She also took on the office of CPAUIA in 1993, holding both posts until she retired in 1996. At the time of their abolition, the offices of CRTUM and CPAUIA were held by the same person, Mr Gerry Corless. See *FAW*, para. 4.30; and J. Lourie, *Fairness at Work Cm 3968*, House of Commons Research Paper 98/99 (London: House of Commons, 1998), 52.

[75] See now TULRCA 1992 s. 254.

[76] Lourie, n.74 above, at 53; C. Barrow, *Industrial Relations Law* (London: Cavendish, 1997), 24.

[77] See G. Pitt, *Employment Law* (3rd edn., London: Sweet & Maxwell, 1997), 8.

[78] TULRCA 1992 s. 45.

[79] See TULRCA 1992 s. 80.

[80] TULRCA 1992 s. 103.

[81] TULRCA 1992 s. 25.

[82] TULRCA 1992 ss. 37A–E.

[83] An enforcement order can then be made to the High Court. Appeal lies to the Employment Appeal Tribunal (EAT).

age. CPAUIA has assisted only one, which did not lead to a court case."[84] It appears that it was on this basis that section 28 of the Employment Relations Act 1999 provided that CRTUM and CPAUIA were to "cease to exist".[85] Their abolition was presented as not a matter of principle, but a strategy of rationalisation of state resources. It was estimated that £321,000 may be saved annually.[86]

Even though CPAUIA has been abolished, the right of a member of the public to seek an injunction in respect of unlawful industrial action is preserved.[87] Moreover, "the Commissioner for the Rights of Trade Union Members is not being abolished, except in a formal sense, because some of its powers are being given to the Certification Officer".[88] The CO is to hear complaints involving most aspects of the law where CRTUM was empowered to provide assistance.[89] The White Paper contemplated that this would prompt people to consider alternatives to court proceedings and would "enable trade union members to secure their rights more easily and effectively".[90]

Schedule 6 to the ERelA 1999 enhanced the CO's existing powers. Where a trade union has breached one of a number of statutory duties (or its own rules), the CO now has the power to issue "enforcement orders" rather than mere declarations. These orders will be enforced as if they were court orders. The CO's powers have been extended to areas where the CO previously had no competence. For the first time, complaints can be made to the CO regarding access to trade union accounting records,[91] regarding application of funds for political objects,[92] and breach of trade union rules.[93]

An applicant has the option to bring a complaint before the CO or a court.[94] In this manner, individual choice is preserved. However, if the applicant chooses the former route, appeal against the CO's decision is possible only on points of law.[95] To enable an applicant to bring the same claim before both "would obviously be a waste of public funds".[96] This is consistent with the Government's stated aim of encouraging "potential litigants—in any branch of the civil law—

---

[84] *FAW*, para. 4.31.

[85] This resulted in various consequential amendments, namely the repeal of TULRCA 1992 Part I, Chap. VIII, and ss. 235B, 235C, 266–271.

[86] See DTI, *The Employment Relations Bill: Regulatory Impact Assessment*, Feb. 1999, Annex, paras. 31 and 34.

[87] TULRCA 1992 s.235A. See also HC Standing Committee E, 4 Mar. 1999, col. 280, per Mr Wills.

[88] HL Hansard, 10 May 1999, col. 1047, per Lord McIntosh of Haringey.

[89] *FAW*, para. 4.31.

[90] *Ibid.*

[91] ERelA 1999 Sched. 6, para. 6 amending TULRCA 1992 s. 31.

[92] ERelA 1999 Sched. 6, para. 13 inserting TULRCA 1992 s. 72A.

[93] ERelA 1999 Sched. 6, para. 19 inserting TULRCA 1992 ss. 108A–C.

[94] Subject to provision made for vexatious litigants now incorporated in TULRCA 1992 s. 256A.

[95] See J. Lourie, *Employment Relations Bill 1998/99*, House of Commons Research Paper 99/11 (London: House of Commons, 1999) at 45. See e.g. TULRCA 1992, new ss. 45D and 56A inserted by ERelA 1999 Sched. 6, paras. 8 and 12.

[96] HC Standing Committee, E 4 Mar. 1999, col. 280, per Mr Wills.

to use practical alternatives to court proceedings to resolve their disputes. This saves court time and often produces quicker, cheaper and more effective remedies for the parties concerned."[97]

There are at least two ways in which these legislative reforms may be useful to trade unions. First, the abolition of CRTUM and CPAUIA indicates an end to state-funded support for actions against trade unions. Secondly, by offering complainants an alternative to the ordinary courts, there is greater opportunity to bypass judges who lack the expertise in industrial issues which we have come to expect of the CO. However, it seems that these benefits are incidental, for the changes to procedure made by the Employment Relations Act appear to constitute primarily a cost-cutting device. This is a rationale for the abolition of CRTUM and CPAUIA which should appeal to business without alienating organised labour. As an exercise in balancing vested interests, it is hard to fault.

E. CONCLUSION

In order that trade unions may play an effective role within workplace "partnerships", New Labour acknowledges the importance of their independence. Measures have been taken in the Employment Relations Act 1999 which give additional precedence to trade unions which possess this status. However, less is done to restore the autonomy of trade union governance, which was eroded under previous Conservative governments.

The Blair Government remains preoccupied with protecting "individual choice" through rigorous "democratic" mechanisms. The limitations of the Conservative model of "choice" and "democracy" appear to have been ignored. Nothing has been done to alter the law relating to disciplinary action by unions against their members or to restore to unions the right to choose their own members, even though these were measures recommended by the ILO. Nor has much been done to reduce the sheer number of bureaucratic rules which currently burden trade union administration. This seems to stem from New Labour's reluctance to be associated with the popularly understood "mistakes" of past Labour administrations. This Government does not want to be accused of reviving trade union activism, which some believe "brought down" the Labour Government of 1979.[98] Trade unions must be seen to be responsible.

Those reforms which were made seem to stem largely from a desire to cut costs to business and the state. The changes made to the check-off system and the "clarification" of balloting requirements were both justified by *Fairness at Work* in terms of the burdens the previous legislation placed on business. Their impact on trade unions was not mentioned. The abolition of the two Commissioners has been explained by the Government in terms of government

---

[97] HC Standing Committee, E 4 Mar. 1999. See ERDRA 1998, discussed above in Chap. 2 at 29.
[98] See e.g. HL Hansard, 10 May 1999, col. 985, discussed above in Chap. 1 at 6–8.

expenditure. The new role given to the Certification Officer is designed to ensure that the actions of trade unions will still be subject to special scrutiny in a manner which is cost-efficient not only for the state but also for the complainant. This is consistent with the aim, expressed by New Labour in the White Paper, of creating a "flexible and efficient labour market".[99] It also seems designed to demonstrate the capacity of this Labour Government to be fiscally responsible.[100] In short, the legislative changes outlined in this chapter have little to do with the conferment of "collective rights" on trade unions.

[99] *FAW*, para. 2.10.
[100] See above Chap. 1 at 8–11.

4

Trade Union Recognition and Derecognition

A. INTRODUCTION

RECOGNITION IS CENTRAL to British industrial relations. Not only does recognition confer on unions certain basic statutory entitlements,[1] but it is regarded as the door to collective bargaining and consultation rights.

Traditionally, the key to this door has been held by employers. An employer has had the choice whether to recognise and has determined the form such recognition will take. For example, the employer might decide on recognition of a particular trade union for purposes of consultation (perhaps merely as regards health and safety).[2] In the alternative, an employer might be more generous, extending recognition to collective bargaining on a broad range of subjects. Where a trade union has been representative of a large part of the employer's workforce, employers have tended to grant recognition for certain purposes, but they have not been obliged to do so. A trade union could seek to influence this decision by calling for industrial action,[3] but, given the consequences of doing so,[4] this has not commonly been viewed as a desirable option.

During the 1970s statutory experiments with compulsory recognition departed from this voluntaristic tradition, but on entry into government in 1979 the Conservatives returned to the familiar model which centred on employer choice. This was consistent with their general hostility to trade union representation and insistence on the protection of managerial prerogative in "free" labour markets. Initially, the trade union movement was not particularly alarmed by this restoration of a *laissez-faire* approach to recognition. This was, after all, part of their heritage. Trade unions did not doubt that many managers valued their contribution to communication and co-ordination within the workplace.[5]

Despite other incursions into collective rights, the TUC was fairly sanguine on the subject of recognition, until the 1990s when a worrying trend was

---

[1] See e.g., on disclosure of information, TULRCA 1992 ss. 181–185. On time off for trade union duties and activities, see TULRCA 1992 ss. 168–170 and the *ACAS Code of Practice (No. 3) Time Off for Trade Union Duties and Activities* (1991).

[2] See W. Brown, S. Deakin, M. Hudson, C. Pratten and P. Ryan, *The Individualisation of Employment Contracts in Britain* (London: DTI, 1998) at 33–4.

[3] TULRCA 1992 s. 244(1)(g).

[4] E.g., dismissal of workers could follow from industrial action: see above Chap. 1 at 39–43.

[5] As noted in *FAW*, para. 4.7: "of the 50 largest UK companies, 44 recognise trade unions".

observed.[6] Managers were increasingly pursuing deliberate or "purposive" derecognition tactics.[7] In 1984, unions were recognised in 66 per cent of workplaces. By 1998, that figure had fallen to 42 per cent.[8]

We can only speculate on why this trend developed at this stage, but it could well be due to various (and potentially interlinking) factors. These may include the Conservative campaign to discredit trade union representation,[9] the development of post-Fordist manufacturing practices which challenged conventional modes of managing industrial relations[10] and the increasing emphasis on consultation of workers which often took place through internal representative structures.[11]

Whatever the reasons for this managerial strategy, trade unions found it difficult to resist, for they had no legal right to be recognised and no legal right to maintain any existing recognition arrangements.[12] Even EC provision made for collective representation in the context of information and consultation requirements did not help unions to secure legal recognition.[13] It has also been observed that "explicit or implicit threats of derecognition, aided by the knowledge of derecognition elsewhere, contributed to undermining the bargaining position of trade unions at firms that retained recognition".[14]

The TUC became genuinely concerned and soon embarked on a campaign for statutory reform to reverse the trend towards derecognition.[15] Their publication, *Your Voice at Work*, argued that there should be compulsory recognition where the majority of those voting in a workplace ballot were in favour, leading to an award of recognition through a new "Representation Agency".[16] Yet it was not only "recognition" *per se* that interested the TUC, but what flows from this status. Conventionally, but not inevitably, this has been collective bargaining. The TUC sought the enactment of legislation which would not only make

---

[6] P. Gregg and A. Yates, "Changes in Wage-Setting Arrangements and Union Presence in the 1980s" (1991) 29 *BJIR* 361; P. Smith and G. Morton, "Union Exclusion and the Decollectivisation of Industrial Relations in Contemporary Britain" (1993) 31 *BJIR* 97; P. Smith and G. Morton, "Union Exclusion in Britain: Next Steps" (1994) 25 *IRJ* 3; Brown *et al.*, n.2 above, at 17–18.

[7] *Ibid.*

[8] M. Cully, S. Woodland, A. O'Reilly and G. Dix, *Britain at Work: As Depicted by the 1998 Workplace Employee Relations Survey* (London/New York: Routledge, 1999) at 238.

[9] See above Chap. 1 at 7.

[10] See above Chap. 1 at 5.

[11] In part, this may be attributed to the influence of EC Dirs. on collective redundancies and transfers of undertakings, discussed below in Chap. 6 at 155–9.

[12] Other than in the unlikely scenario that the recognition agreement was legally enforceable. See K.D. Ewing, "Trade Union Derecognition and Personal Contracts" (1993) 22 *ILJ* 297 at 298.

[13] See Cases C–382/92 and 383/92 *Commission* v. *UK* [1994] ECR I–2435 and 2479 and Lord Wedderburn, "British Labour Law at the Court of Justice: A Fragment" (1994) 10 *IJCLLIR* 339. See also *R.* v. *Secretary of State for Trade and Industry ex parte UNISON* [1996] IRLR 438 discussed in P. Skidmore, "Workers' Rights—A Euro-Litigation Strategy" (1996) 25 *ILJ* 225.

[14] Brown *et al.*, n.2 above, at p. iii and 67.

[15] See Cully *et al.*, n.8 above, at 106.

[16] TUC, *Your Voice at Work* (London: TUC, 1995), 11 and 29–38. See also for a brief analysis of these proposals M. Hall, "Beyond Representation and EU Law" (1996) 25 *ILJ* 15 at 19–21.

recognition compulsory but which would also make explicit the connection between recognition and collective bargaining; ensuring that the one flowed from the other.

The TUC extended its campaign to the international stage when it brought a complaint regarding trade union recognition before the ILO Committee on Freedom of Association (CFA).[17] The case concerned the Co-Steel Plant at Sheerness, where a substantial majority of the workforce had opted for trade union representation through collective bargaining, but was allegedly threatened with dismissal if it did not sign individual contracts. The CFA condemned the absence of legislation protecting the workers' rights in that case, considering that this amounted to a violation of freedom of association, guaranteed under ILO Convention No. 98.

In the period leading up to the General Election of 1997, New Labour faced a dilemma. The Party needed to present its policies as a departure from those of recent Conservative governments, so as to maintain the support of the trade union movement and "Old Labour". Indeed, this was a political imperative. Simultaneously, Blair wanted to attract the voters of "middle England" who lay beyond traditional Labour heartlands. This could be done only by distancing the Labour Party from popular associations, such as the 1970s "Social Contract" with trade unions.[18]

The Government therefore needed to be both careful and selective in its policy agenda. The key concession to trade union demands in Labour's 1997 election manifesto was the pledge that "where a majority of the relevant workforce votes in a ballot for the union to represent them, the union should be recognised".[19] We assume that the reason for this pledge was that, by then, a compulsory recognition procedure was central to the TUC campaign for reform of British labour law.[20] Other areas of collective labour rights ripe for reform were not mentioned. On entry into government in 1997, Labour informed the ILO of its commitment to the introduction of a statutory recognition procedure, involving a ballot of worker opinion, as a means by which to ensure that a representative trade union would be given the opportunity to bargain on behalf of workers.[21] The Government then set about considering how best to draft such a procedure.

The obvious problem was that this electoral promise was going to be difficult to fulfil, given the Blair Government's other policy objectives. How was promotion of collective bargaining to be reconciled with the emphasis which New

---

[17] Case No. 1852 (UK) *304th Report of the ILO Committee on Freedom of Association* (1996), para. 474 at 493.

[18] See above Chap. 1 at 11–12.

[19] Labour Party, *New Labour Because Britain Deserves Better* (London: Labour Party, 1997), 17. See also Labour Party, *Equipping Britain for the Future* (London: Labour Party, 1997), 11.

[20] See B. Towers, "'. . . the most lightly regulated labour market . . .' The UK's Third Statutory Recognition Procedure" (1999) 30 *IRJ* 82 at 92–3.

[21] Case No. 1852 (UK) *309th Report of the ILO Committee on Freedom of Association* (1998), para. 308 at para. 337.

Labour places on individual rights (and choice) as an aspect of "fairness"? How could a statutory scheme with an essential coercive element be reconciled with the notion of a voluntary "partnership"? Moreover, how could such regulation be reconciled with New Labour's commitment to a "lightly regulated labour market" and protection of managerial prerogative on grounds of economic efficiency?[22]

This chapter examines the extent to which Schedule A1, inserted by the ERelA 1999 into TULRCA 1992, responds to these conflicting demands. We do not pretend that this task is straightforward. This is a skilfully drafted statutory scheme. It is lengthy, finely nuanced and brimming with apparent contradictions.

This chapter takes a two-pronged approach to this difficult task. We begin by analysing the key influences on the Government's policymaking in this field: the historical and political context within which the ERelA 1999 was enacted. This involves examination of past experiments with statutory recognition, for we consider that Schedule A1 must be understood, at least in part, as a response to this legacy. It also entails further consideration of the TUC and CBI "Joint Statement" on trade union recognition. We consider that this expression of union interests and business concerns had a profound effect on the drafting of Schedule A1. Deference to the latter accounts for a number of the limitations inherent in the statutory scheme.

This is the foundation on which we build the second stage of our analysis: a study of the content of Schedule A1, consisting of four parts. We start by examining the procedures according to which recognition and its twin, derecognition, are to be achieved. Our next step is to investigate the consequences of statutory recognition for collective bargaining. We then go on to consider the extent to which collective agreements arising under Schedule A1 are enforceable and can thereby improve workers' terms and conditions of employment. We end by outlining how the roles of ACAS and the CAC have been revised under this scheme and considering what this tells us about the Government's intentions.

Having traversed this material, we reach a conclusion which we find alarming, namely that the new recognition procedure will seldom prove beneficial to trade unions. While some employers may make moves to recognise unions, so as to avoid becoming enmeshed in the statutory scheme, Schedule A1 is remarkably ineffective as a means by which to secure recognition of representative independent unions and effective collective bargaining. This legislative device is crafted to create the illusion of respect for "collective rights", while actually giving precedence to the interests of management. It is a very clever political decoy, but that is the full extent of its merits.

---

[22] *FAW*, Foreword and Chap. 2. See also above Chap. 1 at 8–11.

1. "Mistakes of the past": the historical legacy

Within the voluntarist tradition of collective *laissez-faire*, recognition could only be acquired with the consent of the employer, although the trade union might use the artillery of industrial action to persuade the employer to give such consent. During the 1970s, two distinctive pieces of legislation departed from this tradition, providing for conditions in which employers would be obliged to recognise trade unions. The first was enacted by a Conservative government, the second by a Labour administration. Neither proved successful, but both have been influential in determining the manner in which Schedule A1 has been drafted.

This influence has been largely negative, for these two statutory recognition procedures engendered tremendous hostility. Unions strongly opposed the first of these measures, while employers took active steps to diminish the efficacy of the second. We outline the major features of these two statutory initiatives and consider why they provoked such antagonism.

a. the Industrial Relations Act (IRA) 1971: trade union resistance

The Industrial Relations Act (IRA) 1971 constituted an important departure from the standard British model of collective bargaining. Until that time, many unions had managed to achieve recognition as collective bargaining representatives "without any significant help from the law",[23] but the ongoing lack of legislative support was beginning to cause concern.

The Donovan Commission Report of 1968 had been critical of the extent of industrial conflict caused by recognition disputes and the inconsistency of collective bargaining coverage in the UK, suggesting that legislative action be taken.[24] The then Labour Government had responded to these concerns by establishing a Commission on Industrial Relations (CIR) to consider recognition claims by trade unions and investigate means of improving industrial relations in particular firms or industries.[25] The Conservative Government elected in 1970 drew its industrial relations policy from these developments. Yet its agenda extended beyond the promotion of collective bargaining.[26] The IRA 1971 offered trade

---

[23] O. Kahn-Freund, *Labour Relations: Heritage and Adjustment* (Oxford: OUP, 1979), 68.

[24] *Royal Commission on Trade Union and Employers' Associations 1965–1968 (Donovan Commission Report)* Cmnd 3623 (London: HMSO, 1968), paras. 213–224.

[25] *In Place of Strife: A Policy for Industrial Relations* Cmnd 3888 (London: HMSO, 1969), paras. 56–59.

[26] The Conservative Government of the time did claim that its policy was aimed at increasing "the strength and size of trade unions", but whether this was its genuine objective is doubtful: M. Mellish and L. Dickens, "Recognition Problems under the Industrial Relations Act" (1972) 1 *ILJ* 229 at 229 citing HC Hansard, 14 Dec. 1970, col. 962.

unions certain benefits, such as entitlement to compulsory recognition, but only if they were prepared to submit to a new scheme of registration. This was regarded as an attempt to tame and control the trade union movement.

i. provision for recognition and derecognition under sections 44–50 of the IRA 1971

Under sections 44–50 of the IRA 1971, independent registered unions[27] were able to apply to the National Industrial Relations Court (NIRC) for recognition as a "sole bargaining agent" in respect of a "bargaining unit". This obviously posed questions as to what constituted a "bargaining unit" in the circumstances of the case, whether a sole bargaining agent was appropriate and who this should be. Such questions could be referred to the CIR, although final determination of whether this would promote a "satisfactory and lasting settlement" lay with the NIRC.[28]

If an employer did not accept the award made by the CIR, a ballot of the bargaining unit could be called and, where a simple majority of those voting asked for recognition of a particular trade union as sole bargaining agent for purposes of collective bargaining, an order would be made by the NIRC to this effect.[29] If the employer still failed to comply, this constituted an "unfair labour practice" actionable before the NIRC.[30] In such circumstances, unions could make a claim for a legally binding award on terms and conditions from the Industrial Arbitration Board (IAB). Therefore, the eventual sanction was a "substantive change in individual contracts".[31] There was also scope for derecognition under this procedure.[32]

ii. the trade union campaign for repeal of the IRA 1971

The Conservative Government of the time presented these provisions as an attempt to import the supposedly successful US model of recognition into UK industrial relations. This is evident from such features as the introduction of an exclusive bargaining agent and use of the term "unfair labour practice".[33] Yet entry to this statutory scheme depended upon registration, which meant that trade unions had to submit their rules to a Registrar for scrutiny, thereby placing trade union activities under statutory constraints.[34] This strategy was

---

[27] That is, unions registered under the IRA 1971, Part IV.

[28] IRA 1971 ss. 46–48.

[29] IRA 1971 ss. 49–50.

[30] IRA 1971 s. 54.

[31] See Lord McCarthy, *Fairness at Work and Trade Union Recognition: Past Comparisons and Future Problems* (London: Institute of Employment Rights, 1999) at 10.

[32] IRA 1971 s. 51.

[33] B. Towers, *Developing Recognition and Representation in the UK: How Useful is the US Model?* (London: Institute of Employment Rights, 1999) at 3.

[34] For critical views of this legislation, see Lord Wedderburn, "The Legal Framework of Industrial Relations and the Act of 1971" in Lord Wedderburn, *Labour Law and Freedom: Further Essays in Labour Law* (London: Lawrence & Wishart, 1995); and Mellish and Dickens, n.26 above, at 229–41.

unlikely to appeal to trade unions affiliated to the TUC which, embedded in a voluntarist tradition, were suspicious of this form of state intervention.

The unions which benefited from this development were the new breed of professional and staff associations, which were independent but deliberately moderate in their aims. For example, the United Kingdom Association of Professional Engineers (UKAPE), founded in 1969, indicated that it would be registered as a trade union but would not behave like one, as it would operate in a more "responsible" fashion. By the route of statutory recognition, moderate professional associations like UKAPE sought to compete with TUC-affiliated trade unions for negotiation rights with employers.[35] The IRA 1971 did not so much promote collective bargaining as provide scope for the more "responsible" unions to undermine existing patterns and models of bargaining representation.

These concerns, combined with the " fairly peremptory approach to consultation . . . about the details of the proposed legislation", had alienated the TUC, which embarked upon a campaign for non- registration.[36] TUC-affiliated trade unions did not utilise the compulsory recognition provisions.[37] Too few references were made to the CIR to begin to test the efficacy of the recognition procedure.[38] By 1974, the 1971 Act had been discredited by mass protest, industrial action, imprisonment of shop stewards,[39] the refusal of trade unionists to serve on the NIRC and withdrawal of trade union nominees from industrial tribunals.[40] As a minority government in 1974, Labour fulfilled its electoral promises repealing the IRA 1971.[41]

b. the Employment Protection Act (EPA) 1975: employer resistance

After the second election of 1974 in which it secured an overall majority, Labour began to pursue its own distinctive agenda, which involved positive state intervention to promote collective bargaining. With the consent of the unions, efforts to secure union recognition were to have the support of legal institutions.[42]

---

[35] Mellish and Dickens, n.26 above, 230–1 and 236–40.

[36] P. Davies and M. Freedland, *Labour Legislation and Public Policy* (Oxford: Clarendon Press, 1993), 275–82 and 303–5.

[37] Mellish and Dickens, n.26 above, at 230.

[38] See J. Lourie, *Fairness at Work Cm 3968*, House of Commons Research Paper 98/99 (London: House of Commons, 1998), 32 and McCarthy, n.31 above, at 20–1. For an example of the procedure in action see R.J. Price, "Union Recognition: General Accident Fire and Life Assurance Corporation Ltd (Second Report)" (1973) 3 *ILJ* 58–9.

[39] See e.g. the *Pentonville Five* case: *Midland Cold Storage* v. *Turner* [1972] ICR 230 (NIRC). See also Davies and Freedland, n.36 above, at 309–10.

[40] R. Taylor, *The Trade Union Question in British Politics: Governments and Unions since 1945* (Oxford: Blackwell, 1993) at 193–202; J. Clark and Lord Wedderburn, "Modern Labour Law: Problems, Functions and Policies" in Lord Wedderburn, R. Lewis and J. Clark (eds.), *Labour Law and Industrial Relations: Building on Kahn-Freund* (Oxford: Clarendon Press, 1983), 180.

[41] See the TULRA 1974.

[42] See Kahn-Freund, n.23 above, at 69.

The first step in this direction was the creation of the Advisory Conciliation and Arbitration Service (ACAS) in 1974. The second crucial development was the enactment of the Employment Protection Act (EPA) 1975, which gave ACAS a special role in the context of a second scheme designed to promote recognition of trade unions.[43] This was a very different procedure from that introduced under the IRA 1971, in that the applicant union had to be independent but did not have to be registered. It therefore had the support of the trade union movement, but failed to anticipate the potential for employer resistance.

i. promotion of recognition under sections 11–16 of the EPA 1975

Under sections 11–16 of the EPA 1975, a recognition issue could be referred by an independent union to ACAS.[44] The requirement that the union be certified independent to be eligible for an application was more welcome than the previous requirements for registration, but still allowed for applications from smaller, less representative, workers' associations, such as UKAPE.[45] There remained scope for potential conflict between a TUC and a non-TUC union, and such disputes could not be settled under the Bridlington procedure.[46]

ACAS was to examine the issue, consult all parties affected and seek to assist settlement by conciliation.[47] ACAS was also to make inquiries to "ascertain the opinions of the workers to whom the issue relates by any means it thinks fit, including the holding of a ballot".[48] Where settlement proved impossible, ACAS would provide a written report setting out its findings and recommendation as regards recognition for collective bargaining purposes.[49] "Collective bargaining" was defined by section 126 of the EPA 1975 as negotiations relating to or connected with one or more matters set out in section 29(1) of the Trade Union and Labour Relations Act 1974 and therefore could cover a wide range of issues, beyond pay, hours and holidays.[50]

---

[43] EPA 1975, Sched. 1. This tripartite body would outlast both this Labour administration and the periods of Conservative government which followed. See Taylor, n.40 above, at 228. See also below, this chap. at 119–21.

[44] EPA 1975 s.11.

[45] EPA 1975 s. 8. See above this chap. at 67. See also *EMA* v. *ACAS* [1980] IRLR 164 (HL) and *UKAPE* v. *ACAS* [1980] IRLR 124 (HL). This was discussed extensively in R. Lewis and B. Simpson, *Striking a Balance? Employment Law After the 1980 Act* (Oxford: Martin Robinson, 1981), 142–5.

[46] The Bridlington rules were designed to resolve disputes between trade unions within the TUC relating to contested membership. These procedures therefore applied only to TUC members. See for comments on the repercussions of the challenge mounted by trade unions outside the umbrella of the TUC L. Dickens, "ACAS and the Union Recognition Procedure" (1978) 7 *ILJ* 160 at 165–7; and *ACAS Annual Report 1980* (London: HMSO, 1981) at 74.

[47] EPA 1975 s. 12.

[48] EPA 1975 s. 14.

[49] EPA 1975 s. 12(4)–(7).

[50] See S. Wood and J. Godard, "The Statutory Recognition Procedure in the Employment Relations Bill: A Comparative Analysis" (1999) 37 *BJIR* 203 at 210–11. Compare with the subject matter for collective bargaining under Schedule A1 discussed below this chap. at 110–13.

If the employer failed to abide by the ACAS recommendation, provision was made for further ACAS conciliation.[51] The union could also refer the matter to the Central Arbitration Committee (CAC) which would impose an "appropriate" award of terms and conditions of employment, to be incorporated in the individual contract of employment.[52] This award would provide a basic minimum, enforceable in the county courts, which could be improved upon by negotiation between the employer and the individual worker.[53] The problem with this sanction was that the non-compliant employer who already provided appropriate basic terms had nothing to fear. In such circumstances, there was no effective inducement to engage in collective bargaining.[54]

ii. employer non-co-operation and judicial review

The EPA 1975 was a much more effective mechanism than the IRA 1971 for the promotion of recognition and collective bargaining. It was greeted with enthusiasm by the TUC and even non-affiliated trade unions. This was reflected in the huge swathe of applications which initially flooded into ACAS. 1,610 applications were made under section 11 of the EPA 1975 between 1976 and 1980.[55] Although this arguably placed considerable strain on ACAS resources, it was a mark of union confidence in this initiative.

Securing employer co-operation proved more problematic. During the period 1975–9, a significant number of employers voluntarily conceded recognition to unions "either for the first time or in respect of employees hitherto outside collective negotiations".[56] In this way, employers could "avoid the public scrutiny which would result from a reference under the statutory procedure".[57] However, others took a more definite non-co-operative stance.

Employers used various methods of resistance. They refused ACAS access to their workers, which meant that ACAS was unable to ascertain their views on recognition.[58] Even when ACAS was allowed access, employers used negative propaganda to deter their workers from voting for recognition in a ballot, which was difficult for unions to counter.[59] Some employers sent letters which

[51] EPA 1975 s. 15.

[52] EPA 1975 s. 16.

[53] EPA 1975 s. 16(7).

[54] Dickens, n.46 above, at 176; Lord Wedderburn, "The Employment Protection Act 1975: Collective Aspects" (1976) 39 *MLR* 169 at 183; B. Doyle, "A Substitute for Collective Bargaining? The Central Arbitration Committee's Approach to Section 16 of the Employment Protection Act 1975"(1980) 9 *ILJ* 154 at 158; P.L. Davies, "Failure to Comply with Recognition Recommendation" (1979) 8 *ILJ* 55–60.

[55] Lourie, n.38 above, at 33.

[56] Lewis and Simpson, n.45 above, at 146. See also *ACAS Annual Report 1980* (London: HMSO, 1981), 100.

[57] L. Dickens and G. S. Bain, "A Duty to Bargain? Union Recognition and Information Disclosure" in R. Lewis (ed.), *Labour Law in Britain* (Oxford: Basil Blackwell, 1986) at 93.

[58] See the facts of *Grunwick* v. *ACAS* [1978] IRLR 38 (HL). See also ACAS Annual Report 1978 (London: HMSO, 1979) at 29.

[59] "The very nature of the situation means that an employer has ready access to the employees in a way an unrecognised union does not": Dickens, n.46 above, at 168.

intimated that the business would be sold were the majority of workers to come out in a ballot in favour of recognition, while others interviewed each worker individually to convey the management's opposition to trade union recognition.[60] Moreover, lack of managerial co-operation could lead to delays,[61] meaning that cases could take over a year to reach determination by the CAC. Over one-fifth of cases took 18 months or more to reach this stage.[62] Such behaviour made it difficult for unions to sustain interest in the recognition request, as workers became exasperated with the lack of results.[63]

The drafters of the EPA 1975 had not made provision for such conduct. The brevity of the statutory provisions also meant that the detailed implementation of the procedure had to be decided by ACAS.[64] The EPA 1975 did not make it clear how the bargaining unit was to be demarcated,[65] what was to happen in the event of conflicting applications by independent trade unions,[66] what level of support was to be determinative of recognition,[67] or what powers ACAS could exercise in the face of non-co-operation by an employer.

ACAS nevertheless felt obliged to resist the attempts of certain employers to evade the procedure and took steps accordingly. Where ACAS had notice that an employer had been using negative propaganda to dissuade workers from supporting recognition, ACAS dealt with this by interpreting the stated support for the union, which was low, in the light of the employer's actions.[68] The willingness of ACAS to act on its own initiative led to "fierce controversy over the recognition, criteria and procedures used by ACAS. It was widely asserted, by employers and their representatives, that ACAS was acting in a biased and partisan way".[69] Indeed, ACAS became concerned that its reputation as "provider of independent and impartial conciliation and advice" would begin to tarnish as a consequence.[70]

While the EPA 1975 provided no right of appeal from ACAS decisions, employers soon began to challenge the actions of ACAS by judicial review. They

---

[60] Dickens, n.46 above, at 168.

[61] *ACAS Annual Report 1980* (London: HMSO, 1981), 79.

[62] *Ibid.*, 80.

[63] Dickens, n.46 above, 175; H.A. Clegg, *The Changing System of Industrial Relations in Great Britain* (Oxford: Blackwell, 1979), 142, cited in McCarthy, n.31 above, at 28. See also P.B. Beaumont, "Time Delays, Employer Opposition and White Collar Recognition Claims: The Section 12 Results" (1981) 19 *BJIR* 238. This has also been identified as a concern in the USA. See M. Hart, "Union Recognition in America—the Legislative Snare" (1978) 7 *ILJ* 201 at 205 and 207; and W.B. Gould, *Agenda for Reform: The Future of Employment Relationships and the Law* (Cambridge, Mass.: The MIT Press, 1996), 158.

[64] *ACAS Annual Report 1977* (London: HMSO, 1978), 45–8.

[65] McCarthy, n.31 above, at 31.

[66] *Ibid.*, 25. See *UKAPE*, n.45 above.

[67] Dickens, n.46 above, at 171.

[68] *Ibid.* Of course, this response could only be used in the most blatant cases of abuse; more covert or subtle forms of influence which were often used were harder to detect.

[69] *Ibid.* at 172–3; and McCarthy, n.31 above, at 37.

[70] *ACAS Annual Report 1978* (London: HMSO, 1979) 27 and *ACAS Annual Report 1979* (London: HMSO, 1980) 29. See also R. Townshend-Smith, "Trade Union Recognition Legislation—Britain and America Compared" (1981) 1 *LS* 190 at 211.

found the courts a willing ally in their mission to reduce the discretion of ACAS and render the recognition provisions of the EPA 1975 ineffective. For example, during the *Grunwick* dispute, the employer refused to provide ACAS with even the names and addresses of their workers, so as to avoid a postal ballot.[71] ACAS decided, in the face of such behaviour, to recommend recognition. However, here the employers displayed their trump card: judicial review. The courts found that, in the absence of a full investigation of the views of the workers, such a recommendation lay outside the body's statutory powers.[72] The result was that ACAS felt itself unable to make recommendations in a number of subsequent cases where employer non-co-operation hindered its ability to ascertain worker opinion on recognition.[73]

Indeed, it became obvious that the entire scheme for recognition had awakened serious concerns amongst the judiciary. For example, members of the judiciary considered that the CAC had been granted powers akin to compulsory acquisition of property, constituting "an interference with individual liberty", which "could hardly be tolerated in a free society unless there were safeguards against abuse".[74] Judicial attitudes of this kind played a significant role in undermining the statutory recognition procedure created by the EPA 1975.[75]

The EPA 1975 statutory recognition procedure was abolished in the Employment Act 1980, following concerns expressed by the Chairman of ACAS in a letter sent to the Secretary of State.[76] By this time, the number of references made under section 11 had declined and their usefulness had been called into question.[77] Although union membership and collective bargaining increased during this period, only approximately 16,000 workers were eventually granted recognition by virtue of a recommendation made by ACAS under the EPA 1975.[78] While some believe that the procedure should have been strengthened rather than repealed,[79] the experiment was widely viewed as a failure.

We shall see that New Labour seeks to distinguish the content of Schedule A1 from that of its predecessors. This is done in various ways, which are examined below. One obvious example is the decision to make detailed provision for various eventualities in a schedule which extends to 172 paragraphs. This could not

[71] See B. James and R. Simpson, " *Grunwick* v. *ACAS* " (1978) 41 *MLR* 573. For discussion of this problem, see *ACAS Annual Report 1980* (London: HMSO, 1981), 77.

[72] *Grunwick,* n.58 above. This seems to be symptomatic of the courts' general reluctance to look behind managerial prerogative so as to give force to workers' claims. See e.g. *Moon* v. *Homeworthy Furniture (Northern) Ltd* [1976] IRLR 298 (EAT).

[73] *ACAS Annual Report 1980* (London: HMSO, 1981), 77.

[74] *Grunwick*, n.58 above, at 268, *per* Lord Salmon.

[75] The Sept. 1979 Working Paper on Trade Union Recognition observed that "the government sees no grounds in this situation for criticism of the courts", but ACAS was more critical of the judicial role played in undermining the efficacy of their actions and the legislation. It was discussed in Lewis and Simpson, n.45 above, at 144.

[76] See *ACAS Annual Report 1979* (London: HMSO, 1980) Appendix C.

[77] Lewis and Simpson, n.45 above, at 146.

[78] *ACAS Annual Report 1980* (London: HMSO, 1981), 99–100.

[79] Lewis and Simpson, n.45 above, at 146.

be more different from the brief provisions contained in sections 11 to 16 of the EPA 1975. Yet the key lesson which New Labour seems to have learnt from the 1970s is not so much concerned with the niceties of drafting, as with pragmatism. This is the necessity of securing the support of both unions and business if such a scheme is to be successful.

2. The "Joint Statement" of the TUC and CBI: the political trade-off

The "Joint Statement" produced by the TUC and CBI on trade union recognition is intriguing for two reasons. The first is why such negotiations ever took place at all. The second is how this document, which reflects an absence of consensus, came to be given a title which suggests that agreement was reached between the two sides of industry.

a. why did these negotiations take place?

Labour's landslide victory in the 1997 General Election might have suggested that the Government had the mandate to implement all its electoral promises, including those relating to compulsory union recognition. However, Blair was more hesitant. The experience of the 1970s had been sufficient to establish that such an initiative was doomed, unless the co-operation of both management and labour was secured. The TUC had campaigned for and supported this reform, but the CBI had already voiced its opposition to such an initiative.[80]

The strategy adopted by the Government was to ask the TUC and CBI to discuss the matter and attempt to reach a common solution.[81] This was not a "tripartite" discussion in the style established by the ILO. The Government did not sit down with both sides of industry and attempt to achieve a compromise which suited the needs of all three factions. Instead, the Government's initiative can be regarded as akin to European-style "social dialogue". The social partners were to achieve their own solution and then the executive was to decide whether it should be given legal force.[82]

The CBI remained opposed in principle to such legislation, but took a strategic decision to co-operate with this process. Although the CBI must have been reluctant to legitimate this measure by participation in these discussions, it seems that business could see the point in putting forward their views on its implementation. In this manner, the CBI sought to undermine the efficacy of a statutory recognition procedure and dilute its effect. It is even possible that the

---

[80] It was reported that the CBI wrote to the Government opposing the introduction of compulsory statutory recognition, reminding it of Labour's failure to introduce effective legislation during the 1970s. See "Labour Plan Raises Concern", *Financial Times*, 18 Mar. 1997. Also see Lourie, n.38 above, at 35.

[81] *FAW*, para. 4.14.

[82] See above Chap. 1 at 11–12.

CBI was encouraged by the Government's decision to ask the two sides to meet and fight it out. This time there was no sign of a "Social Contract" between the unions and Government.[83]

Throughout the process of consultation over *Fairness at Work*, it is evident that New Labour actively sought an accommodation between trade union, worker and employer interests. This accommodation (or compromise position) has often been justified in terms of "rights and responsibilities" or even "partnership". In the consultation procedure that followed the White Paper, and during the passage of the Employment Relations Bill, worker and employer representatives were expected to present their views independently, through parallel lobbying, not social dialogue. Therefore, the special initiative taken by the Government as regards the question of trade union recognition is notable. It appears that this was such a controversial subject that it required special treatment.

b. the limited content of the agreement

The "Joint Statement", issued in December 1997, stated that the TUC and CBI welcomed "the Government's commitment to partnership at work".[84] This was unsurprising, for opposition to the overall catch-phrase of "partnership" was unlikely.[85] However, the "Joint Statement" reflected little other genuine agreement. The CBI did not even agree in principle with statutory trade union recognition, holding to the view that collective bargaining was impracticable where one partner was unwilling.[86]

Realising that a statutory recognition procedure was about to be foisted upon them, the CBI did clarify its preferences for the form that such a procedure should take, sometimes in agreement with the TUC; but there were major points of difference. For example, the TUC and CBI could not agree on the appropriate thresholds for a valid application for trade union recognition,[87] the manner in which a bargaining unit should be defined,[88] the level of support for recognition which had to be shown in a ballot,[89] the subject matter of collective bargaining,[90] the question of "automatic recognition",[91] whether individuals should be able to contract out of collective agreements reached through the statutory procedure[92] and whether unions should be able to take industrial

---

[83] *Ibid.*

[84] "Statutory Trade Union Recognition Joint Statement by TUC and CBI", Dec. 1997, para. 1. Available both in (1998) 647 *IRS Employment Trends* 3—4 and at http://www.tuc.org.uk/.

[85] See above Chap. 1 at 13–15.

[86] "Joint Statement" n.84 above, para. 2.

[87] *Ibid.*, para. 6.

[88] *Ibid.*, paras. 9, 12–13.

[89] *Ibid.*, para. 14.

[90] *Ibid.*, para. 17.

[91] *Ibid.*, para. 14.

[92] *Ibid.*, paras. 20–21.

action to secure recognition where a statutory procedure for recognition exists.[93]

In *Fairness at Work*, the Government claimed to be indebted to the joint efforts of the TUC and CBI, which had provided the foundation for their legislative proposals in this field.[94] Yet, in truth, the extent of disagreement apparent in the so-called "Joint Statement" meant that the process of lobbying was far from over, as was evident from submissions made on the White Paper by the CBI and TUC.[95] After the spread of rumours and much media speculation came the statement made by Peter Mandelson, as Secretary of State for Trade and Industry, on 17 December 1998. Even when the Bill was presented in January 1999, Schedule 1 containing the statutory recognition procedures was still far from finalised. The Government continued to make amendments in Committee. Some of these were said to be "technical improvements" while others were "in response to suggestions that were made after the Bill was published".[96] The Government's efforts to pacify the CBI illustrate how far trade union influence on the Labour Party has declined. As we shall see, this decline is reflected in the content of the resultant legislation.[97]

C. THE CONTENT OF SCHEDULE A1

In *Fairness at Work*, the Government said that the "prime purpose" of the recognition procedure was "to offer greater protection and security at work for the vulnerable".[98] It was to provide access to collective bargaining where this was wanted by a majority of the relevant workforce. Yet, Schedule A1 has also been shaped by other interests. The statutory recognition procedure was also advertised in the White Paper as a means by which to achieve "dispute resolution" and establish "partnership".[99] As such, it would be good not only for workers but for business. We consider that commercial interests, outlined in the CBI contribution to the "Joint Statement" and elsewhere, have been determinative of the final form this procedure has taken, such that it is of little practical use to union applicants seeking recognition.

We aim to demonstrate this thesis by close examination of the four major facets of Schedule A1. These are:

1. the procedures for achieving trade union recognition and derecognition;
2. the consequences statutory recognition has for collective bargaining;

---

[93] *Ibid.*, para. 22.
[94] *FAW*, para. 4.14.
[95] Summarised in Lourie, n.38 above, 40–1.
[96] HC Standing Committee E, 16 Mar. 1999, col. 344, *per* Mr Wills.
[97] B. Towers, n.20 above, at 93–4; R. Undy, "New Labour's 'Industrial Relations Settlement': The Third Way?" (1999) 37 *BJIR* 315 at 330–1.
[98] *FAW*, para. 4.11.
[99] *FAW*, paras. 4.11–4.13.

3. the lack of change to the current law governing enforcement of collective agreements;
4. the roles of the institutional actors in the statutory recognition procedure.

In this context, we admit that there would be considerable value in a comparative analysis. Indeed, there has been some excellent and extensive work done on comparisons with US and Canadian models.[100] However, while we refer to some of this literature, we do not pretend to provide such an analysis here. Our chief concern lies with how, on the subject of trade union recognition, the present Labour Government has responded both to the heritage of earlier British legislative initiatives and to the particular dynamics of British industrial relations.

The New Labour response has been to make the procedure designated for the acquisition of trade union recognition and bargaining rights as difficult and complex as possible. In part, this can be linked to the legacy of collective *laissez-faire* and a deep-seated belief in the value of voluntary settlement of disputes between management and labour. Schedule A1 is designed to get the parties to meet, speak and agree their own solutions, not resort to the statutory default mechanism provided. Such a strategy fits neatly within the Government's conception of a consensual, non-conflictual "partnership".[101] Yet this can also be regarded as an evasive, pacifying device which pretends to offer trade unions more than it actually delivers.

1. Procedures for achieving trade union recognition and derecognition

The procedures by which recognition (and derecognition) can be achieved are lengthy, detailed and complex. Given this, it is not practical here to outline in detail the precise workings of all aspects of these procedures or to provide a commentary on each section. Such a task will no doubt be undertaken elsewhere. Instead, our aim is to identify the key features of the procedure through which recognition (and derecognition) may be achieved under Schedule A1 and subject these to scrutiny. The key features identified are:

a. the voluntary and compulsory elements of the statutory recognition procedure;
b. the criteria for CAC acceptance of an application for recognition;
c. the numerical requirements which must be satisfied to establish workplace support for recognition;
d. the means by which employer co-operation is to be secured.

---

[100] See e.g. R.J. Adams, "Why Statutory Union Recognition is Bad Labour Policy: The North American Experience" (1999) 30 *IRJ* 96; Hart, n.63 above; Towers, n.33 above and n.20 above; Townshend-Smith, n.70 above; Wood and Godard, n.50 above.
[101] See above Chap. 1 at 17–18.

Discussion of the consequences of recognition for collective bargaining follows below.[102]

a. voluntary and compulsory elements of the recognition and derecognition procedures

The new statutory procedure for union recognition and derecognition has, despite its compulsory aspects, been presented by New Labour as an exercise in the promotion of co-operative communication. Their ostensible aim is that the parties should meet, talk and attempt to resolve their differences themselves. In this respect, ACAS is at hand to play a facilitative role, distinct from that which it performed under the Employment Protection Act 1975; and stages are set out during which the parties are encouraged to bargain. The idea seems to be that, through dialogue, the employer and workers can establish a "partnership".

However, the parties do not bargain freely but in the shadow of the law. Once the requisite time periods have expired, the CAC will intervene, playing a quasi-judicial, evaluative and coercive role. What the CAC can and will do when it intervenes inevitably influences the content of the parties' negotiations. We consider the road to recognition to be so difficult and the capacity of Schedule A1 to promote collective bargaining so limited, that unions in their attempt to gain some form of recognition may well feel forced to make extensive concessions at this early stage. The apparent entitlement of a representative trade union to collective bargaining over pay, hours and holidays is therefore unlikely to be realised. Moreover, the delays inherent in the negotiation procedures set out in Schedule A1 are most likely to work to the benefit of employers, for extensive delay is one way in which unions have been known to lose the support of members frustrated by the lack of results.[103]

i. voluntary agreement and the rhetoric of "partnership"

In their "Joint Statement", the TUC and the CBI both stated their wish that "agreements on trade union recognition be voluntary wherever possible". They were agreed that "where the parties themselves cannot reach agreement, there should be a period for voluntary conciliation under the auspices of ACAS to explore the scope for agreement".[104] This preference is reflected in Schedule A1 and was justified in Standing Committee, on the basis that "voluntary agreements are the best way to build partnerships between workers and employers".[105]

The procedure created by the Employment Relations Act takes the parties through various stages, each of which offers the possibility of negotiation and a

---

[102] See below this chap. at 101–115.
[103] See above this chap. at 70.
[104] "Joint Statement", n.84 above, at para. 3.
[105] *FAW*, para. 4.15; HC Standing Committee E, 16 Mar. 1999, *per* Mr Wills at col.346; and HL Hansard, 10 May 1999, col. 1044, *per* Lord McIntosh. See also above Chap. 1 at 16–17.

route to "partnership". It is only when these procedures have been followed and the parties are still not in agreement that the CAC will ultimately be able to impose recognition (or derecognition), and only then if the requisite support in the workplace has been demonstrated. As Wedderburn has observed, these procedures "try, above all, to edge the parties into voluntary, collective agreements without resort to legal sanction—a traditional tactic of collective *laissez-faire*".[106] The Regulatory Impact Assessment (RIA) observed that "the procedure has been designed so that few cases are likely to reach the final stage".[107] This is likely to cut costs both for the parties and the Government.

ii. the mechanisms for enforced negotiation

Under paragraphs 1–4 of Schedule A1, an independent trade union (or unions) seeking recognition for purposes of collective bargaining[108] on behalf of a group of workers must make a request to the employer concerned.[109] The employer has an initial negotiating period of ten working days to respond to the request.[110] If the employer agrees to recognise the union (or unions), then the attention of the parties is to turn to agreement on a bargaining procedure.[111] If the employer does not accept the request but is willing to negotiate, then a second period of negotiations may commence.[112] This period will extend for 20 working days or such longer time as the parties agree. A request may be made by either party to ACAS to assist in conducting the negotiations.[113] If the employer makes such a request and the union(s) will not co-operate within ten working days, no request can be made to the CAC for compulsory recognition.[114] It is only if the parties fail to reach agreement during this second period, or the employer refuses to respond or negotiate by the end of the first period, that the union(s) may apply to the CAC to decide two questions. The first is whether the proposed bargaining unit is appropriate or whether some alternative unit would be more appropriate. The second is whether the applicant union(s) have the support of a majority of the workforce within the unit.[115] It may be that agreement has already been reached on the first question in the course of negotiations. If so, the CAC will be called on to determine only the second.[116]

---

[106] Lord Wedderburn, "Collective Bargaining or Legal Enactment: The 1999 Act and Union Recognition" (2000) 29 *ILJ* 1 at 2.

[107] DTI, *The Employment Relations Bill: Regulatory Impact Assessment* (London: DTI, 1999), Annex, 4, para. 14.

[108] This is collective bargaining of a very limited scope. See TULRCA 1992, Sched. A1, para. 3, discussed below this chap. at 110–13.

[109] More will be said later about the form of the request and who is entitled to make it. See below this chap. at 80–7.

[110] TULRCA 1992, Sched. A1, para. 10(1) and (6).

[111] See TULRCA 1992, Sched. A1, Part II.

[112] TULRCA 1992, Sched. A1, para. 10(2) and (3).

[113] TULRCA 1992, Sched. A1, para. 10(5).

[114] TULRCA 1992, Sched. A1, para. 12(5).

[115] TULRCA 1992, Sched. A1, paras. 11 and 12.

[116] TULRCA 1992, Sched. A1, para. 12(3) and (4).

Even once the CAC accepts the application,[117] there is further potential for a solution to be reached by agreement between the parties. The CAC is obliged to facilitate agreement on the appropriate bargaining unit, over an "appropriate period" of at least 20 working days. This period may last for longer if the CAC so specifies.[118] It is only if the parties have not reached agreement by the end of this period that the CAC will intervene to determine the appropriate bargaining unit.[119] If the CAC then decides that the application is valid and proceeds on this basis, then either there may be automatic recognition[120] or a secret ballot to test workplace support for recognition may be held.[121] This means that at least 50 days of negotiation are envisaged, just to reach the stage where a ballot on workplace support for recognition is held. Moreover, there remains a residual option for an employer and unions to reach a joint accommodation to prevent CAC intervention, if they so inform the CAC before any declaration of automatic recognition is made or within ten working days of the CAC's notification to the parties that a ballot will be held.[122] Parallel and equally lengthy procedures apply in respect of derecognition.[123]

The chief consequence of statutory recognition is that the parties must then adopt a bargaining procedure. This second stage of the recognition procedure will be discussed below,[124] but again, in this context, considerable emphasis is placed on the parties' capacity to make their own arrangements without interference by a third party.[125]

iii. bargaining in the shadow of the law

The provision made for negotiations in Schedule A1 reflects the Government's emphasis on "partnership" and voluntary accords. However, such negotiations necessarily take place "in the shadow of the law". What is "agreed" is likely to be dependent upon the perceived consequences of a failure to reach a settlement. In this sense, agreement is potentially illusory, as the Conservative Opposition was swift to observe.[126]

The Government has sought to reassure business that the statutory recognition scheme is not, at root, coercive. It has been pointed out that the only

---

[117] This is in itself a convoluted process: see TULRCA 1992, Sched. A1, paras. 13–17.

[118] This must be done by a notice to the parties "containing reasons for the extension". See TULRCA 1992, Sched. A1, para. 18.

[119] This must be done by the CAC within ten working days or a longer period where the CAC specifies to the parties the reason for the time extension. See TULRCA 1992 Sched. A1, para. 19(2) and (3).

[120] TULRCA 1992, Sched. A1, para. 22. Although, for reasons given below, this is a relatively unlikely contingency. See below this chap. at 92–3.

[121] TULRCA 1992, Sched. A1, para. 23.

[122] TULRCA 1992, Sched. A1, paras. 17 and 24. Compare this with the explanation of the trade union's option to withdraw an application provided in HL Hansard, 7 June 1999, col. 1185, *per* Lord McIntosh.

[123] TULRCA 1992, Sched. A1, Parts IV–VI.

[124] See below this chap. at 101–15.

[125] See TULRCA 1992, Sched. A1, paras. 30, 69 and 78, discussed below this chap. at 103.

[126] HC Hansard, 30 Mar. 1999, col. 885.

consequence of statutory recognition is more "dialogue", namely "a duty to meet and to try to negotiate".[127] At most, should the parties fail to reach agreement and recognition be imposed, the CAC can only ultimately impose a bargaining procedure on the parties. This is "a procedure for holding talks only; the parties will not be required to reach agreement for the simple reason that people cannot be forced to agree".[128] There will be no "imposed agreement on terms and conditions which might produce a momentary benefit for employees, but . . . nothing for the long-term relationship in the workplace".[129] Here the Government has sought to distinguish the recognition procedure set out in Schedule A1 from that available under the Employment Protection Act 1975.[130]

In doing so, the Government has revealed the very limitations of what Schedule A1 will accomplish. A union which is confident in its ability to take (or threaten) effective industrial action is usually able to persuade an employer to grant recognition. It is the union for which this is not a viable option that is likely to make an application under Schedule A1. What does such a union gain from the procedure and these initial negotiations? If all the union gains is potential access to dialogue with the employer, but no enhanced bargaining power, it is difficult to see what point the procedure serves, unless the terms on which the CAC intervenes enhance the union's bargaining power. We shall argue that numerous facets of statutory recognition procedure in Schedule A1 operate in the employer's favour as opposed to that of the union. This clearly has a detrimental impact on the bargaining power of the applicant union in any initial negotiations relating to recognition.

For the time being, it is sufficient to observe that the delays entailed in the negotiation process do not bode well for the bargaining power of the applicant union. Delays can be lethal to an effective recognition campaign.[131] In their submissions on *Fairness at Work*, the TUC welcomed the introduction of set time limits, which could overcome many of the problems with delay associated with indefinite periods for dispute resolution associated with the EPA 1975 recognition procedure.[132] However, the TUC did express concern that the Government proposed that the CAC would facilitate a second period for discussions where the parties had already negotiated over a lengthy period and failed to reach agreement.[133] It is interesting that, after the release of the White Paper, the

---

[127] HC Standing Committee E, 16 Mar. 1999, col. 346, *per* Mr Wills.

[128] HC Standing Committee E, 16 Mar. 1999, col. 348, *per* Mr Wills. See TULRCA 1992, Sched. A1, paras. 30–32.

[129] HC Standing Committee E, 16 Mar. 1999, col. 348, *per* Mr Wills.

[130] Where an employer did not abide by a recommendation for recognition made by ACAS under the EPA 1975, the CAC was empowered to grant an award of appropriate terms and conditions of employment to be incorporated into the contracts of the relevant workers. See EPA 1975 s. 16, discussed above this chap. at 69. The option of a default award was proposed by Lord McCarthy in HL Hansard, 7 June 1999, cols. 1277–1278, but was rejected by the New Labour Government.

[131] See above this chap. at 70. See also L. Dubinsky, *Resisting Union-Busting Techniques: Lessons from Quebec* (London: Institute of Employment Rights, 2000) at 20–1.

[132] TUC, *TUC Response: Fairness at Work White Paper* (London: TUC, 1998), para. 54.

[133] *Ibid.*

employers appeared to accept that time scales were appropriate, but considered those proposed to be too *short*.[134] This was also the view taken by the Conservative opposition, which wished to extend the period during which an employer had to respond to the request of a union or unions for recognition.[135] It seems that business appreciated that their interests lay in delaying the recognition procedure as long as was possible to gain further bargaining advantage in potential negotiations. The Government has tactically taken the middle ground between the TUC and CBI positions. The result is a procedure that is not so very favourable to a union seeking recognition.

b. formal criteria for requests and applications

Before the CAC can determine the appropriate bargaining unit and whether a ballot should be held, certain other requirements must be satisfied. CAC acceptance of a union's application turns on its findings as to whether the request for recognition is valid in the first place,[136] whether the required negotiating steps were followed,[137] and whether further criteria for admissibility are met.[138] These criteria have to be applied afresh by the CAC where the scope of the bargaining unit has been determined by the CAC and this varies from the union's original proposed bargaining unit.[139] This is further complicated by the Government's tactical decision that "instead of putting the burden of proof sometimes on employers and sometimes on unions, the CAC, in deciding whether the tests are passed, will have to consider evidence given by either party".[140] The application of the various criteria, set out below, seems likely to place notable limitations on the operation of the statutory recognition procedure.

Moreover, these formal requirements send a significant message to unions and employers concerning the form in which the Government expects collective bargaining will take place. Schedule A1 provides a benchmark of single-employer as opposed to multi-employer bargaining. Small firms employing fewer than 21 workers are not expected to engage in collective bargaining at all.[141]

The statutory preference is for bargaining with an independent trade union, but a pre-emptive collective agreement granting recognition to any independent trade union, not necessarily representative of the workers in the bargaining unit, can preclude an application by a more representative union.[142] This means that,

---

[134] Lourie, n.38 above, at 41.
[135] HC Hansard, 31 Mar. 1999, cols. 1170–1173; HL Hansard, 7 June 1999, col. 1181.
[136] TULRCA 1992, Sched. A1, paras. 5–9.
[137] TULRCA 1992, Sched. A1, paras. 11–12. Compare with Sched. A1, para. 15.
[138] TULRCA 1992, Sched. A1, paras. 33–42.
[139] See TULRCA 1992, Sched. A1, para. 20 and therefore paras. 44–50.
[140] HC Standing Committee E, 16 Mar. 1999, col. 362, *per* Mr Wills.
[141] See below this chap. at 82–4.
[142] TULRCA 1992, Sched. A1, para. 35. See below this chap. at 85–7.

just as they threatened to do under the EPA 1975, professional associations which may not be affiliated to the TUC have the potential to undermine the bargaining position of TUC-affiliated unions.[143] This threat may arise even where the professional association is less representative of the workforce than its TUC-affiliated counterpart.

i. request for recognition to one lone employer

In 1968, the Donovan Commission, identifying the tension between formal and informal systems of collective bargaining, advocated a shift from formal industry-level bargaining to single-employer bargaining (through a combination of company and "factory" agreements).[144] The result was intended to be the extension of collective bargaining.[145] Recent studies indicate the continuation of a trend away from multi-employer bargaining without any enhancement of collective bargaining at the company or plant level.[146] Employers appear to have rejected sectoral bargaining in conjunction with other employers,[147] possibly because they are acutely aware of business competition and the potential to undercut competitors through cutting labour costs.[148]

In Schedule A1, there are various requirements which relate to the form of the request that must be made by the applicant union,[149] the most important being that it is made to one lone employer. Schedule A1 "deals solely with relations between an individual employer and his or her employees".[150] The possibility still exists for voluntary recognition agreements between employers' associations and unions if they so wish, but the legislation follows and perpetuates established trends. This limitation to single- employer bargaining was defended in Standing Committee as stemming from the CBI and TUC in their "Joint Statement".[151] Such a view can be drawn from a careful reading of this document's discussion on the definition of the "bargaining unit".[152] Certainly, it follows from patterns of collective bargaining already established in the UK.

In 1998, commenting on the proposals in *Fairness at Work*, Lord Wedderburn observed that this was a sensible choice. If recognition at the level of the single

---

[143] See above this chap. at 68.

[144] *Donovan Commission Report*, n.24 above, at paras. 67–68.

[145] *Ibid.*, chap. 5.

[146] Cully *et al.*, n.8 above, at 106. See also W. Brown, "The Contraction of Collective Bargaining in Britain" (1993) 31 *BJIR* 189 at 195.

[147] Brown, n.146 above, at 198.

[148] A development highlighted briefly in R. Hyman, "Industrial Relations in Europe: Crisis or Reconstruction?" in T. Wilthagen, *Advancing Theory in Labour Law and Industrial Relations in a Global Context* (Amsterdam: North-Holland, 1998) at 188.

[149] TULRCA 1992, Sched. A1, para. 8. Under para. 9, further procedural forms may be specified by statutory instrument. See also para. 5 which specifies that it must be received by the employer to be valid.

[150] HC Standing Committee E, 16 Mar. 1999 at col. 358, *per* Mr Wills.

[151] *Ibid.*

[152] "Joint Statement", n.84 above, paras. 12–13: "[b]oth the TUC and CBI recognise that whereas this procedure does not relate to national industrial agreements, the framework is intended to be compatible with such agreements".

firm can be "got right", then "a version might be worked out for associated employers, company groups and perhaps even more easily transnationals and MNCs".[153] This remains a possibility, but there is no sign in the Employment Relations Act 1999 that the present Government has plans in this direction.

What is more promising is that no employer is excluded from the coverage of Schedule A1. The Conservatives argued that exceptions be made in particular cases, such as that of the Plymouth or Exclusive Brethren who, for reasons of religious conscience, refuse to recognise trade unions. The Government was presented with an uncomfortable stand-off between two established human rights: freedom to manifest one's religion or beliefs and the right of workers to be represented by a trade union. The former is protected to some extent under Article 9 of the European Convention on Human Rights, while the latter arguably arises under both Article 11 of the Convention and Articles 5 and 6 of the European Social Charter.[154] The Government came out on the side of collective representation, stating that the Brethren would be unable to use their religious beliefs to evade recognition through the statutory procedure.[155] In this instance, the Government seemed to take a strong line on collective representation of workers, but any admiration for this stance is likely to diminish on closer investigation of the other limitations inherent in Schedule A1.

ii. the exclusion of "small firms"

In their "Joint Statement", the TUC and CBI expressed their differences on the subject of "small firms". The CBI believed that "a recognition procedure would have a disproportionate effect on small businesses and that a minimum threshold should apply". The TUC could not support such a proposal "as it would exclude significant and increasing numbers of employees from statutory rights to union recognition".[156] It was the CBI view which prevailed with the New Labour Government.

Exclusion of small firms from this procedure was canvassed in *Fairness at Work*:

> Many small companies recognise trade unions already. Many do not. In many small firms, employment relations are managed not just on an individual, but on a personal level. In these circumstances statutory requirements on trade union recognition would be inappropriate. So the provisions will not apply to companies below a set threshold.[157]

---

[153] Lord Wedderburn, "A British Duty to Bargain—A Footnote on the End-Game" (1998) 27 *ILJ* 253 at 253.

[154] See J. Hendy and M. Walton, "An Individual Right to Union Representation in International Law" (1997) 26 *ILJ* 205 and J. Hendy, *Every Worker Shall Have the Right to be Represented at Work by a Trade Union* (London: Institute of Employment Rights, 1998).

[155] See discussions in HC Standing Committee E, 16 Mar. 1999, cols. 393–397, *per* Mr Boswell, Mr Collins and Mr Wills.

[156] "Joint Statement", n.84 above, at para. 9.

[157] *FAW*, para. 4.17.

This argument was repeated by the Government in debates relating to the Employment Relations Bill,[158] which subsequently set the 21—worker threshold.[159] If, at any time, the employer decides to reduce the workforce to fewer than 21 workers, the employer may apply for derecognition.[160]

A request for recognition will not be valid unless the employer, taken together with any associated employer or employers, employs either at least 21 workers on the day the employer receives the request or an average of at least 21 workers in the 13 weeks ending with that day. This ensures that employers cannot artificially evade statutory coverage, either by reliance on the corporate veil[161] or by varying the number of workers in their employ according to demand within a three-month period.[162] Nevertheless, there have been suggestions that "employers are willing to split up their operations into smaller franchised units to defeat the purpose of the legislation".[163]

Reference to "workers" rather than "employees" makes the legislation more inclusive and these rights more universal. The Conservative Opposition sought to amend the Employment Relations Bill to exclude from the definition of "workers" the directors, company secretary and other persons who are regarded as "officers of the company", shareholders in any private limited company or company whose shares are not quoted on any recognised stock exchange, and members of a partnership.[164] There could be "no logical reason to include such persons in the quorum required to trigger the recognition procedure". After all, if such persons were included as workers, this could cut against the union's claim for recognition, as the board of a company inclined to resist trade union recognition would vote against the claim, leaving the union with "an assured X number of votes against it".[165] However, the Government Minister observed that the application of section 296 of TULRCA 1992 ensured that "most directors, and particularly non-executive directors, will not normally be workers". The danger of the Conservative amendment would have been that employees owning shares in the business would be excluded from counting as a worker for the purposes of Schedule A1, and this could not be countenanced by the Government.[166] Here we may be witnessing the remnants of New Labour's past

---

[158] In HC Standing Committee E, 16 Mar. 1999, Mr Wills stated at col. 347 that: "[t]he Government recognize that small firms may be different in that they are often managed on a personal basis and collective bargaining may be inappropriate". However, he acknowledged that some small firms already recognised trade unions voluntarily and that he was "sure they will continue to do so".

[159] See TULRCA 1992, Sched. A1, para. 7.

[160] TULRCA 1992, Sched. A1, paras. 99–103.

[161] See for the definition of "associated employer" TULRCA 1992 s. 297.

[162] See for how the average is to be determined TULRCA 1992, Sched. A1, para. 7(2).

[163] *Employment Rights Building on Fairness at Work* (London: Institute of Employment Rights and Press for Union Rights, 2000), 11, para. 9.7.

[164] HL Hansard, 8 July 1999, cols. 1048–1049, *per* Baroness Miller.

[165] *Ibid.*

[166] HL Hansard, 8 July 1999, col. 1051, *per* Lord McIntosh.

enthusiasm for "stakeholding" as a means by which to promote "partner-ship".[167]

The 21-worker threshold is likely to preserve the status quo, namely minimal collective bargaining in small firms. In 1998, statistical evidence from the WERS Survey indicated that union recognition was much more common among large workplaces.[168] Moreover, in small workplaces, "the indicators of a healthy employment relationship are mixed". Workers in these small businesses tend to have relatively high levels of job satisfaction, but at the same time they find themselves lowly paid, and industrial tribunal applications are also relatively high in respect of such workers.[169] This raises certain questions about what the impact of Schedule A1 will be, for it seems likely to exclude those most in need of the assistance it can provide.

In the House of Lords, the Government minister conceded that the exclusion of these small workplaces would exclude 8.1 million people or 31 per cent of the total workforce from the statutory recognition provisions.[170] The Government does not appear concerned by the lack of access to collective bargaining which this threshold entails. Nor was it willing to respond to TUC concerns that this exclusion is likely to have a discriminatory impact, as more women than men work in small workplaces.[171]

This threshold seems relatively arbitrary, when one makes comparisons with other pieces of legislation. For example, the Government has amended the Disability Discrimination Act 1995, lowering the threshold number of employees necessary for a firm to be covered by the legislation from 20 to 15.[172] One member of the Opposition described the number as having been "plucked out of the air".[173] She and others argued for a threshold of 50 workers, thereby seeking to exclude greater numbers of workplaces from these provisions.[174]

The Government itself has provided its own legislative loophole, which allows the Secretary of State to move this numerical threshold up or down.[175] Government ministers indicated that they would do so if this proved "necessary".[176]

[167] See above Chap. 1 at 14.

[168] Cully *et al.*, n.8 above, at 239–40.

[169] *Ibid.* at 27.

[170] See HL Hansard, 8 July 1999, col. 1045. The TUC has placed this estimate more conservatively at approximately five million. See Motion C2 on Employment Rights and Fairness at Work, carried at 1999 TUC Congress.

[171] TUC, *TUC Response: Fairness at Work White Paper* (London: TUC, 1998), paras. 38–47.

[172] Disability Discrimination Act 1995 s. 7(1) as amended by SI 1998/2618, in force from 1 Dec. 1998.

[173] HL Hansard, 7 June 1999, col. 1161, *per* Baroness Miller.

[174] See HL Hansard, 30 Mar. 1999, cols. 884–916; HL Hansard, 10 May 1999, cols. 1038–1040; HL Hansard, 7 June 1999, cols. 1160–1175; HL Hansard, 8 July 1999, cols. 1040–1046; HL Hansard, 15 July 1999, cols. 567–571; HC Hansard, 26 July 1999, cols. 41–48. Their arguments reflect submissions made by the CBI, British Chambers of Commerce (BCC) and Federation of Small Businesses (FSB). Lourie, n.38 above, at 41.

[175] TULRCA 1992, Sched. A1, paras. 7(6)–(8).

[176] HC Standing Committee E 16 Mar. 1999, cols. 406–407; HL Hansard, 7 June 1999, at col. 1176 and 8 July 1999, col. 1045; and HC Hansard, 26 July 1999, col. 48.

iii. limitations placed on applicant unions

All unions which make a request for recognition under Schedule A1 must be independent.[177] This means satisfying the Certification Officer that the union meets the criteria set out in section 5 of TULRCA 1992. This is desirable, given the importance of independence under ILO standards. It is also consistent with the emphasis placed on "independence" in past UK legislation.[178]

It is still open to employers to opt for recognition of a non-independent or "sweetheart" union. "If workers are happy to be represented by a union without a certificate of independence, there is no problem."[179] Nevertheless, this cannot ultimately be used as a device by which to defeat access of independent unions to recognition under the statutory procedure. Workers can seek derecognition of a non-independent trade union under Schedule A1, so as "to ensure that an employer cannot frustrate the wishes of his workforce by recognising a non-independent trade union".[180] The main problem for the workers is the nuisance and delay arising from the necessity to make such an application.[181]

More important are the screening devices which ensure that there will be no conflicting or overlapping applications to the CAC.[182] This may seem an overly elaborate way in which to address issues of potentially overlapping applications, but these have been designed to ensure that "there will be no return to . . . the damaging demarcation disputes of the past".[183] These rules apparently reflect TUC concerns over cases like *UKAPE*,[184] but the way in which the actual provisions have been drafted means that they can also be used to thwart the acceptance of applications from the most representative trade union within a bargaining unit.

Schedule A1 requires that the bargaining unit in an application must not overlap with that in an application which the CAC has already accepted,[185] or be substantially the same as that which the CAC has accepted in the past three years.[186] Moreover, applications cannot relate to substantially similar matters in respect of which the CAC has already made a declaration or decision relating to non-recognition[187] or derecognition in the past three years.[188] This is consistent with the understanding that, in general, a recognition agreement or

---

[177] TULRCA 1992, Sched. A1, para. 6. Also, where a trade union loses its certificate of independence, the agreed or imposed bargaining arrangements shall cease to have effect. See TULRCA 1992, Sched. A1, Part VII, paras. 149–154.

[178] See above Chap. 3 at 48–9.

[179] HC Standing Committee E, 16 Mar. 1999 at col. 348, *per* Mr Wills.

[180] *Ibid.* See also TULRCA 1992, Sched. A1, Part VI, paras. 134–148.

[181] See below this chap. at 95–6.

[182] TULRCA 1992, Sched. A1, para. 14. Compare with paras. 38–51.

[183] HC Standing Committee E, 16 Mar. 1999 at col. 347, *per* Mr Wills.

[184] See above this chap. at 68.

[185] TULRCA 1992, Sched. A1, para. 38.

[186] TULRCA 1992, Sched. A1, para. 39.

[187] TULRCA 1992, Sched. A1, para. 40.

[188] TULRCA 1992, Sched. A1, para. 41.

declaration of recognition by the CAC has a currency of three years. This is designed to provide a measure of industrial stability.[189]

Joint applications by more than one union are admissible, but the unions must be able to show that "they will co-operate with each other in a manner likely to secure and maintain stable and effective collective bargaining arrangements", and that "if the employer wishes, they will enter into arrangements under which collective bargaining is conducted by the unions acting together on behalf of the workers constituting the relevant bargaining unit".[190]

Where two or more relevant applications have been made, at least one worker falls within both proposed bargaining units and the CAC has not yet accepted any of the applications, then a 10 per cent test may be applied. If only one of the applicants has 10 per cent membership at that workplace, it will succeed while the others will not. If the 10 per cent test is satisfied in respect of more than one application or none of the applications, the CAC will send all the applicants away.[191] This means that a competing application from an independent trade union (such as a professional association similar to UKAPE) with over 10 per cent membership, but which is not representative of the majority of the workforce, can thwart an application by a much more representative trade union. This is significant, given that more than half of unionised workplaces have two or more unions present.[192] It is possible that such a scenario will force TUC-affiliated unions to consider alliances with non-affiliated unions; indirectly placing pressure on them to adopt a more moderate negotiating stance.

Similarly, an application must not cover any workers in respect of whom a union is already recognised by the employer in question (voluntarily or otherwise).[193] There are only two exceptions to this rule. One is where the applicant union is the one already recognised and the existing recognition agreement does not cover pay, holidays or hours.[194] The other is where the recognised union has no certificate of independence, was previously recognised in respect of the same (or substantially the same) bargaining unit and ceased to be recognised three years prior to the application.[195]

A canny employer may therefore choose to pre-empt the statutory recognition procedure by recognising the trade union which is independent but which poses the least threat to its management agenda. This choice of the employer can preclude a more representative union bringing a claim for recognition. The

---

[189] This was a period agreed upon by the TUC and CBI in their "Joint Statement", n.84 above, para. 7. See also Wedderburn, n.106 above, at 38, who is less than impressed by the stability this is supposed to confer on bargaining arrangements. We are tempted to agree with his views, given the potential for employer-led changes in the bargaining unit, discussed below this chap. at 89–90.

[190] TULRCA 1992, Sched. A1, para. 37. See HC Hansard, 26 July 1999, col. 39, *per* Mr McCartney.

[191] TULRCA 1992, Sched. A1, para. 14.

[192] Cully *et al.*, n.8 above, at 93.

[193] TULRCA 1992, Sched. A1, paras. 11–12 and para. 35.

[194] TULRCA 1992, Sched. A1, para. 35(2).

[195] TULRCA 1992, Sched. A1, para. 35(4).

employer's decision to do so may also lead, in turn, to a deterioration in the membership of that (once more representative) trade union. In such circumstances, workers are more likely to join the union which, being recognised by the employer, has some influence, as opposed to another which sits entirely outside the bargaining process.[196] Therefore, in the name of "choice", the new procedures for workers' determination of their collective bargaining representative can be undermined. In July 1999, reports were leaked that regional media employers were already planning to use recognition for "non-traditional independent unions" as a means by which to avoid the effects of the statutory recognition procedure.[197]

The issue of demarcation disputes was discussed by the TUC and CBI in the context of their "Joint Statement". They agreed that an Agency (now the CAC) "should have the power not to proceed with an application until the matter had been resolved", on the basis that this would encourage the unions to resolve their differences between themselves. There was also agreement that "it is for the TUC, rather than the legislation, to settle disputes involving its affiliates by recourse to its own established rules and procedures".[198] The problem is that the capacity for an employer to engage in a strategy of pre-emptive recognition of the independent union of its choice means that it will often be actually the employer, rather than the TUC, which resolves demarcation disputes.

There is potential for correction if the Government is concerned by the manner in which the CAC applies these provisions or their effect when they are placed in operation. Where two or more applications are made to the CAC in circumstances where each application is relevant and relates to the same bargaining unit, such that the CAC cannot accept either application, the Secretary of State may make a direction as to the order in which the CAC will consider the admissibility of the applications.[199] This is potentially desirable, but is one facet of the legislation which undermines what once was the independence of the CAC.[200] There are no indications yet of how this residual discretion will be exercised, if at all.

c. numerical thresholds for establishing workplace support

It is not only the rhetoric of "partnership" but also that of "free choice" that is reflected in Schedule A1. Workers may exercise their "choice" as to their preferred bargaining representative through "democratic" procedures according to certain numerical thresholds. However, the bargaining unit within which the workers will be balloted is to be determined by the CAC primarily with reference to the need for "effective management". It is therefore the employer which

---

[196] See *Donovan Commission Report*, n.24 above, at para. 219.

[197] S. Milne, "Newspapers Plot to Circumvent Union Law", *Guardian*, 27 July 1999.

[198] "Joint Statement", n.84 above, at para. 11.

[199] TULRCA 1992, Sched. A1, para. 169.

[200] See below this chap. at 121–6 for discussion of the transformation of the role of the CAC.

is in fact likely to determine the "electorate" for any ballot. Employers also retain managerial discretion to restructure, thereby undermining established bargaining units and recognition agreements. For this reason it is *managerial* choice that is likely to prevail.

Moreover, the threat of derecognition hovers in the background. Business is provided with the weaponry to end dealings with a union recognised under the statutory procedure. In an even-handed show of parity of treatment, almost exactly the same procedures can be used to derecognise as to recognise a union. There is no pretence here that the Government's aim is simply to extend collective bargaining.[201] This is a matter of "choice" for the interested "partners" in the working relationship: the employer and the workers.

Finally, the logistics of the automatic recognition procedure and the costs and inconvenience of balloting are likely to ensure that a union does not embark on the statutory recognition process without considerable confidence in a positive outcome. This may mean that, in many workplaces, there will be no initiatives taken to secure union recognition, because the procedure itself operates as a deterrent. Unions will be more willing to compromise early in the course of bargaining, rather than bear the expenses and suffer the delays that the negotiating procedure, the application procedure and the balloting procedure entail. This does not bode well for effective and credible union representation of workers.

i. the rhetoric of "choice" and "democracy"

The election commitment given by New Labour was that unions should be recognised "if that was what the majority of the workforce wanted".[202] The justification for this promise is the protection of individual choices. *Fairness at Work* acknowledged that, "while many employers and employees will continue to choose direct relationships without the involvement of third parties", in certain cases the workforce might choose collective representation.[203] In order to claim legitimacy, workers' choices are to be made through "democratic" procedures.[204] Where the union can establish substantial support by such means, employers are not to deny trade union recognition.[205] This is, in part, out of respect for individual choices, but also because to do so makes sense in business terms.[206]

---

[201] Compare with the claims made by the Heath Government as regards the IRA 1971, discussed above this chap. at 65. See Mellish and Dickens, n.26 above, at 229.

[202] HC Standing Committee E, 16 Mar. 1999 at col. 344, *per* Mr Wills.

[203] *FAW*, para. 1.9.

[204] Lord McIntosh in HL Hansard, 7 June 1999, col. 1196, observed that "[w]e want these decisions to have clear democratic legitimacy". See also, for another example of the use of "democratic" rhetoric, comments made by Baroness Turner in HL Hansard, 10 May 1999, col. 1009.

[205] *FAW*, para. 2.6.

[206] "The key to better relationships between workers and employers, to better morale and to greater profitability is to respect workers' wishes—that is what recognition is about. The schedule stands for partnership, not conflict": HC Standing Committee E, 16 Mar. 1999 at col. 349, *per* Mr Wills.

This might appear to be a significant incursion into the traditional sphere of managerial prerogative, which has conventionally included the employer's choice whether to recognise a trade union; yet the statutory requirements designed to assess workers' support for recognition deviate significantly from those imposed in the general democratic process. The scope of those balloted in the "bargaining unit" is likely to be determined largely with reference to the interests of management rather than labour. Arguably, this is akin to allowing one political party to determine the boundaries of constituencies. In addition, the threshold baseline of support necessary for a valid application is unusually high. It can be compared to requiring a political party to demonstrate that it can win an election before it is allowed to stand for office. Moreover, the numerical thresholds required to achieve either automatic recognition or recognition through a ballot make it more difficult for a trade union to achieve statutory recognition than it is for a political party to win a general election. There is no respect at all for the principle that individual workers should be given a choice to select a trade union as their bargaining agent, regardless of the views of the majority of the workforce.[207]

ii. determination of the bargaining unit

Determination of the bargaining unit is crucial to the efficacy of a statutory recognition procedure because this is likely to affect the level of support for trade union recognition, in terms both of the preliminary "baseline support" which must be established and the outcome of any ballot. It is most likely to matter where a workplace contains a mixture of staff performing very different tasks and belonging to different unions.

In the "Joint Statement", the TUC considered that if the union and employer were in dispute about the "bargaining unit", the "Agency" should make a ruling on what is appropriate, deciding each case on its merits. The TUC asked that a range of factors be taken into account in determining the bargaining unit including "the nature of shared interests and similar work; group awareness; the wishes of the workforce concerned; the organisation and location of work; the relative financial autonomy of the group; and the need to avoid disrupting existing arrangements for collective bargaining". The CBI acknowledged the significance of these factors but believed that "the key consideration is the nature of the business".[208]

Fairness at Work denied that there would be any difficulty with determination of the bargaining unit, which would be "clearly defined to avoid disagreements".[209] This was an ambitious claim. Schedule A1 envisages an ideal

---

[207] This is a principle established by the ILO in cases such as *Case No. 1698 (New Zealand)* 292nd Report of the ILO Committee on Freedom of Association (1994) para. 675 at paras. 689–695. See for further discussion of its implications for the UK, Hendy and Walton, n.154 above, and Hendy, n.154 above.

[208] "Joint Statement", n.84 above, at para. 13.

[209] *FAW*, para. 4.17.

scenario in which the employer and union parties agree on the bargaining unit, in their preliminary negotiations.[210] However, agreement may not be forthcoming. If so, it falls for the CAC to determine what bargaining unit is appropriate.[211] Whether the definition set out in the Employment Relations Act is precise enough to avert the danger of disagreement is debatable. This provision nods in the direction of managerial prerogative without settling disputes about the application of subsidiary criteria for the determination of the bargaining unit.

In deciding the appropriate bargaining unit, the CAC must take into account, primarily, "the need for the unit to be compatible with effective management" and five other factors, "so far as they do not conflict with that need".[212] These other factors are: the views of the employer and of the union (or unions); existing national and local bargaining arrangements; the desirability of avoiding small fragmented bargaining units within an undertaking; the characteristics of workers falling within the proposed bargaining unit and of any other employees of the employer whom the CAC considers relevant; and the location of workers.[213] The CAC must give notice of its decision to the parties, but in this case is not under any direct statutory obligation to give reasons, although it may wish to do so to protect its decisions from judicial review.[214]

This central emphasis on compatibility with effective management reduces the chances of broader-based bargaining and gives precedence to the employer's preferences. This was what the CBI asked for in the "Joint Statement" and ultimately what it got.[215] The Government has claimed that this is a "modern definition of recognition", "tailored for single-status, single-table bargaining workplaces, if that is what the employer wants".[216] In this way, New Labour managed to distance itself from trade union demands and reassure business. The employer will therefore have considerable influence in determining the scope of the workforce balloted for recognition.

iii. the baseline of support

In the "Joint Statement", the CBI set out its view that a union claim for recognition should be accompanied by a demonstration of 30 per cent support from the workers to whom the claim relates.[217] The TUC did not support this idea "for a number of reasons, not least that the issue of support is inextricably tied up with the definition of the bargaining unit".[218] Nevertheless, *Fairness at Work* indicated that a "baseline of support" was necessary,[219] stating that a union

---

[210] TULRCA 1992, Sched. A1, para. 10.
[211] TULRCA 1992, Sched. A1, paras. 11–12 and 18–19.
[212] TULRCA 1992, Sched. A1, para. 19(3).
[213] TULRCA 1992, Sched. A1, para. 19(4).
[214] See on judicial review of the EPA 1975, above this chap. at 69–71.
[215] "Joint Statement", n.84 above, at para. 12.
[216] HC Standing Committee E, 16 Mar. 1999, col. 347, *per* Mr Wills.
[217] "Joint Statement", n.84 above, at para. 6.
[218] *Ibid.*
[219] *FAW*, para. 4.17.

applying for statutory recognition would have to present evidence to the CAC, possibly in "the form of membership records or a petition signed by a sufficient number of employees". The employer could also submit evidence.[220] The reason given was that this would "deter insubstantial claims".[221] The Government's aim may have been to avoid the large bulk of applications which hampered the operation of the statutory recognition procedure under the Employment Protection Act 1975.[222]

Schedule A1 now requires that members of the applicant union (or unions) must constitute at least 10 per cent of the workers in the relevant bargaining unit and the CAC must be satisfied that a majority of workers in that unit must be likely to favour recognition of the union for collective bargaining purposes.[223] The CAC must give reasons for this decision.[224]

The 10 per cent threshold is not too great a barrier to overcome; it compares favourably with the CBI's initial proposal of 30 per cent membership. The problem lies with the second limb of the test, for it may be more difficult to convince the CAC that the majority of workers would favour recognition. This could be done by evidence of over 50 per cent union membership but, in a workplace where the trade union is not recognised, this may be difficult to achieve. As Dickens observed, when commenting on the operation of the statutory recognition procedure under the Employment Protection Act 1975, "where it is thought the employer is opposed to union membership (and the fact that there are no unions may be so interpreted), an employee may feel union membership would jeopardise his career or employment prospects".[225] At present, there is no properly developed legal concept of privacy whereby an employee can keep such information hidden from the employer, although it is arguable that this may develop under the Human Rights Act 1998.[226]

If evidence of support for trade union recognition is not to be achieved by membership records of the applicant union then, as the Government might have suggested in the White Paper, the union may have recourse to a petition. However, a union which lacks recognition may well find it difficult to gain access to the workplace to tout for signatures. Access is provided for the unrecognised trade union in the context of preparations for a recognition ballot, but not at this initial preliminary stage.[227] Individual trade union members could try to persuade fellow-workers to sign a petition during breaks, but they

---

[220] *FAW*, Annex 1.
[221] *FAW*, para. 4.17.
[222] Discussed above this chap. at 69–70.
[223] TULRCA 1992, Sched. A1, para. 36.
[224] *Ibid.*
[225] Dickens, n.46 above, at 173.
[226] See M. Forde, *Surveillance and Privacy at Work* (London: Institute of Employment Rights, 1998). Note also the move towards protection of the names of trade union members in the context of industrial action ballots under the ERelA 1999. See below Chap. 5 at 145–7.
[227] See the apparently limited requirement of access under TULRCA 1992, Sched. A1, para. 26(3), discussed below this chap. at 99–100.

might be reluctant to expose themselves to the employer's displeasure in this fashion.[228] Alternatively, trade union members could seek to canvass support by word of mouth for a meeting off the employer's premises, where signatures could be provided. In either case, achieving proof of this baseline of support is not likely to be easy.

iv. automatic recognition

Automatic recognition is based on the assumption that the primary reason for joining a trade union is that people want to be represented collectively. However, employers have refused to share this conviction. They have argued that workers may want to be trade union members "for reasons other than the desire to be covered by collective bargaining", such as individual representation or financial services.[229] The result was that the White Paper proposal for automatic recognition was watered down in the subsequent December 1998 policy statement, and again in the Employment Relations Act. Provision is made for automatic recognition where "the CAC is satisfied that a majority of workers constituting the bargaining unit are members of a union".[230] However, the CAC's obligation to grant recognition in these circumstances is subject to three important "qualifying conditions". If any of these conditions are fulfilled, the CAC cannot grant automatic recognition and must hold a ballot. These conditions arise where:

> (a) the CAC is satisfied that a ballot should be held in the interests of good industrial relations; (b) a significant number of the union members within the bargaining unit inform the CAC that they do not want the union (or unions) to conduct collective bargaining on their behalf; and (c) membership evidence is produced which leads the CAC to conclude that there are doubts whether a significant number of the union members within the bargaining unit want the union (or unions) to conduct collective bargaining on their behalf.[231]

In all likelihood, the most problematic of these three conditions for automatic recognition is the first, because it is so open-ended. It could be argued that imposing automatic recognition on an employer, who refuses to regard the union as representative in the absence of ballot, would not enhance "good industrial relations".

The relevant Government minister in Standing Committee suggested a much narrower role for this catch-all exception. It was to ensure that "only genuine and current members should be counted". While union membership is "a matter of fact", determined by the union rule book, the CAC must be able to take account of evidence which would cast doubt on union claims for support within the unit for collective bargaining. "If, for example, the employer can show that

---

[228] See above Chap. 2 at 32–9 for discussion of the limits of protection from discrimination on grounds of trade union membership and activities.
[229] Lourie, n.38 above, at 40–1.
[230] TULRCA 1992, Sched. A1, paras. 22 and 87.
[231] TULRCA 1992, Sched. A1, para. 22(4).

a significant number of union members have recently cancelled their check-off authorisations and appear to be leaving the union, that might prompt the CAC to hold a ballot."[232]

As regards factors (b) and (c), in Standing Committee the minister explained that "a significant number" in this context merely meant "a number capable of affecting the result". There was "no reason for the CAC to take account of a small number of workers who do not want to be represented if it is clear that a majority do so wish. But if the number who oppose recognition means that the majority is in doubt, then there should be a ballot. That sensible and practical approach underlies the wording of the clause".[233]

Much depends on how the CAC, and ultimately the courts (if the CAC's decision is challenged by judicial review), interpret these factors. In this respect, guidance may be given by the Secretary of State and the CAC must take such guidance into account.[234] If the CAC expresses concern that present provisions for automatic recognition have an "unsatisfactory effect" and represents that they should be amended, the Secretary of State is empowered to make amendments by statutory instrument which would rectify that effect.[235] This is consistent with various "safety net" amendment clauses contained in Schedule A1,[236] which allow the Government a measure of flexibility in its handling of industrial relations.

v. "majority support" in a ballot

From Labour's 1997 Election Manifesto, it might have seemed that in order to win recognition a union would merely have to achieve a bare majority in a workers' ballot. This is, after all, the standard requirement established in ballots as regards industrial action and election of trade union representatives.[237] This mistaken impression was corrected by the White Paper, which stated that "a majority of those voting and at least forty per cent of those eligible to vote" had to support recognition.[238] This qualification to New Labour's electoral promises was stated to be justified for two reasons:

> First, without real and substantial support amongst employees, collective bargaining simply will not work. Second, since collective bargaining has an impact on all

---

[232] HC Standing Committee E, 16 Mar. 1999 at cols. 388–9, *per* Mr Wills.

[233] *Ibid.*

[234] TULRCA 1992, Sched. A1, para. 167. This may compromise the traditional independence of the CAC. See below this chap. at 121–6.

[235] This is subject to the affirmative resolution procedure. However, the Secretary of State is free to amend paras. 22 and 87 "in such way as he thinks fit, and not necessarily in a way proposed by the CAC (if it proposes one)": TULRCA 1992, Sched. A1, para. 166.

[236] Other examples include TULRCA 1992, Sched. A1, paras. 7(6) and 7(7) which allows the Secretary of State to amend the threshold of workers for small firms; para. 29 which allows the Secretary of State to alter the numbers of favourable votes which unions require for success in a recognition ballot; and para. 169 which allows the Secretary of State to give directions to the CAC in situations where there are overlapping applications for recognition.

[237] See above Chap. 3 at 51 and below Chap. 5 at 141–5.

[238] *FAW*, Annex I.

employees, not just those claiming union representation, it is right that it should be granted only in circumstances where substantial support is demonstrated.[239]

These are curious arguments which, if applied to the political sphere, would undermine the Government's own credibility. One might observe that, without real and substantial support from the populace, government will not work. Moreover, since government has an impact on all citizens, not just those who vote, should they not also be able to show "substantial support", namely from 40 per cent of the electorate? Yet, as has been observed elsewhere, "if these conditions had applied at the general election . . . there would scarcely be an MP in Westminster".[240]

The Government's statement is also inconsistent with New Labour's apathy on the subject of voluntary recognition, for an employer remains free to recognise a union regardless of the degree of support such a union can muster in the workplace. This is a state of affairs maintained by Schedule A1, which even allows an employer's decision to recognise a non-representative trade union to preclude an application for statutory recognition by a more representative union.[241] The consequences for the individual worker in such a situation are at least as problematic, if not more so, than the circumstances of the individual worker in a workplace where statutory recognition is granted by virtue of a bare majority.

The Government did resist Conservative proposals for an even more stringent test; that of an affirmative vote by 50 per cent of those eligible to vote.[242] Mr Wills thought it sufficient that "strong opposition will lead to losing the ballot and lack of support will fail the forty per cent test".[243] The Government has however made statutory provision for voting thresholds to be revised by Order, either upwards or downwards.[244]

The case for revising this threshold seems to be strong. "In any forty per cent rule, the dead, those who are ill and those who abstain are all considered to have been against the proposition and to have voted no. All of them will add to the 40 per cent barrier whether or not that was their true intention."[245] A "yes" vote from forty per cent of the electorate is more than the Labour Government achieved in the 1997 general election, which was widely regarded as a landslide victory.[246]

[239] *FAW*, para. 4.16.

[240] N. Cohen, "The Fat-Cat Lawyers are Licking Their Lips", *Observer*, 4 June 2000.

[241] See above this chap. at 85–7.

[242] HC Standing Committee E, 16 Mar. 1999, cols. 405–406.

[243] HC Standing Committee E, 16 Mar. 1999, cols. 406–407, *per* Mr Wills.

[244] TULRCA 1992, Sched. A1, para. 29. See also HC Standing Committee E, 16 Mar. 1999, cols. 406–407.

[245] HC Hansard, 31 Mar. 1999, col. 1179, *per* Mr Welsh.

[246] Lourie, n.38 above, at 41. See also HC Hansard, 31 Mar. 1999, col. 1180.

vi. the level of support required for derecognition

Even where recognition is granted, if it appears that worker support for the union has deteriorated, statutory *derecognition* becomes possible.[247] The White Paper invited submissions on how this should work.[248] By December 1998, the Government was clear that this would be a feature of the new regime, thereby satisfying the demands of the CBI.[249]

Part IV of Schedule A1 provides that, three years after a CAC declaration of recognition, an employer can seek derecognition, as can any worker or group of workers within the bargaining unit.[250] An application will not be considered admissible unless the equivalent threshold to be met for recognition is met here, in reverse. So it is necessary for the applicant to demonstrate that at least 10 per cent of the workers constituting the bargaining unit favour an end to the bargaining arrangements and that a majority of the workers constituting the bargaining unit would be likely to favour an end to the bargaining arrangement.[251] Arguably, it will be much easier for the employer, who has ready access to the workforce, to produce this kind of evidence than it was for the union applying for recognition.[252]

If, after the necessary time for negotiations has passed, the CAC accepts a request for derecognition, then there is scope for a ballot to test support for recognition.[253] For a derecognition ballot to succeed, the proposition that bargaining arrangements should be ended must be supported by a majority of the workers voting and at least 40 per cent of the workers constituting the bargaining unit.[254]

Where the recognition was automatic, the employer can, after three years, request to end bargaining arrangements, but the CAC will not accept the application unless it is evident that "fewer than half of the workers constituting the bargaining unit are members of the union (or unions)".[255] It is only in those circumstances that a ballot will be held for derecognition. Derecognition will be granted where a majority of those voting and at least 40 per cent of the workers constituting the bargaining unit favour derecognition.

Where the employer has recognised a union that is not independent, workers have the ability to make an application to end bargaining arrangements. This is consistent with the general emphasis in TULRCA 1992 and the Employment

---

[247] *FAW*, para. 4.17.

[248] *FAW*, para. 4.18.

[249] J. Lourie, *Employment Relations Bill 1998/99 Bill 36*, House of Commons Research Paper 99/11 (London: House of Commons, 1999), 12.

[250] See in particular, TULRCA 1992, Sched. A1, paras. 104–116.

[251] TULRCA 1992, Sched. A1, para. 110(1) and para. 114(1). Again, reasons must be given for these decisions and other admissibility requirements met.

[252] See above this chap. at 90–2.

[253] TULRCA 1992, Sched. A1, paras. 117–121.

[254] TULRCA 1992, Sched. A1, para. 121(3).

[255] TULRCA 1992, Sched. A1, para. 131(1).

Relations Act 1999 on preferential treatment for independent trade unions.[256] However, this application will not be admissible if an application has already been made to the Certification Officer (CO) for a certificate of independence and the decision of the CO is still pending.[257] Also, if at all during the period allowed for negotiations the union is found to be independent, the application will be treated as not having been made.[258] If the union is definitely not independent, the matter is still not straightforward. Once again, *prima facie* evidence will have to be produced to demonstrate that at least 10 per cent of the workers in the bargaining unit do favour and that a majority of workers would be likely to favour an end to extant bargaining arrangements.[259] If after the period allowed for negotiations no agreement is reached between the parties, a ballot must be held with the standard thresholds required for derecognition.[260]

Derecognition is also potentially possible, not simply by reason of loss of employee support for representation by a particular union (or unions), but also for reasons associated with managerial choice. There are two ways in which the employer can seek to achieve derecognition even though the three year period has not expired.[261] The first is by reducing the workforce in the bargaining unit below the number qualifying for statutory recognition; the second entails claiming that the bargaining unit has ceased to exist. If at any time the employer decides to reduce the workforce to fewer than 21 workers, the employer may apply for derecognition.[262] In such circumstances, the choices of the workforce become irrelevant. The employer can also choose to alter the nature of the bargaining unit by restructuring the business, changing the activities pursued in the course of business or changing substantially the number of workers employed.[263] It is then for the CAC to decide whether the original bargaining unit still exists and, if not, what it may be replaced with.[264] In this situation derecognition may arise because support for union representation has splintered or defused, for example being apportioned across two new bargaining units. If it is decided that the bargaining unit has ceased to exist, there is also a prospect of effective derecognition.[265] The stability that the three year rule confers is potentially undermined by the discretion conferred on management under these provisions.

---

[256] See above Chap. 3 at 48–9.

[257] TULRCA 1992, Sched. A1, para. 140. Note that the application for a certificate of independence must have been made before the application for derecognition. The Government considered it "important to prevent unscrupulous employers using an application for a certificate of independence by a sweetheart union which they control to delay a perfectly fair application under Part VI". See HL Hansard, 8 July 1999, col. 1070, *per* Lord McIntosh.

[258] TULRCA 1992, Sched. A1, para. 146.

[259] TULRCA 1992, Sched. A1, para. 139(1) and the CAC must give reasons for its decision that this requirement is satisfied.

[260] TULRCA 1992, Sched. A1, para. 147.

[261] See above this chap. at 95

[262] TULRCA 1992, Sched. A1, paras. 99–103.

[263] TULRCA 1992, Sched. A1, para. 70(3), recognised in *FAW*, Annex 1 at 44.

[264] TULRCA 1992, Sched. A1, para. 70(4) and (5).

[265] TULRCA 1992, Sched. A1, paras. 74–77.

vii. the costs and logistics of balloting

Once the CAC decides to proceed with a ballot, various procedural obligations are placed on it. These are designed to secure "democratic legitimacy", to the extent that they secure impartiality. Nevertheless, the entire balloting procedure is not just an exercise in careful impartiality, but an event which raises the spectre of significant costs.

The ballot "must be conducted by a qualified independent person appointed by the CAC".[266] It must be carried out in a way which does not skew the result, but which is sensitive to the costs involved. It may be held at a workplace (or workplaces) decided by the CAC or by post, or even by a combination of these methods.[267] This is a significant departure from the legislative formula used in other contexts, where balloting of trade union members is legitimate only if conducted by post, for example in relation to elections of trade union officials[268] and balloting for industrial action.[269]

In deciding which method is most appropriate, the CAC must have regard to:

(a) the likelihood of the ballot being affected by unfairness or malpractice if it were conducted at a workplace or workplaces;
(b) costs and practicality;
(c) such other matters as the CAC considers appropriate.[270]

A combination of methods is to be avoided "unless there are special factors making such a decision appropriate". Such special factors can include "factors arising from the location of workers or the nature of their employment" and factors which the employer or union(s) identify and put to the CAC.[271] This arguably plays into familiar assumptions that workplace ballots are somehow more likely to be subject to "improper interference" than postal ones.[272] Yet, the potential for a variety of methods of balloting is to be welcomed.

In Standing Committee the minister indicated how these factors might be applied in practice:

> A workplace ballot may be cheaper than a postal ballot, and may lead to a higher turnout, although neither is necessarily the case. In the case of split sites or shift working, a workplace ballot can be more expensive and more difficult to organise than a postal ballot. However, workplace ballots may lead to victimisation of workers who vote against the employer or to intimidation or [*sic*] workers who vote against the union. On the other hand, a postal ballot is relatively difficult to interfere with and is less obtrusive than a workplace ballot. It may, therefore, be more appropriate in the

---

[266] TULRCA 1992, Sched. A1, para. 25(2) and (7). Compare with TULRCA 1992 ss. 49, 75 and 226B which contain similar provisions relating to appointment of an independent scrutineer.
[267] TULRCA 1992, Sched. A1, para. 25(4).
[268] TULRCA 1992 s. 51.
[269] TULRCA 1992 s. 230 (with the exception of merchant seamen).
[270] TULRCA 1992, Sched. A1, para. 25(5).
[271] TULRCA 1992, Sched. A1, para. 25(6).
[272] See McCarthy (1999) n.31 above, at 40.

case of a highly emotive dispute over recognition. It is said that postal ballots produce lower turnouts than workplace ballots, but again, that is not always true. Some evidence suggests that turnout is higher in postal ballots if the issue is one that directly affects workers, rather than a national issue such as an election or a political fund.[273]

The gross costs of the ballot are to be borne half by the employer and half by the union (or unions[274]). The imposition of costs on the parties to a recognition dispute, as opposed to the state, is significant for two reasons. First, it reduces the burden on state coffers. Secondly, the apportionment of balloting costs equally between employers and the applicant union (or unions) can be linked to the Government's determination to achieve voluntary recognition wherever possible. In Standing Committee, the minister explained that it had been hoped that this:

> would be an incentive and an encouragement for both parties to reach a voluntary agreement if they were faced with paying ballot costs. We hope that both parties will endeavour to avoid a ballot.[275]

This aim fits neatly with the provision made for the employer and union parties to reach a joint accommodation within ten days of the CAC's notification to the parties that a ballot will be held.[276] It is therefore apparent that the balloting procedure is not only a "democratic" means by which to ascertain workers' preference for their bargaining agent, but also is to operate as a deterrent which will encourage the parties to reach a voluntary agreement regarding recognition.

d. securing employer co-operation

One of the lessons New Labour learnt from the Employment Protection Act 1975 was that, if a statutory recognition procedure is to be effective, steps must be taken to ensure that employers act in a co-operative fashion. In this section, we examine the measures taken in Schedule A1 to ensure that the employer co-operates with the ballot, provides access and gives the independent scrutineer the workers' details to enable the ballot to be held. Finally, we consider the sanction imposed on the non-co-operative employer.

i. the employer's three duties: co-operation, access and provision of workers' details

One of the chief failings of the EPA 1975 was that, employers took various measures to thwart the operation of an investigation into recognition. They refused to allow ACAS access to their workers to ascertain their views on recognition

---

[273] HC Standing Committee E, 16 Mar. 1999, cols. 391–393, *per* Mr Wills.

[274] TULRCA 1992, Sched. A1, para. 28(2). The presumption is that where the application is made by more than one union, they will either bear the financial burden in equal shares or will jointly indicate how they will share the costs. See para. 28(3).

[275] HC Standing Committee E, 16 Mar. 1999, col. 403, *per* Mr Wills; a similar explanation was provided in HL Hansard, 7 June 1999, col. 1210, by Lord McIntosh.

[276] TULRCA 1992, Sched. A1, paras. 17 and 24.

and withheld the names and addresses of their workers to avoid a postal ballot. Even when apparently co-operative, employers could spread propaganda or intimidate workers to skew the outcome of the ballot. There was nothing in the EPA 1975 which allowed ACAS to take action to prevent such conduct; and when ACAS attempted to impose recognition without carrying out a full investigation, the courts found their actions to be *ultra vires*.[277]

Schedule A1 places three crucial duties on an employer in the course of balloting. First, the employer is obliged to "co-operate generally, in connection with the ballot, with the union (or unions) and the person appointed to conduct the ballot". This is a useful catch-all provision, although how it will be interpreted is uncertain. More specific provision is also made to prevent an unco-operative employer from mistreating workers who are involved in supporting an application for statutory recognition.[278]

Secondly, the employer is to give the union or unions reasonable access to the workplace.[279] However, such access is envisaged only after the recognition procedure has been initiated; not before. An employer is under a duty to give the union (or unions) only "such access to the workers constituting the bargaining unit as is reasonable to enable the union (or unions) to inform the workers of the object of the ballot and to seek their support and their opinions on the issues involved".[280] This limited provision for access does not adhere to ILO standards.[281] The ILO Committee on Freedom of Association made it clear in the *Co-Steel Sheerness* case that a trade union should have basic rights of access to the workplace and to management representatives, regardless of recognition.[282] Moreover, the lack of access prior to the balloting stage makes it difficult to achieve the support necessary to meet the preliminary threshold which requires that an applicant union (or unions) demonstrate 10 per cent membership and produce evidence that a majority would be in favour of recognition.[283] It is only once this preliminary criterion is established that a ballot can be held, suggesting that statutory access comes too late in the process.

A Code of Practice governing access came into force with Schedule A1 on 6 June 2000.[284] This is consistent with the Government's determination to produce codes on various areas of industrial relations, as opposed to "detailed regulation". These codes make recommendations on good practice. "Most importantly, they can be taken into account by tribunals and courts, particularly when

---

[277] See above this chap. at 69–71.

[278] TULRCA 1992, Sched. A1, paras. 156 and 161. However, the sufficiency of these provisions is questionable, as was observed above in Chap. 2 at 38–9.

[279] TULRCA 1992, Sched. A1, para. 26(3). Compare with *FAW*, para. 4.19.

[280] TULRCA 1992, Sched. A1, para. 26(3).

[281] See Case No. 1852 (UK) *304th Report of the ILO Committee on Freedom of Association* (1996), para. 474. See above this chap. at 63.

[282] *Ibid.* at 493.

[283] See above this chap. at 90–2.

[284] *Code of Practice: Access to Workers During Recognition and Derecognition Ballots*, issued by the Secretary of State under TULRCA 1992 s. 203.

they have to decide whether the behaviour of either party, the employer or the employee, is reasonable in the circumstances."[285]

The Code emphasises the importance of parity of employer and union access to the workforce.[286] It is envisaged that not only will unions have access but employers should be able to address workers directly on the subject of union representation. It is interesting to note that in Canada, the employer's ability to speak to workers on such a subject is strictly circumscribed. They may present only factual information, which must not be conveyed in such a way as to create a perception of "anti-union animus or intimidation".[287] The Canadian approach would counteract the problems relating to employer propaganda experienced during the operation of the EPA 1975 statutory recognition procedure.[288] The Code and the Employment Relations Act 1999 do not.[289] In part, this may be due to New Labour's emphasis on compliance with the European Convention of Human Rights, especially Article 10, which guarantees "freedom of expression". However, the proviso to Article 10 allows restriction of free speech for protection of the rights of others and it was arguably open to the Government to curtail the speech of employers in these circumstances.

The third duty is specifically designed to counter problems experienced under the EPA 1975. The employer is obliged to give to the CAC (within ten days of CAC notification that a ballot is required) the names and home addresses of all the workers constituting the bargaining unit.[290] The CAC will pass this information on to the person conducting the ballot.[291] This also enables the union(s) to send information to affected workers via the person conducting the ballot,[292] provided that the union(s) bear the cost of doing so.[293]

ii. the sanction for an employer's failure to comply with the three basic duties

The key purpose of these provisions is to ensure that the employer cannot frustrate the holding of the ballot. The difficulties experienced by ACAS during the operation of the EPA 1975 recognition procedure are not to be repeated. If the employer fails to fulfil any of these three duties and the ballot has not been held, the CAC may order the employer to "take such steps to remedy the failure as the CAC considers reasonable and specifies in the order" within a particular and reasonable time period.[294] If the employer does not abide by this order and the

---

[285] HC Hansard, 30 Mar. 1999, col. 928, *per* Mr Byers. See TULRCA 1992 s. 207.

[286] *Code of Practice: Access to Workers During Recognition and Derecognition Ballots*, n.284 above, paras. 28, 41 and 45.

[287] Wood and Godard, n.50 above, at 217–18. See for a thorough discussion of the issues, D.C. McPhillips, "Employer Free Speech and the Right of Trade-Union Organization" (1982) 20 *Osgoode Hall Law Journal* 139.

[288] See above this chap. at 69–70.

[289] See B. Simpson, "Fairness at Work" (1998) 27 *ILJ* 245 at 247.

[290] TULRCA 1992, Sched. A1, para. 28(4).

[291] TULRCA 1992, Sched. A1, para. 26(5).

[292] TULRCA 1992, Sched. A1, para. 26(6).

[293] TULRCA 1992, Sched. A1, para. 26(7).

[294] TULRCA 1992, Sched. A1, para. 27(1).

ballot has still not been held, the CAC "may issue a declaration that the union is (or unions are) recognised as entitled to conduct collective bargaining on behalf of the bargaining unit".[295] If the CAC issues a declaration of this nature "it shall take steps to cancel the holding of the ballot; and if the ballot is still held it shall have no effect".[296] The penalty for a lack of co-operation is *de jure* recognition.

The legislation does not address one problem; namely what happens if the ballot is held, but it later emerges that the employer's conduct was reprehensible. As it stands, these provisions appear to place an onus on the union to make a complaint to the CAC before the ballot is held or suffer the consequences.

Moreover, the significance of a declaration of recognition depends on the benefits which this status can confer on the trade union. The second stage of the statutory recognition procedure relates to the establishment of a procedure for collective bargaining. It is perhaps the employer's co-operation at this later stage which is even more important.

2. The consequences for collective bargaining

Fairness at Work stated that recognition achieved under the statutory procedure would have consequences over and above those currently contingent on voluntary recognition. An employer would be obliged to follow a procedure for negotiations with the statutorily recognised trade union.[297] The subsequent negotiations would cover at least the minimum of pay, hours and holidays.[298] *Prima facie*, such measures might seem designed to promote collective bargaining. We shall argue that, if this was the aim of the Government, the manner in which Schedule A1 implements this policy means that it is unlikely to be achieved. In the trade-off between employer and union interests, the efficacy of these provisions was undermined.

The scope for enforcement of the bargaining procedure is limited. Moreover, the restricted range of subject matter designated for collective bargaining is problematic. Despite calls for unions to adjust to modern developments in industry by bargaining with employers over a broader range of issues, such as organisation of work and equal opportunities policies, Schedule A1 suggests that recognition will not necessarily lead to negotiation on such matters. The Government seems more interested in providing the recognised trade union with an entitlement to information and consultation rights.

---

[295] TULRCA 1992, Sched. A1, para. 27(2). This can be contrasted with the lack of a sanction of recognition for non-co-operation under the EPA. See above this chap. at 69–72.

[296] TULRCA 1992, Sched. A1, para. 27(3).

[297] *FAW*, para. 4.18.

[298] The Government also invited views on whether this list of subject-matter should also include training. See below this chap. at 110–15.

a. the obligation to establish a method of bargaining

Prior to the entry into force of Schedule A1, where an employer voluntarily recognised a trade union, no collective bargaining necessarily took place. Recognition was often granted for purposes of information and consultation over matters such as health and safety or business transfers, as opposed to collective bargaining.[299] Even where recognition was granted in respect of collective bargaining, there was no guarantee that the union would get the employer to the bargaining table or persuade the employer to reach any kind of collective agreement. The recommendations for recognition issued by ACAS under the EPA 1975 were designed to promote bargaining, but failure to comply led only to the imposition of terms and conditions of employment by the CAC, which did not punish a failure to bargain on the part of an employer whose workers enjoyed such terms already.[300]

The TUC was determined to depart from this position and sought to ensure that an obligation to engage in collective bargaining would flow from statutory recognition. The "Joint Statement" suggested that a model procedure could be developed in order to facilitate such bargaining. The TUC said that it had "no wish to see punitive sanctions for non-compliance" but specifically requested that there be an "effective remedy for workers who are denied the right to have a union negotiate on their behalf".[301]

The White Paper appeared to take this suggestion on board. The employer and the union would be expected to "try to reach a procedure agreement to give effect to recognition and set out how they will conduct collective bargaining".[302] If agreement could not be reached, the newly recognised union could apply to the CAC either to facilitate agreement or impose a default procedure, legally binding on both parties.[303] In this section, we examine how the commitment to instituting a procedure for collective bargaining is achieved under Schedule A1. In our view, it is unsatisfactory in various respects.

i. bargaining over the procedure agreement

Schedule A1 provides that where there is compulsory recognition of a trade union, via a declaration from the CAC, the parties must adopt a method of collective bargaining. This is a procedure to be followed by the relevant employer and the recognised union (or unions) in the course of their negotiations.[304] Even when recognition is voluntarily conceded, the employer cannot evade the obligation to establish a collective bargaining method, as long as recognition was given after a formal request made in compliance with the statutory proce-

---

[299] See above this chap. at 61.
[300] See above this chap. at 69. Discussed in Davies, n.54 above, at 55–60.
[301] "Joint Statement", n.84 above, at para. 18.
[302] *FAW*, Annex 1.
[303] *FAW*, Annex 1.
[304] TULRCA 1992, Sched. A1, para. 30.

dure.[305] In this context, the boundaries between voluntary and compulsory recognition become blurred. Both constitute statutory recognition for the purpose of Schedule A1.

The ideal scenario is apparently that the parties will agree a method of collective bargaining between themselves. From the date of a CAC declaration of recognition or the date recognition was agreed, they are given an initial "negotiation period" of 30 working days to reach agreement on a bargaining procedure. This period may be extended further by mutual consensus.[306] If no agreement is achieved during the "negotiation period",[307] either party may apply to the CAC, which will seek to facilitate agreement during an "agreement period".[308] This second period lasts for 20 working days or such longer period as the CAC may decide with the consent of the parties.[309] Any bargaining which takes place during the "negotiation" or the "agreement" periods does so "under the shadow of the law", or at least against the backdrop of arbitral intervention.

ii. imposition of the default procedure agreement by the CAC (and the
  Secretary of State)

During the "agreement" period the parties can request jointly that the CAC not intervene and, if they do so, the CAC must comply with this request.[310] Otherwise, if no agreement is reached and no such request is made, the CAC "must specify to the parties the method by which they are to conduct collective bargaining".[311] This is described in *Fairness at Work* as a "default procedure agreement" (DPA) and will be referred to as such here.[312] This arbitral intervention differs from that imposed under the Employment Protection Act 1975.[313] The DPA which can eventually be imposed by the CAC is not an award of substantive terms and conditions of employment, but rather a procedure to be followed. It may not bring any substantive benefits to the workers in question,[314] but is to promote the actual process of bargaining. This however appears to be exactly what the TUC wanted and envisaged.

---

[305] TULRCA 1992, Sched. A1, paras. 52 and 58. This latter procedure is more complex, for the CAC must firstly consider whether there was an agreement for recognition and whether certain threshold criteria for statutory recognition (such as the size of the workforce) would be satisfied. See also Sched. A1, paras. 55 and 60.

[306] TULRCA 1992, Sched. A1, para. 30(4) and (5). In respect of a bargaining method for voluntary agreement, the period is calculated from the date of the recognition agreement. See para. 58(4) and (5).

[307] Or if agreement is reached but not adhered to by one of the parties. See TULRCA 1992, Sched. A1, para. 32.

[308] TULRCA 1992, Sched. A1, paras. 30(3), 31(2), 58(3) and 63(1).

[309] TULRCA 1992, Sched. A1, paras. 31(8) and 63(8).

[310] TULRCA 1992, Sched. A1, paras. 31(7) and 63(7). Also, in the case of voluntary recognition, the applicant is free to withdraw the request for CAC intervention within the agreement period. See para. 63(6).

[311] TULRCA 1992, Sched. A1, paras. 31(3) and 63(2).

[312] In TULRCA 1992, Sched. A1, it is simply referred to as "the method". See e.g. para. 31.

[313] See above this chap. at 69.

[314] Note Lord McCarthy's observations relating to the absence of any recourse to a substantive award at HL Hansard, 7 June 1999, cols. 1278–1279.

Although the CAC has the ultimate discretion in crafting a procedure to suit the parties' needs, it must also take into account the method of bargaining specified by the Secretary of State.[315] On the very same date that Schedule A1 of TULRCA 1992 came into force,[316] so too did the Trade Union Recognition (Method of Collective Bargaining) Order (TURM).[317] The Schedule to TURM, which sets out the "Specified Method" to be incorporated into the DPA, tells us how New Labour expects collective bargaining to take place following statutory recognition.

TURM provides a detailed prescription of an annual bargaining procedure and seeks to establish a model body which will conduct such bargaining.[318] While the CAC "may depart from the specified method to such extent as it thinks appropriate in the circumstances of individual cases", TURM is likely to be highly influential in setting the parameters of the DPA.[319] TURM states that it is not intended that this method be "applied as a model for voluntary procedural agreements" and does not expect that these need be as "prescriptive" as the specified method,[320] but, given that this is what is likely to be imposed if the parties do not reach agreement, TURM may well shape the form and substance of any "voluntary" agreement reached.

For this reason, the specified method provided by the Government is a matter for concern. Its content reflects a political compromise which once again operates to the benefit of employers rather than unions. Despite an appearance of even-handedness, TURM privileges employer interests; it gives the recognised trade union no new rights to information from an employer; it imposes no explicit requirement that the parties negotiate with a view to reaching agreement; and it fails to acknowledge the need to ensure that the employer does not undermine the collective bargaining process by providing inducements to workers to enter into individual contracts. These features of TURM are discussed below.

—even-handed treatment of employer and union interests?   The model provided by TURM requires the employer and union to establish a "Joint Negotiating Body" (JNB).[321] The JNB is to comprise equal numbers of employer and union representatives, so as to provide equal representation of employer and union interests.[322] Each "Side" is to select one of its members to act as its Chairman

---

[315] After consultation with ACAS: TULRCA 1992, Sched. A1, para. 168.

[316] 6 June 2000.

[317] SI 2000/1300. See *Trade Union Recognition: Public Consultation on a Code of Practice on Access to Workers During Recognition and Derecognition Ballots and a Method of Conducting Collective Bargaining*, URN 99/1256 (London: DTI, 2000) at 20 *et seq.*

[318] SI 2000/1300, Sched., para. 14.

[319] SI 2000/1300, Preamble to the Schedule.

[320] *Ibid.*

[321] SI 2000/1300, Sched., para. 4. This title seems to be inspired by the "Special Negotiating Body" (SNB) contemplated under the European Works Councils Dir. (EWCD). See Dir. 94/45 [1994] OJ L254/64, Article 5. See below Chap. 6 at 162.

[322] SI 2000/1300, Sched., para. 5. Paras. 6 and 7 list who is qualified to act as a representative for either the employer or the union within the JNB.

and another as its Secretary.[323] For the first 12 months, the meetings of the JNB are to be chaired by the Chairman of the Employer Side and chairmanship will alternate at intervals of 12 months.[324] This seems even-handed until one recalls that statutory recognition has a duration of only three years, in which case it is the Employer Side that will chair the meeting for two-thirds of the meetings in addition to the advantage associated with setting the key ground rules as the initial chair. The Secretary of the JNB will *always* be the Employer Side Secretary. Although this Secretary must liaise with the Union Side Secretary, ultimate control over the minutes of the meetings thereby resides with the employer.

A "staged procedure" is set out, under which the union must take the first step, submitting its claim in respect of pay, hours and holidays at least a month in advance of the "common review date".[325] If the union does not meet this deadline, there will be no procedure for the bargaining round in question (unless the union's claim has been delayed because the CAC is determining a complaint relating to the employer's failure to disclose information for collective bargaining purposes).[326] It therefore becomes unlikely that bargaining will take place. This is in stark contrast to the position of the employer, which may initiate bargaining concerning variation of contractual terms affecting pay, hours and holidays at any time.[327] If the employer does so, the standard procedures apply. These provisions reflect rather than redress the current imbalance of bargaining power.

—*access to information*   The remainder of the procedure, namely the next five steps, revolves around time limits within which the parties will meet and exchange documentation.[328] In particular, the employer must set out "all relevant information" in its possession to explain its response to the union's claim.[329] Also, the employer must, in at least one meeting, be available to explain its response and answer any reasonable questions according to the best of its ability.[330]

These look like promising requirements, but it is explicitly stated that the employer is under no greater obligation than is generally imposed under

---

[323] The same person may do both. See SI 2000/1300, Sched., para. 9.

[324] SI 2000/1300, Sched., para. 10.

[325] SI 2000/1300, Sched., para. 15, Step 1. The "common review date" is the established annual date where the employer reviews the pay, hours and holidays of workers. If there is no established annual date, the union is to submit its first claim within three months of the DPA being imposed (and by the same date in subsequent rounds).

[326] SI 2000/1300, Sched., para. 15, Step 1. This is at least an improvement on the draft Method of Collective Bargaining circulated for consultation, which concerned no such exception to this rule. See *Trade Union Recognition: Public Consultation on a Code of Practice on Access to Workers During Recognition and Derecognition Ballots and a Method of Conducting Collective Bargaining,* URN 99/1256 (London: DTI, 2000) at 24.

[327] SI 2000/1300, Sched., para. 17.

[328] These time limits may always be varied where the employer and union agree. See SI 2000/1300, Sched., para. 30.

[329] SI 2000/1300, Sched., para. 15, Step 3.

[330] SI 2000/1300, Sched., para. 15, Step 4.

sections 181 and 182 of TULRCA 1992 to disclose information for the purposes of collective bargaining.[331] This pre-existing statutory requirement for disclosure to recognised trade unions was introduced under the Employment Protection Act 1975[332] and, despite proposals for its repeal in 1996,[333] has survived unamended. Its survival may be attributable to the fact that this limited obligation "falls far short of what would be required to give employees an effective say in high level decision making".[334] Accordingly, this is not a very promising foundation for a prescribed method of bargaining following statutory recognition.

—no duty to bargain with a view to reaching agreement   The method set out in TURM seems designed to promote mutual settlement of the parties' claims. For example, there is the potential to involve ACAS in the settlement of the parties' differences through conciliation.[335] Also, obligations are placed on the employer as regards provision for workers to have time off for meetings and to provide certain facilities. This is crowned by the requirement that the employer and the union "take all reasonable steps to ensure that this method to conduct collective bargaining is applied efficiently and effectively".[336]

There is however no requirement that the parties conduct collective bargaining "with a view to reaching agreement". This is surprising, given that EC Directives on Acquired Rights[337] and Collective Redundancies[338] require the inclusion of this formula in domestic legislation.[339] Nevertheless, the Government explicitly rejected an amendment to the Employment Relations Bill which would have introduced such a provision.[340] It is compliance with the *procedure* which is emphasised by the Government, not commitment to the potential outcome of a collective *agreement*. An employer that is unwilling to bargain can follow the statutory procedure to the letter, attend meetings, write the prescribed communications and provide the desired facilities but need do no more than go through the motions. This would be highly inconvenient for the employer, due to the time and costs involved, but larger employers may be able to bear such inconvenience with relative equanimity.

---

[331] SI 2000/1300, Sched., para. 15, Step 3. Subject to the requirement in para. 27 of the Sched. that both the employer and union shall have regard to the ACAS Code of Practice on the Disclosure of Information to Trade Unions for Collective Bargaining Purposes.

[332] See EPA 1975 ss. 17–21. See also H. Gospel, "Disclosure of Information to Trade Unions" (1976) 5 *ILJ* 223 and H. Gospel and G. Lockwood, "Disclosure of Information for Collective Bargaining: The CAC Approach Revisited" (1999) 28 *ILJ* 233.

[333] *Industrial Action and Trade Unions*, Cm 3470 (London: HMSO, 1996).

[334] Gospel, n.332 above, at 235.

[335] SI 2000/1300, Sched., para. 15, Step 6.

[336] *Ibid.*, Sched., para. 29.

[337] EC Dir. 77/187 [1977] OJ L61/26, Art. 6(2).

[338] EC Dir. 98/59 [1998] OJ L225/16, Art. 2(1).

[339] See Cases C–382/92 and 383/92 *Commission v. UK* [1994] ECR I–2435 and 2479; also TULRCA 1992 s. 188(2) and TUPE Reg. 10(5).

[340] See the debate between Lord Wedderburn and Lord McIntosh, HL Hansard, 7 June 1999, cols. 1272–1276, discussed in Wedderburn, n.106 above, at 38–9.

the potential to undermine collective bargaining by incentives offered to individual workers   TURM states that, apart from the JNB, "no other body or group shall undertake collective bargaining on the pay, hours and holidays of these workers, unless the employer and union so agree".[341] In this manner, it recognises that if the employer simultaneously engages in collective bargaining with another union or body, this would undermine the DPA and thereby the recognition procedure. Yet the Government makes no provision for the scenario where the employer seeks to undermine collective bargaining by making direct approaches to workers, offering them incentives if they will enter into individually negotiated contracts. Indeed, there is reference to "the rights of individual workers to discuss, negotiate or agree with their employer terms of their contract of employment".[342] This is problematic, given that employers have used incentives for individual contracts as a key tactic to avoid engagement in collective bargaining.

This practice of offering incentives is regarded by the ILO as constituting discrimination against those workers who insist on representation through collective bargaining.[343] However, under Conservative government this tactic received legal endorsement.[344] Where there is evidence that the employer's purpose is to "further a change in his relationship with all or any class of his employees", a complaint of discrimination on grounds of trade union membership is excluded, unless the action was such as no reasonable employer would take. In response, the Employment Relations Act gives powers to the Secretary of State to make regulations to protect workers from detriment and dismissal where they refuse to enter into an individual contract which does not include collectively negotiated terms and conditions of employment.[345] At the time of writing, no such regulations have yet been drafted or laid before Parliament; nor do we consider that they are likely to be in the near future.[346]

The present Labour Government's reluctance to act on this front,[347] combined with the failure to address and limit this practice in TURM, is a matter for concern, since it suggests that this employer tactic will continue to be used to thwart effective collective bargaining, even under the statutory recognition procedure.

[341] SI 2000/1300, Sched., para. 4.

[342] *Ibid.*, Preamble to the Schedule.

[343] Case No. 1730 (UK) *294th Report of the ILO Committee on Freedom of Association* (1994) para. 161; Case No. 1852 (UK) *309th Report of the ILO Committee on Freedom of Association* (1998) para. 308 at 342; *Report of the ILO Committee of Experts* (1998) ILC, 86th Session.

[344] See s. 13 of TURERA 1993 which inserted a new subs. (3) into s. 148 of TULRCA 1992; and *Associated Newspapers* v. *Wilson* and *Associated British Ports* v. *Palmer* [1995] IRLR 258 (HL). Both are discussed in K.D. Ewing, "Dancing with the Daffodils?" (2000) 50(1) *Federation News* 1—22. See also above Chap. 2 at 32–7.

[345] See T. Novitz, "International Promises and Domestic Pragmatism: To What Extent will the Employment Relations Act 1999 Implement International Labour Standards Relating to Freedom of Association" (2000) 63 *MLR* 379 at 389–93.

[346] See above Chap. 2 at 32–7.

[347] The failure to repeal TULRCA 1992 s. 148(3) was identified and criticised by the ILO: see *Report of the ILO Committee of Experts* (2000) ILC, 88th Session.

b. enforcement of the bargaining procedure

If the bargaining procedure is voluntarily agreed between the parties,[348] it will not be expected to be legally binding.[349] The DPA imposed by the CAC will have effect "as if it were a legally enforceable contract made by the parties",[350] unless the parties themselves decide otherwise. If they agree in writing, they can vary the method or determine that it will not be legally enforceable or enforceable in part only.[351] Given that the DPA has *prima facie* contractual status, one might expect a broad range of remedies to be available to the nominal parties to the agreement (the employer and union parties) and those whom the agreement is likely to affect (namely the workers). Nevertheless, Schedule A1 places strict limitations on the means by which the DPA is to be enforced.

i. the unrealistic remedy of specific performance

"Specific performance" is stated to be "the only remedy available for breach of anything which is a legally enforceable contract" by virtue of these provisions.[352] This is an astonishingly unrealistic mechanism for enforcement which arguably amounts to a significant departure from the commitment that a DPA would be enforceable.

In the first version of the Bill, a CAC order could be registered in a county court to ensure that there would be an immediate finding of contempt if the employer repeated the wrongdoing.[353] This has gone. The remedy as it stands in its final incarnation, within Schedule A1, is entirely discretionary. It is as if judicial attitudes in cases relating to statutory recognition decided under the Employment Protection Act 1975 have been forgotten.[354] No account is taken of the courts' traditional hostility to enforced collective bargaining.

To enforce a procedure agreement through specific performance departs from the traditional common law and legislative approach to the enforcement of collective agreements. The presumption is that such agreements are not legally binding unless they meet the criteria set out in section 179 of TULRCA 1992. In addition, the courts have been notoriously reluctant to incorporate the terms of a collective agreement into an individual employment contract.[355] To suppose that the High Court would readily order specific performance, turning the table on employers, and subjecting them to sanctions for contempt, "strains credibility beyond breaking point".[356]

---

[348] They are said to be concluded "in a climate of trust and co-operation", but how true this is of an agreement concluded after the statutory recognition procedure has been utilised is doubtful.

[349] This is explicitly stated in SI 2000/1300, Preamble to the Sched.

[350] TULRCA 1992, Sched. A1, paras. 31(4) and 63(3).

[351] TULRCA 1992, Sched. A1, paras. 31(5) and 63(4).

[352] TULRCA 1992, Sched. A1, paras. 31(6) and 63(5).

[353] Wedderburn, n.106 above, at 40.

[354] See above this chap. at 69–71.

[355] The key example being *Alexander* v. *Standard Telephones (No. 2)* [1991] IRLR 286; and see below this chap. at 117–18. See Wedderburn, n.153 above, at 255–6.

[356] Simpson, n.289 above, at 248.

Moreover, as Lord Wedderburn has observed, specific performance is a technical legal remedy, which requires consideration of whether damages are an adequate redress for the wrong suffered. He notes that Schedule A1 "sets a puzzle by refusing any damages at all", going on to pose the question whether the court will now have to decide whether damages *would have been* an adequate remedy if their award were possible.[357] Also, specific performance as an equitable remedy carries certain collateral legal principles, such as the maxim: "he who comes to equity must come with clean hands".[358] It will be interesting to see how courts interpret this requirement where trade unions have engaged in any form of industrial action during collective bargaining, as they are otherwise entitled to do under TULRCA 1992.[359]

ii. alternative remedies in tort

There are potential remedies in tort which may serve as alternatives to specific performance. This possibility was identified by Lord Wedderburn. A third party, unable to make any claim for specific performance, could seek compensation for damage which sprang from the breach of the procedure agreement or even an injunction to secure its enforcement.[360]

One potential form of action could be for breach of statutory duty.[361] This could be said to arise where the plaintiff suffers loss because a party breaches the DPA imposed by the CAC under Schedule A1, but this is difficult, given that the obligations which the statute confers appear to be solely contractual. Moreover, Lord McIntosh asserted on behalf of the Government that the statement that "specific performance shall be the only remedy" would exclude any action by a third party for breach of statutory duty.[362]

Lord Wedderburn has subsequently considered other scenarios in which liability in tort might arise, such as where a parent company induces its subsidiary not to talk with the union, thereby committing the tort of inducing breach of contract.[363] This would however require active extension of the limited weaponry of enforcement provided by Schedule A1. Although this is not beyond the capacity of the British judiciary, we consider it unlikely that they will depart from their established scepticism of statutory protection of collective bargaining. These cases may be fought, but are unlikely to be won.

Labour has clearly backed down from its earlier stand on enforcement of the DPA. We can only speculate on the reasons. The likeliest scenario would seem to us to be that suggested by Lord Wedderburn, namely that the Government was eager to broker agreement with the TUC and CBI with all the potential

---

[357] Wedderburn, n.106 above, at 39.

[358] *Ibid.* at 39–40. See also HL Hansard, 10 May 1999, col. 1017, *per* Lord Wedderburn.

[359] See TULRCA 1992 ss. 219 and 244; and below Chap. 5.

[360] HL Hansard, 7 June 1999, col. 1157, *per* Lord Wedderburn. See also Wedderburn, n.153 above, at 257.

[361] HL Hansard, 7 June 1999, col. 1156, *per* Lord Wedderburn.

[362] *Ibid.*, col. 1159, *per* Lord McIntosh.

[363] Wedderburn, n.106 above, at 40–1.

compromises that might entail. New Labour does not want to jeopardise its endeavour to create a co-operative climate and voluntary agreement within industrial relations. The Government is therefore reluctant to contemplate any legal sanctions for non-compliance which might create "martyrs".[364] This does not bode well for the future efficacy of the statutory recognition procedure.

c. the narrow scope of designated subject matter for collective bargaining

The promise that statutory recognition would lead to collective bargaining was also diminished by the narrow scope for bargaining contemplated in Schedule A1. The Government's approach is particularly disappointing, given increasing recognition of the importance of equal opportunities in the workplace and the challenges presented by changing modes of work. Both suggest that the traditional ambit of bargaining issues should be widened rather than narrowed.[365]

i. the initial policy stance of interested parties

The Government's ambitions in this sphere were always fairly modest. In a policy document issued a year before the General Election, Labour indicated that collective bargaining issues covered by the statutory recognition procedure would be at least "pay, hours and holidays and training".[366] The TUC considered this list to be "rather simplistic", but conceded that there "might be a case for specifying some minimum list that must be subject to collective bargaining". The CBI wanted training dropped from such a list.[367]

By the time *Fairness at Work* was published, the Government was proposing that the CAC fall-back procedure would "provide for collective bargaining to cover pay, hours and holidays as a minimum".[368] There was less certainty whether "training should be included".[369] TUC submissions on the White Paper argued hard for its inclusion, noting that this was one of the Government's commitments in its Election Manifesto and citing research which showed that "union involvement in training adds value to quality and quantity".[370] They were unsuccessful. Instead, the employer lobbyists won out.[371]

ii. a comparison with the current content of section 178 of TULRCA 1992

One can see immediately why representatives of the TUC might view this list of topics for bargaining as "rather simplistic". It does not cover collective bargain-

---

[364] *Ibid.* at 40.

[365] See above Chap. 1 at 5–6 and below this chap at 111–12.

[366] Labour Party, *Building Prosperity—Flexibility, Efficiency and Fairness at Work* (London: Labour Party, 1996).

[367] "Joint Statement", n.84 above, at para. 17.

[368] *FAW*, Annex I.

[369] *Ibid.*

[370] TUC, *TUC Response: Fairness at Work White Paper* (London: TUC, 1998), paras. 55–60.

[371] Lourie, n.249 above, at 11 and 41.

ing of the breadth envisaged by section 178 of TULRCA 1992. The protected subject matter for collective bargaining is listed as:

(a) terms and conditions of employment, or the physical conditions in which any workers are required to work;
(b) engagement or non-engagement, or termination or suspension of employment or the duties of employment, of one or more workers;
(c) allocation of work or the duties of employment between workers or groups of workers;
(d) matters of discipline;
(e) a worker's membership or non-membership of a trade union;
(f) facilities for officials of trade unions;
(g) machinery for negotiation or consultation and other procedures, relating to any of the above matters, including the recognition by employers or employers' associations of the right of a trade union to represent workers in such negotiation or consultation or in the carrying out of such procedures.[372]

By comparison, the short list of "pay, hours and holidays" looks tawdry. The TUC wanted consideration to be given to a wider coverage of subjects which merited explicit inclusion in such a list. Those identified in their submissions included occupational pensions and equal opportunities.[373] We expect that the former will be encompassed by pay.[374] Bargaining over equal opportunities is likely to continue to pose problems. For example, under-representation of certain racial groups within certain jobs and their treatment within the workplace seem to be excluded.[375]

We would however argue that bargaining over "family friendly" policies should be possible, as this is covered by "hours" and "holidays". To take the view that maternity or parental leave lies outside the minimum list of subject matter for collective bargaining would be inconsistent with recent developments relating to the implementation of EC directives. The Working Time Directive makes specific provision for derogations to be made from certain standards contained therein by means of "collective agreements".[376] This is translated into the provision made in the Working Time Regulations 1998 for "collective and workforce agreements" which can modify or exclude the application of certain regulations.[377] The Parental Leave Directive follows a similar model, making explicit provision for norms to be set by collective agreement as opposed to the

---

[372] TULRCA 1992 s. 178(2).

[373] TUC, n.370 above, at para. 61. A strong case for inclusion of these matters on a trade union bargaining agenda is also made by A. Morris, "Workers First, Women Second? Trade Unions and the Equality Agenda?" in A. Morris and T. O'Donnell (eds.), *Feminist Perspectives on Employment Law* (London: Cavendish, 1999).

[374] Case 170/84 *Bilka-Kaufhaus GmbH* v. *Karin Weber von Hartz* [1986] ECR 1607; and Case C–262/88 *Barber* v. *Guardian Royal Exchange Group* [1990] ECR I–1889.

[375] See K. Monaghan, *Challenging Race Discrimination at Work* (London: Institute of Employment Rights, 2000) who argues for trade union engagement with these issues.

[376] EC Dir. 93/104 [1993] OJ L307/18, Art. 17.

[377] SI 1998/1833, reg. 23.

legislative intervention of Member States.[378] The Maternity and Parental Leave Regulations 1999 provide default provisions, which apply only if the employee in question is *not* covered by a collective or workforce agreement.[379] It seems that collective bargaining is specifically envisaged in relation to these measures. It would therefore be bizarre if "hours of work" were not broadly interpreted and if maternity and parental leave did not come within the minimum list of collective bargaining envisaged by Schedule A1 to TULRCA 1992.

iii. the standard content of recognition agreements

Given concerns over the limitations a minimum list places on trade unions' bargaining agendas, the TUC's ultimate acceptance of the potential practicality of a "minimum list" seems anomalous. It can best be understood by an examination of current industrial relations practice surrounding recognition.

Where recognition has been granted, it has never needed to be in respect of all of the topics listed in section 178 of TULRCA 1992. The employer has always had complete discretion concerning the scope of recognition.[380] The 1998 Workplace Employment Relations Survey (WERS) tells us that, where recognition is given, "the scope of bargaining appears to be quite narrow".[381] It is "mostly confined to negotiations over the handling of grievances (43 per cent), pay (30 per cent) and health and safety (22 per cent)".[382]

In this context, the requirement that statutory recognition negotiations cover a minimum of pay, hours and holidays might seem promising. It creates potential for the parties to extend the scope of the subject matter further. Statutory recognition therefore appears to increase the ambit of present *de facto* topics for collective bargaining, even if it does not encompass the range envisaged by section 178. The problem is that the implementation of a statutory recognition procedure through Schedule A1 has effectively replaced a minimum with a maximum list.

iv. the minimum/maximum problem

When lobbying for the minimum list, the expectation of the trade union movement was that such a list would operate as a minimum level for collective bargaining. The problem is that the way in which Schedule A1 is designed makes it likely that this list will operate as a maximum. This is due to the incentives given to the parties not to follow the statutory recognition procedure to its bitter end,

---

[378] EC Dir. 96/34 [1996] OJ L145/9, Annex, cll. 2 and 3.

[379] SI 1999/3312, reg. 16. See also Scheds. 1 and 2. It is possible for employees to enter a workforce agreement only where they are not covered by a collective agreement. See SI 1999/3312, Sched. 1.

[380] See the reference to recognition "to any extent" for the purpose of collective bargaining in TULRCA 1992 s. 178(3).

[381] M. Cully, A. O'Reilly, N. Millward, J. Fortii, S. Woodland, G. Dix and A. Bryson, *The 1998 Workplace Employee Relations Survey: First Findings* (London: DTI, 1999), 17.

[382] *Ibid.*

but to compromise and enter an agreement which does not give full statutory recognition rights.

Schedule A1 encourages applicant unions to accept such a compromise by various means. For example, this is done by imposing periods of negotiation before intervention by the CAC, which lead to delays that can compromise union support.[383] The costs and inconvenience of the ballot may also operate as a deterrent to union applicants.[384] Moreover, unions are likely to compromise once they realise that the statutory recognition procedure is also biassed in the employer's favour. For example, it is the employer whose views are likely to determine how the CAC views the scope of the bargaining unit.[385] The employer is also permitted to recognise a non-representative independent trade union[386] and restructure or lay off staff[387] to avoid the requirement to recognise. As the new Chair of the CAC has acknowledged, "the procedure laid down by Parliament is long and complex and unions will not want to enter into it lightly".[388]

If the statutory recognition procedure were unbiassed and straightforward, when negotiating with an employer for recognition representative unions would expect recognition over pay, hours and holidays as a minimum and would seek to bargain for more than this. However, as Schedule A1 gives trade unions little incentive to run the gauntlet to its very end, they have less bargaining power and will make more concessions to an employer. What was presented as a minimum list of topics for collective bargaining has arguably become a maximum.

In the House of Lords, Lord McCarthy appeared to identify this problem, arguing that the CAC should be able, at its discretion, to add to the subjects for which recognition was given.[389] This would ensure that "pay, hours and holidays" operated as a minimum, as New Labour had initially promised, and not as a maximum. The amendment was rejected by the Government, on the basis that there existed opportunities "for other matters to be covered in collective bargaining as a result of agreement between employers and employees".[390] The Minister refused to acknowledge the context within which such an agreement would be reached. This is another major failing of New Labour's implementation of their electoral promises.

d. consequences for the consultative status of trade unions

Training was ultimately excluded from the core subject matter of collective bargaining under Schedule A1. This was clearly a concession to employers'

---

[383] Both before and after recognition is granted. See above this chap. at 76–80 and 103.
[384] See above this chap. at 97–8.
[385] See above this chap. at 89–90.
[386] See above this chap. at 85–7.
[387] See above this chap. at 96.
[388] Statement released on 6 June 2000. See "recent press notices issued by the CAC", available at http://www.cac.gov.uk/recent_press_notices/press_notice/.
[389] HL Hansard, 7 June 1999, col. 1145, *per* Lord McCarthy.
[390] HL Hansard, 7 June 1999, col. 1147, *per* Lord McIntosh.

demands and one which is interesting, given the interest in employability and active training policies in the UK,[391] the EU and internationally.[392]

Workers have a compelling interest in ongoing training and self-development to ensure future employability outside the employer's workplace, which the employer cannot be expected to share. There is a strong argument that workers (through their union) should be able to participate actively in collective negotiation over the type of training they can expect to receive and how it will be delivered.[393] Moreover, from a functional economic perspective, the inclusion of unions in this process is conducive to long-term planning, "driving the training system towards meeting long term skill requirements rather than employers' immediate needs".[394]

Nevertheless, the Government has taken a different tack. Where a trade union is recognised under Schedule A1 and a method of collective bargaining has been specified by the CAC, that union is to be *consulted* over the employer's policy on training.[395] This seems to follow from the emphasis which EC directives have placed on information and consultation requirements as opposed to collective bargaining.[396] It also connects with the Labour Government's insistence that recognised trade unions have a role to play within such a framework.[397] However, consultation places unions in a more passive role than they assume in a collective bargaining scenario. We are therefore concerned by the implications of this shift in policy.

In 1998, 37 per cent of the union representatives surveyed in WERS reported that they received no information about training.[398] The obvious question is whether the new statutory requirement of consultation over training will change this position.

To us it seems doubtful that many trade unions will acquire the new statutory right to consultation over training conferred by Schedule A1. For the reasons given above, we expect that relatively few trade unions will utilise the new statutory recognition procedure and only those which do so (and are successful) can

---

[391] As discussed in E. Keep and H. Rainbird, "Training" in P. Edwards (ed.), *Industrial Relations: Theory and Practice in Britain* (Oxford: Blackwell, 1995) at 515–42. See for the Labour Government's recognition of this, *The Learning Age*, Cm 3790 (London: TSO, 1998); and "Knowledge 2000: Conference on the Knowledge Driven Economy", programme and speeches available at http://www.dti.gov.uk/knowledge2000/programme.htm. See also above Chap. 1 at 10–11.

[392] See e.g. M. Freedland, "Employment Policy" in P. Davies, A. Lyon-Caen, S. Sciarra and S. Simitis (eds.), *European Community Labour Law: Principles and Perspectives: Liber Amicorum Lord Wedderburn* (Oxford: Clarendon Press, 1996); European Commission, *Towards a Europe of Knowledge*, COM(97)563 final; and ILO, *World Employment Report 1998—99: Employability in the Global Economy: How Training Matters* (Geneva: ILO, 1998).

[393] TUC, n.370 above, paras. 55–60.

[394] Keep and Rainbird, n.391 above, at 516.

[395] ERelA 1999 s.5 inserts ss. 70B and 70C into TULRCA 1992. The details of this procedure are outlined below in Chap. 6 at 153–5.

[396] See above Chap. 1 at 18.

[397] See e.g. SI 1999/1925, also below Chap. 6.

[398] Cully *et al.*, n.381 above, at 18.

claim this entitlement. Therefore, we assume that the Government does not intend a large number of trade unions to claim the new statutory right.

Rather, it appears that the purpose of this provision is not to effect a direct legal change in status in a large number of cases, but rather to set up a model of good practice which, through its statutory endorsement, may permeate UK industrial relations. This is consistent with New Labour's notion that law can seldom provide a solution to a problem but can be used as a tool to "reflect a new culture, . . . enhance its understanding and support its development".[399] It is also consistent with the Government's emphasis on a voluntary partnership wherein parties will take rational decisions in their own best interests, adopting sensible modes of communication. If this works, we may expect a very gradual shift towards information and consultation over training.

So far, so good. Yet if this model of best practice is genuinely the Government's aim, then it seems to be sending the implicit message that consultation rather than collective bargaining over training is sufficient. This seems to us to be alarming, given that it is linked in with a statutory recognition procedure which is ostensibly designed to extend rather than diminish the scope of collective bargaining.

3. Enforcement of the collective agreement relating to terms and conditions of employment

One further concern is what will happen if a collective agreement is concluded under the statutory recognition procedure. What force will it have, and to what extent is it likely to have a positive effect on workers' terms and conditions of employment? If such an agreement is likely to have no effect, then the statutory recognition procedure would seem to have no merit at all.

The barriers to enforcement are familiar to the labour lawyer. The first is the standard difficulty associated with the ability of any party to a collective agreement, be it the employer or the union, to secure its legal enforcement. The second is rather more complex, as it relates to the ways in which a collective agreement may determine the content of the individual employment contract. Altogether, it seems that, unless a recognised trade union is exceptionally fortunate or has considerable bargaining power for reasons extraneous to the statutory recognition procedure,[400] the eventual outcome of the process may not be at all rewarding for the workers whom the union seeks to represent.

---

[399] *FAW*, Foreword. See above Chap. 1 at 17.
[400] E.g., due to the threat of effective industrial action which would have a genuine economic impact on the employer. See below Chap. 5.

a. legal enforcement of collective agreements

There is a common law[401] and (at present) a legislative presumption[402] that collective agreements are not intended by the parties to be legally enforceable. "This was the principle proposed in 1954, adopted in the Donovan Report 1968, applied by the High Court in 1969, overturned in 1971 but restored three years later."[403]

A collective agreement[404] will not be legally enforceable unless it is in writing and contains a provision which states that the parties intend it to be a legally enforceable contract. It is possible that only part of the agreement may be designated to be legally binding. To meet these requirements, it is not enough for the parties merely to state that the agreement is "binding"; they must show that they have directed their minds to the question of legal enforceability and have decided in its favour.[405]

TURM considers briefly the treatment of collective agreements which arise from the bargaining process. It states that all such agreements affecting the pay, hours and holidays of workers in the bargaining unit "shall be set down in writing and signed by the Chairman of the Employer Side and by the Chairman of the Union Side or, in their absence, by another JNB member on their respective Sides".[406] Therefore, if the method in TURM is applied by the CAC or voluntarily by the parties, one of the two crucial requirements for legal enforcement of a collective agreement should be met.

However, TURM does not in any way indicate that the parties should state such an agreement to be legally enforceable. Instead, the clear message is that the parties should respond to any alleged breach by engaging in further meetings and discussions:

> If either the employer or union consider that there has been a failure to implement the agreement, then that party can request in writing a meeting of the JNB to discuss the alleged failure. A quorate meeting shall be held within five working days of the receipt of the request by the JNB Secretary. If there is a failure to resolve the issue at that meeting, then meetings shall be arranged, and steps shall be taken. . . .[407]

It is not said whether this prescribed method is intended to be the exclusive method of dealing with such a breach and will therefore preclude industrial action. We assume that this is not the Government's intention and that the provision will not be interpreted in such a manner. In earlier Parliamentary debates, the Government minister stated that it would not allow the statutory recogni-

---

[401] *Ford Motor Co* v. *AUEW* [1969] 2 QB 303.
[402] TULRCA 1992 s. 179.
[403] Lord Wedderburn, *Labour Law and Freedom: Further Essays in Labour Law* (London: Lawrence and Wishart, 1995), 213.
[404] As defined in TULRCA 1992 s. 178.
[405] *National Coal Board* v. *National Union of Mineworkers* [1986] IRLR 439 at 449 *per* Scott J.
[406] SI 2000/1300, Sched., para. 19.
[407] *Ibid.*, para. 20.

tion procedure as an excuse further to limit the right to strike.[408] Nor need it be assumed that TURM is meant to prevent legal enforcement of the collective agreement, if this was what the parties expressly agreed. It appears that the Government merely recognises that this is unlikely to arise in practice.[409]

b. incorporation of the terms of a collective agreement into the individual contract of employment

It is also possible to argue that all or part of a collective agreement is legally enforceable, in so far as it has been incorporated into an individual employment contract. In *Fairness at Work*, it was observed that:

> The terms of agreements resulting from collective bargaining are normally incorporated into individual employees' contracts either explicitly or by custom and practice and thus set the minimum terms and conditions for all employees in the bargaining unit.[410]

However, this is not as straightforward a process as the White Paper suggested.

In other European States, standards set by collective agreements are regarded as inderogable. The employer may not contract with an individual worker for less.[411] In certain countries, this is due to the fact that the courts subscribe to an "agency model" whereby the trade union is regarded as concluding agreements as the agent of the employee/member.[412] In others, it can be accounted for by the extension of collective agreements by public authorities to certain employers and workers.[413] Neither system operates in the UK. In order for there to be incorporation of provisions in a collective agreement into the individual contract, there has to be an express "bridging term" identifying the provisions in question and the external source from which they are to be taken. Moreover, the particular term relied on by the party must be considered appropriate for incorporation in the individual employment contract. The case law in this area is not altogether consistent and can lead to considerable uncertainty for both the employer and worker.[414] Nothing has been done by the Employment Relations Act 1999 to remedy this situation. The current legal position is such that the collective agreement which arises from statutory recognition will not necessarily be incorporated into the employment contracts of relevant workers.

Moreover, in *Fairness at Work*, it was expressly acknowledged that whatever the terms of the collective agreement which was negotiated following statutory recognition, the employer and worker would remain free to agree different

---

[408] HL Hansard, 7 June 1999, col. 1282, *per* Lord McIntosh. See below Chap. 5 at 140–1.

[409] S. Deakin and G. Morris, *Labour Law* (2nd edn., London: Butterworths, 1998), 770–1.

[410] *FAW*, Annex 1.

[411] Wedderburn, n.403 above, at 215–16.

[412] S. Anderman, "Collective Agreements and Contracts of Employment in the UK" in R. Blanpain and M. Weiss (eds.), *The Changing Face of Labour Law and Industrial Relations: Liber Amicorum for Clyde W. Summers* (Baden-Baden: Nomos Verlagsgesellschaft, 1993) at 280.

[413] Wedderburn, n.403 above, at 221.

[414] See for an excellent overview Anderman, n.412 above, and Deakin and Morris, n.409 above, at 258–66.

terms. "Since the current law allows flexibility and works well, the Government sees no reason to change it."[415] The danger identified by Lord Wedderburn was that "in many cases the employer will be able to sell significantly 'different terms' to vulnerable workers which suit him better than the collective agreement". He argued for "banning the descent of individual employment conditions below the bargained minima",[416] but did not succeed in persuading the Government to do so.

TURM explicitly states that the fact that a method is imposed by the CAC does not prevent discussions between individual workers and their employers as regards contractual terms "which differ from the terms of any collective agreement into which the employer and the union may enter as a result of collective bargaining conducted by this method".[417] In this context, the Government seems to have entirely forgotten the statement that prefaces the "Collective Rights" section in *Fairness at Work*, which acknowledges that "individual contracts of employment are not always agreements between equal partners".[418] The more vulnerable worker is forgotten and is unprotected. This is a shame for, were collective agreements arising from the statutory recognition procedure to set minimum terms and conditions for the workers covered, this would greatly enhance its credibility.

There also remains the potential for the employer to undermine the collective agreement, by giving additional pay and other benefits to workers who accept personal contracts in preference to collective bargaining.[419] If the Government does not make use of its regulatory powers under the Employment Relations Act to restrict this practice,[420] workers are unlikely to see the point in trade union recognition and collective bargaining as it will effectively diminish their terms and conditions of employment. The long-term result may well be that, once trade unions no longer operate in the workplace or engage in collective bargaining, employers will have no incentive to provide such pleasing terms and conditions of employment, and the standards previously set by collective agreement will be progressively undermined.

4. The institutional actors in the statutory recognition procedure

Both the institutional actors in the recognition procedure, ACAS and the CAC, have their roots in the Employment Protection Act 1975. We have seen that once

---

[415] *FAW*, Annex 1.

[416] Lord Wedderburn, n.153 above, at 258. An example of a comparable practice can be found in the EPA 1975, where the award of terms and conditions made by the CAC set a minimum standard for the individual contracts of workers of the workers it covered. See EPA 1975 s. 16(7)(c) discussed above, this chap. at 69.

[417] SI 2000/1300, Preamble to Sched.

[418] *FAW*, para. 4.2.

[419] See above Chap. 2 at 32–7 and this chap. at 107.

[420] Even though this will be problematic, given the content of the Miller amendment contained in ERelA 1999 s. 17(4). See above Chap. 2 at 36–7.

again, under Schedule A1, they have been drafted in as key players, but the parts they play differ significantly from those under the old statutory regime. Changes have been made to ensure that the more obvious "mistakes of the past" are not repeated. This section considers how this feat has been accomplished at an institutional level. We argue that these developments reveal New Labour's deep ambivalence towards collective labour rights and their protection under the Employment Relations Act 1999.

a. the Advisory Conciliation and Arbitration Service (ACAS)

In 1974 ACAS came into being and was soon given official statutory powers under the EPA 1975.[421] It is directed by a Council consisting of a full-time chair and nine other members, representative not only of government but also employer and union interests. While its essential form has not changed since that date, the introduction of a new statutory recognition scheme has the potential to present new challenges for this longstanding institution.

The crucial developments in the Employment Relations Act concerning ACAS relate to its general statutory aims and its anticipated role within the recognition procedure. Both can be distinguished from the position under the EPA 1975, indicating that New Labour does not wish to be seen as "going back" to the statutory experiments of the 1970s.

i. the "general duty" of ACAS

Under the EPA 1975, the statutory "general duty" of ACAS was "to promote the improvement of industrial relations, and in particular to encourage the extension of collective bargaining and development and, where necessary, reform of collective bargaining machinery".[422] In 1993, while ACAS preserved its role in promoting the improvement of industrial relations, reference to "collective bargaining" was omitted. This change can be attributed to the Conservative Government's conviction that collective bargaining was not the ideal mechanism for management of industrial relations. Instead, ACAS was required to carry out its statutory role "in particular, by exercising its functions in relation to the settlement of trade disputes under sections 210–212".[423]

Under the Employment Relations Act this duty has been pared away to a more sparse and general requirement "to promote the improvement of industrial relations"[424] without reference to either collective bargaining or dispute resolution.[425] What precisely is meant by this phrase is uncertain. Its ambiguity

---

[421] EPA 1975, Sched. 1. See for a discussion of its beginnings and its evolution from previous advisory and conciliation services E. Armstrong and R. Lucas, *Improving Industrial Relations: The Advisory Role of ACAS* (London: Croom Helm, 1985), 1—3; and Clegg, n. 63 above, at 388- 91.
[422] EPA 1975 s.1(2); later TULRCA 1992 s. 209.
[423] Due to TURERA 1993 s.43 amending TULRCA 1992 s. 209.
[424] ERelA 1999 s. 26 amending TULRCA 1992 s. 209.
[425] HC Standing Committee E, 4 Mar. 1999 at cols. 367–369, *per* Mr Wills.

is considerable.[426] This allows ACAS more flexibility in carrying out its functions, but it is arguably significant that New Labour refused to contemplate a change back to statutory aims which would require ACAS to encourage collective bargaining.[427]

ii. a different part to play in statutory recognition

One might have expected the reputation of ACAS to be scarred by employer hostility to the last statutory recognition procedure and the spate of judicial review proceedings which arose under that legislation. Nevertheless ACAS, with a strong instinct for institutional survival, fought back, informing the Secretary of State that the Service could not satisfactorily operate the EPA 1975 recognition provisions as they stood.[428] It subsequently tried to distance itself from the role it was forced to play within the recognition procedure and focussed on its mediation services, its conciliatory strengths and its capacity to provide guidance through Codes of Practice.[429] In 1997, Labour envisaged that requests relating to recognition would go first to ACAS and then to the CAC,[430] but ACAS resisted this model, fearing that if it took on such a role again this could be as detrimental to its activities and credibility as it was in the past.[431] Now it is apparent that ACAS will have a more familiar function under the statutory recognition procedure, playing a facilitative part, rather than making recommendations which must be obeyed.

For example, during the first 20-day negotiation period, specific provision is made for the employer and unions to request assistance from ACAS.[432] If the employer proposes that ACAS be requested to assist, and the union rejects the proposal or fails to accept the proposal within ten working days, no application may be made to the CAC for recognition.[433] Similarly, where it is the employer who applies to end bargaining arrangements, there is also provision for the parties to request ACAS intervention.[434] If the employer rejects the union's proposal that ACAS assistance be requested, or fails to respond within ten working days, then the employer cannot make a formal application to the CAC for derecognition.[435] The Government has thereby enhanced the role which ACAS plays in achieving dispute resolution. Moreover, ACAS was given new powers to issue Codes of Practice relating to reasonable access of trade unions to the workplace

---

[426] Armstrong and Lucas, n.421 above, Chap. 9.
[427] Noted by Wedderburn, n.106 above, at 6.
[428] *ACAS Annual Report 1979* (London: HMSO, 1980) 30 and Appendix C. See above this chap. at 71.
[429] Both with regard to individual employment rights and collective labour relations.
[430] See Lourie, n.38 above, at 36.
[431] "ACAS resists moves to impose new legal role", *Financial Times*, 18 June 1997.
[432] TULRCA 1992, Sched. A1, para. 10(5).
[433] TULRCA 1992, Sched. A1, para. 12(5).
[434] TULRCA 1992, Sched. A1, para. 104.
[435] TULRCA 1992, Sched. A1, para. 107(3).

during preparations for a recognition or derecognition ballot.[436] Its independence is preserved and its status remains intact. In this way, it seems that the Employment Relations Act utilises ACAS expertise in collective labour relations, without imposing on this body the more strenuous obligations which it undertook under the EPA 1975.[437] While this will have certain practical implications as regards funding and resources,[438] no major changes to the role of ACAS are foreseen.[439] Indeed, ACAS greeted with enthusiasm the Government's emphasis on the voluntary resolution of problems and disputes and the utilisation of its "joint problem solving approach".[440] It also welcomed "the separation of voluntary conciliation from the statutory decision-making element" and the proposal to make the CAC the decision-making body as regards the latter.[441]

b. the Central Arbitration Committee (CAC)

The CAC was established on 1 February 1976, under section 10 of the EPA 1975, as the younger sister of ACAS.[442] "It replaced the Industrial Arbitration Board (previously the Industrial Court) as the standing national arbitration body in the field of industrial relations and was given additional powers to make awards in disputed disclosure of information and trade union recognition cases."[443] Under the statutory recognition procedure introduced by the EPA 1975, the CAC had power to make awards on terms and conditions of employment where an employer failed to abide by a recommendation relating to recognition given by ACAS.[444] Such powers were removed by the Conservative Government.[445] It

---

[436] TULRCA 1992, Sched. A1, paras. 26(8) and 118(8). See also TULRCA 1992 s. 199. However, the Code which has been issued, discussed above this chap. at 99–100, was issued by the Secretary of State as opposed to ACAS.

[437] See above this chap. at 68–71.

[438] *The Employment Relations Bill: Regulatory Impact Assessment* (London: DTI, 1999), 8, paras. 39–40 and Annex, 7, para. 26 recognise that it will be necessary to fund an increase in the collective conciliation work of ACAS. "It is estimated that the number of staff would have to be increased by five, and the annual cost would be £207,000 (including non-wage costs) with additional one-off training costs in the first year of £40,000." Savings from the abolition of CRTUM and CPAUIA will be devoted to this and funding for the CAC. See above Chap. 3 at 56–8. This was the funding requested by ACAS in the *ACAS Response to the Fairness at Work White Paper* in ACAS Annual Report 1998 (London: HMSO, 1999), Appendix A at 110.

[439] Other changes are really only administrative. E.g. the reporting arrangements of ACAS, which will change to cover the financial year, rather than the calendar year. This means that the period covered by the annual report and ACAS accounts will be the same. See ERelA 1999 s. 27 amending TULRCA 1992 s. 253(1). Corresponding reporting requirements have been imposed on the CAC and the Certification Officer. See ERelA 1999 s. 27 amending TULRCA 1992 s.265(1) and ERelA 1999, Sched. 6, para. 24.

[440] *ACAS Response to the Fairness at Work White Paper* in n.438 above, Appendix A at 105–7.

[441] *Ibid.*, 108.

[442] ACAS has a statutory responsibility to provide the CAC with staff, accommodation, equipment and facilities. See TULRCA 1992 s. 259(3).

[443] Lourie, n.249 above, at 38.

[444] See above this chap. at 69.

[445] The trade union recognition and industrial award provisions of the EPA 1975 were repealed by the Employment Act 1980. Also the CAC's functions under the Fair Wages Resolution (FWR) ended when the FWR was rescinded with effect from 21 Sept. 1983.

subsequently dealt with those few disputes which arose relating to disclosure of information for collective bargaining,[446] and provided arbitration to parties who wished their dispute to be settled under its auspices.[447] Although the CAC is widely viewed as an innovative and effective dispute resolution institution,[448] the erosion of its functions under Conservative government meant that it has a fairly low public profile. "For a good number of years, it has been quietly getting on with a limited role."[449]

The Employment Relations Act 1999 is likely to change this. As we have seen, under new Schedule A1 to TULRCA 1992, the CAC will play a central role in the statutory recognition procedure. It will make vital decisions relating to trade union recognition, even though its discretion will be fettered by the detailed statutory provisions contained in Schedule A1 and subsequent regulatory intervention by the Secretary of State. "The CAC seems unlikely to be as free to decide the scope and extent of recognition as their predecessors were."[450] Nevertheless, its activities are central to the success of the new statutory scheme and how the CAC performs its tasks is likely to be controversial. In juggling this "political hot potato",[451] the Labour Government has made some potentially significant changes to the institution of the CAC. These include the creation of a new statutory duty, the making of new appointments, the implementation of new statutory procedures for hearings and new provision for intervention by Government in CAC decision-making.

i. the creation of a new statutory duty

In exercising its functions under Schedule A1, the CAC has a new statutory duty. It must:

> have regard to the object of encouraging and promoting fair and efficient practices and arrangements in the workplace, so far as having regard to that object is consistent with applying other provisions of this Schedule in the case concerned.[452]

Like the more general duty imposed on ACAS, this new provision arguably gives us some clue about the objectives of New Labour. What the Government hopes to accomplish under the new statutory recognition procedure is likely to be closely linked to the statutory remit of the CAC.

It is therefore notable that there is no mention of collective bargaining. This is curious, for one might expect this to be the chief aim of a body responsible for implementing a statutory recognition and bargaining procedure. Instead, the statute refers to "efficiency", suggesting that business needs are to be a key

---

[446] TULRCA 1992 s. 183. See Gospel and Lockwood, n.332 above.

[447] TULRCA 1992, s. 212.

[448] Davies and Freedland, n.36 above, at 395.

[449] Statement by the new CAC Chairman, Sir Michael Burton, on 6 June 2000 in "recent press notices issued by the CAC" available at http://www.cac.gov.uk/recent_press_notices/press_notice/.

[450] McCarthy, n.31 above, at 15. Wedderburn, n.106 above, at 7 makes the same point.

[451] "Political Spotlight Falls on Dormant Recognition Body", *People Management*, 14 Jan. 1999.

[452] TULRCA 1992, Sched. A1, para. 171.

concern of the CAC. This is consistent with various features of Schedule A1, including the deference the CAC must give to "the need for effective management" when determining the scope of the bargaining unit.[453]

It is also interesting that, in the formulation of this statutory duty, the Government has combined the rhetoric of "fairness" with that of efficiency as if the two were mutually compatible. In Standing Committee, the Government Minister defended this formulation on the basis that it summed up exactly the Government's policy:

> We believe that treating people fairly is right in itself, but we also believe that it is good for employees' commitment, morale and productivity—therefore, it is good for business.[454]

This denial of the potential conflict between these two objectives is also arguably inherent in the notion of "partnership", the standard hammer in the rhetorical toolbox of New Labour. This is potentially dangerous, for it does not provide the CAC with a realistic reference point for its decision-making.

Of course, fairness and efficiency are not to be the CAC's sole objectives. They are to be applied only in so far as this is consistent with the application of Schedule A1 provisions to the case in question. What this balancing act may involve is difficult for us to determine. Indeed, it seems to open unnecessarily the prospect of judicial review. The new statutory duty conferred on the CAC seems unlikely to enhance the efficacy of the recognition procedure.

ii. the making of new appointments

The Secretary of State has always had the responsibility of making appointments to the CAC. With the advent of Schedule A1, these appointments were bound to become more politically sensitive. For this reason, the procedure for consultation has been modified. Whereas previously the Secretary of State consulted only ACAS over appointments, it is now permissible to consult with "other persons".[455] In Standing Committee, the Government Minister indicated that "representative organisations and, indeed, any small firm" would have the opportunity to be consulted on CAC appointments.[456] All these appointments are now to be made in accordance with the rules existing on public appointments.[457]

To date, the CAC has been led by a central "chairman" who has expertise in law and industrial relations. This chair has been assisted by deputy chairpersons with similar qualifications. The remainder of the Committee has been made up of "some persons whose experience is as representatives of employers and some whose experience is as representatives of workers".[458] Now the CAC is virtually

---

[453] TULRCA 1992, Sched. A1, para. 19(3). See above this chap. at 89–90.
[454] HC Standing Committee E, 16 Mar. 1999, col. 349, *per* Mr Wills.
[455] TULRCA 1992 s. 260(3A).
[456] HC Standing Committee E, 4 Mar. 1999, col. 251, *per* Mr Wills.
[457] See HC Standing Committee E, 4 Mar. 1999, col. 248.
[458] TULRCA 1992 old s. 260(2), now new s. 260(3).

reconstituted with appointments of a new "chairman", seven new deputy chair-persons and 32 new members.

From 1975 until his retirement in 1999, the position of chair was held by Sir John Wood, Professor of Law at Sheffield University. His strong leadership undoubtedly brought credit to the CAC.[459] As the Minister told the House of Commons Standing Committee, it was envisaged that the new chair would be someone "who commands the respect of both employers and trade unions, and who has substantial managerial and organisational skills, suitable to leading an enhanced CAC".[460] However, it is apparent that the new appointment led to extensive debate and political wrangling between the various sectoral interests. The TUC wanted George Bain who had chaired the Low Pay Commission, but it is understood that the Secretary of State for Trade and Industry, Stephen Byers, settled on Sir Michael Burton as the best compromise candidate. He is a QC who has represented both unions and employers over the years. However, his appointment is rather controversial, given his role in representing strike-breaking Yorkshire miners against the NUM[461] and Sir Rupert Murdoch's News International against the print unions in the Wapping dispute.[462] His approach to his new role is likely to be highly determinative of the utility of the statutory recognition procedure.

iii. new statutory procedures for hearings

To date, CAC hearings have usually been held by the chair or a deputy, flanked by two members.[463] This is a similar format to an employment tribunal, but the CAC has prided itself on avoiding a legalistic approach to its functions. It aims at problem-solving in terms of "sound industrial relations and workable solutions",[464] and is therefore "much more active and interventionist" than an employment tribunal or court.[465] This practice has developed under the guidance of Sir John Wood on a practical basis. However, given the potential for controversy over CAC decision-making the Government was prompted to formalise these procedures.[466]

A new section 263A inserted into TULRCA 1992 sets down in statute the existing arrangements for hearings, requiring that CAC functions under Schedule A1 shall be carried out in panels of three. Each panel shall consist of

---

[459] Wedderburn, n.106 above, at 7 and Davies and Freedland, n.36 above, at 395.

[460] HC Standing Committee E, 4 Mar. 1999, col. 249, *per* Mr Wills. In addition, the appointee must be expert in the relevant law but not necessarily legally qualified.

[461] *Taylor and Foulstone* v. *NUM (Yorkshire Area)* [1984] IRLR 445.

[462] See K. Ewing and B. Napier, "The Wapping Dispute and Labour Law" (1986) 45 *CLJ* 285. See also S. Milne, "New arbitrator made name putting anti-union cases", *Guardian*, 2 Feb. 2000.

[463] Lourie, n.249 above, at 41.

[464] CAC *Annual Report 1976*, para. 5.4, cited in Lourie, n.249 above, at 42.

[465] J. Wood, "The Central Arbitration Committee: A Consideration of its Role and Approach" (1979) 89 *DE Gazette* 9, cited in Davies and Freedland, n.36 above, at 395.

[466] See concerns expressed by the Opposition in HC Standing Committee E, 16 Mar. 1999, cols. 380–381. Moreover, the need for compliance with Art. 6(1) of the European Convention on Human Rights (ECHR) may also have prompted this initiative.

the chair or a deputy chair, a member of the Committee whose experience is as a representative of employers and a member of the Committee whose experience is as a representative of workers. The chair of the Committee is to decide which panel will deal with a particular case and the panel may, at the discretion of its chair, sit in private where this seems "expedient".[467] The matter shall be decided according to the opinion of the majority of the panel. If no majority view can be reached, the chair of the panel shall decide the question. Subject to these provisions, each panel is given the leeway to determine its own procedure.[468]

Arguably, despite the introduction of these new formal requirements, the basic workings of the CAC seem unlikely to change dramatically. Sir Michael Burton has commented that the CAC will "be striving wherever possible to help the parties reach a voluntary settlement since we are acutely conscious that this is an area where the parties will need to have an on-going relationship".[469] This can be read as uncritical subscription to the New Labour philosophy of "partnership" or may simply indicate the continuation of a practical problem-solving approach in which facilitation of a mutually agreed solution is preferred to the imposition of arbitration.[470]

iv. intervention by Government in CAC decision-making

The CAC's functions to date have been performed on behalf of the Crown, but the body has maintained a measure of independence. The CAC has not been "subject to directions of any kind from any Minister of the Crown as to the manner in which it is to exercise its functions".[471] The institution was specifically protected from ministerial directions, had power to interpret its own awards and its decisions were not subject to appeal.[472] This is changed by the advent of the Employment Relations Act 1999.

It seems that the political sensitivity of the recognition process has prompted the Government to take a much more interventionist approach than it had previously. The discretion of the CAC in making decisions under Schedule A1 is carefully fettered. There are lists of factors which the CAC must take into account at each stage and there are time limits they are required to observe.[473]

---

[467] In HC Standing Committee E, 4 Mar. 1999 at col. 260, it was indicated that the Government had no firm views on when private sittings might be appropriate. This was a matter for the CAC. However, Mr Wills gave as an example the case where commercially sensitive information might be revealed. He expected such cases to be very rare, but thought it sensible to give the CAC discretion. Such discretion will no doubt have to be exercised with reference to ECHR Art. 6(1) which sets out permissible exceptions to the general principle that such hearings should be held in public.

[468] ERelA 1999 s. 25 inserting TULRCA 1992 s.263A.

[469] Statement of 6 June 2000. See "recent press notices issued by the CAC", available at http://www.cac.gov.uk/recent_press_notices/press_notice/.

[470] See the description of CAC adjudication provided by Davies and Freedland, n.36 above, at 395–6.

[471] TULRCA 1992 s. 259(2).

[472] R. Benedictus, "Employment Protection: New Institutions and Trade Union Rights" (1976) 5 *ILJ* 12 at 16.

[473] Even if these can potentially be extended by notice to the parties. See above this chap. at 77–8.

These detailed provisions are, ostensibly, designed to prevent the recurrence of actions for judicial review which plagued the statutory scheme for recognition established under the Employment Protection Act 1975. However, these careful attempts to circumscribe CAC discretion can also be regarded as a kind of political containment device, which reflects the desire of the Government to control the effects of the new statutory experiment. This speculative observation seems to be borne out by the Government's insistence on reserving certain regulatory powers under Schedule A1, so that the Secretary of State can give further instructions to the CAC and take action to correct the scheme where it appears to be malfunctioning.

For example, the Secretary of State has the power to issue guidance to the CAC on the three qualifying questions relating to automatic recognition.[474] As yet, no such guidance is forthcoming, but it is a matter of concern that it is contemplated. Such guidance has the capacity to obstruct the grant of automatic recognition and thereby entirely disable this avenue of recourse to statutory recognition. Even if this may not be so dangerous in the hands of a Labour government, this provision could be more problematic in the future when (if only eventually) a Conservative government comes into power.

The *quid pro quo* envisaged by New Labour is that there is provision for the CAC to make representations to the government if it considers that the automatic recognition procedure has an unsatisfactory effect, in order that the Secretary of State may amend it.[475] However, this regulatory flexibility, while apparently convenient, arguably places too much power in the hands of the executive. It also gives the CAC an unprecedented political role (as opposed to its present industrial role) that it will have to exercise with care.

Schedule A1 also provides the Secretary of State with powers to specify a method for collective bargaining to be taken into account by the CAC when imposing a DPA.[476] This option was taken by the Government in TURM, which significantly limits the CAC's discretion. In addition, the Secretary of State is empowered to make rules for how the CAC should treat competing claims for derecognition.[477]

For the statutory recognition procedure to be effective, it is important that the CAC be viewed generally as a credible arbitration body making decisions based on the facts of the case, independently of political factors. If the Government too frequently exercises these regulatory powers, the CAC may come to be seen as a government puppet. To do so would arguably undermine the Government's other efforts to bolster the powers and status of the CAC.

---

[474] TULRCA 1992, Sched. A1, para. 167. See also paras. 22 and 87.
[475] TULRCA 1992, Sched. A1, para. 166.
[476] TULRCA 1992, Sched. A1, para. 168.
[477] TULRCA 1992, Sched. A1, para. 169.

D. CONCLUSION: THE IMPLICATIONS OF SCHEDULE A1

During the passage of the Employment Relations Bill, the Conservative Opposition engaged in a fair degree of scaremongering. It was asserted that Schedule A1 was merely a "coy euphemism for foisting compulsory trade union recognition on unwilling employers and a possible majority of the work-force".[478] The aim of this chapter has been to demonstrate that almost nothing could be further from the truth. The most the employer has to fear from the new statutory scheme is the inconvenience of meetings with applicant unions and the costs of a potential recognition ballot. The stringent levels of support required for compulsory recognition make it impossible that a union seeking such status under the procedure would be successful if this were opposed by a majority of the workforce.

In drafting Schedule A1, the Government has demonstrated its eagerness to learn from the "mistakes of the past". "New Labour" is much more explicitly and openly deferential to employer wishes and needs than "Old Labour" administrations have been in the past. The Government has sought to engage employer representatives in policymaking and responded positively to their interests. This was achieved through the mechanism of the "Joint Statement" and via concessions made to views expressed therein and subsequently. The statutory recognition scheme introduced by this Labour Government can be distinguished from its forbears in that it contains no provision for a default award of terms and conditions of employment but seeks to utilise procedure to promote "partnership" through "voluntary agreement". The applicant union is to be encouraged to enter into dialogue with the employer and the outcome of recognition will be a statutory obligation for both parties to engage in further dialogue. The individual choices made by workers relating to representation by a particular trade union are to be tallied through "democratic" procedures, which should persuade the employer of their authenticity. The idea is apparently to bring employers to the bargaining table where they may "consider the industrial relations and strategic benefits of agreeing recognition".[479] This is ostensibly a non-confrontational model of statutory recognition. The Government has indicated that it expects relatively few applications to be made under the statutory scheme.[480]

It is unlikely that employers will mount the legal challenges to decisions made under this statutory recognition procedure that they did under the Employment Protection Act 1975. This is not, as the Government has claimed, because the lengthy provisions set out in Schedule A1 are so clear and detailed as to be safe

---

[478] See HL Hansard, 10 May 1999, col. 975, *per* Baroness Miller.

[479] C. Wynn-Evans, *Employment Relations Bill: A Practical Summary* (London: Tolley, 1999), 20.

[480] Initially 500 applications *per* year were projected by *The Employment Relations Bill: Regulatory Impact Assessment* (London: DTI, 1999), Annex, 3, para. 11. The estimate now stands at 150. See N. Pandya, "Executive action gives competitive advantage", *Guardian,* 10 June 2000.

from judicial review.[481] The reason is that Schedule A1 provides them with other means by which to evade compulsory recognition. These include refusing applicant unions access to establish the initial threshold requirements, engineering long delays in the negotiating process, denying that the bargaining unit sought by the union is conducive to "effective management", recognising a non-independent or a non-representative independent trade union in place of the applicant union and engaging in covert propaganda which has the effect of subverting a recognition ballot.

Even if statutory recognition is granted, the employer has little to fear subsequently. Upon grant of statutory recognition the employer must engage in bargaining with the trade union, but the scope of such bargaining is limited. Only a narrow range of subject-matter comes within the remit of such bargaining. The default procedure envisaged by the Secretary of State gives precedence to employers' interests. Moreover, enforcement of the procedure agreement (such as it may be) will be difficult to achieve. It even seems that it will still be possible for employers to entice workers to sign individual contracts, offering them more favourable terms and conditions of employment, while engaging in collective bargaining with the trade union that has acquired statutory recognition. Moreover, any collective agreement will still not set minimum terms and conditions of employment for the workers it purports to cover.

When employers were still anticipating legislation on compulsory recognition, the number of voluntary recognition agreements increased considerably. "From July 1997 to February 1998, recognition deals outpaced derecognitions, in terms of numbers of employees, affected by 45 to one."[482] ACAS reported that this mood of anticipation had led in one case to solution of a recognition dispute through a balloting procedure, following a version of the proposed statutory procedure in *Fairness at Work*.[483] In Standing Committee, the Government minister observed that it was "especially heartening that the Bill is having a positive effect even before it has become law".[484] However, many employers have been adopting a "wait and see" approach pending the new legislation[485] and others may well lose their inclination to recognise once they realise the actual limitations of Schedule A1. Just as the EPA 1975 initially led to a spate of voluntary recognition agreements which died away as the paucity of the legislative provisions became apparent, so too we predict the same trend here. The reason is that the compulsory recognition procedure set out in Schedule A1, the very lynchpin of New Labour's collective labour rights policy, is largely a sham.

---

[481] As observed in Simpson, n.289 above, at 247 there is still considerable scope for judicial review of CAC decisions; e.g. as regards the ambit of the bargaining unit, the award of automatic recognition and the terms of the DPA.

[482] Lourie, n.38 above, at 32, citing TUC, *Trade Union Trends: Focus on Recognition* (London: TUC, 1998).

[483] ACAS *Annual Report 1998* (London: HMSO, 1999), 24.

[484] HC Standing Committee E, 16 Mar. 1999 at col. 345, per Mr Wills.

[485] ACAS *Annual Report 1998* (London: HMSO, 1999), 26.

5

Industrial Action

A. INTRODUCTION

INDUSTRIAL ACTION MAY take various forms, from the complete withdrawal of labour in an all-out "strike" to the partial disruption caused by a "go-slow" or "work to rule". All forms affect the ability of the employer to supply goods or services. The aim of such action is to counteract the *de facto* power held by employers, by demonstrating the potential of labour to inflict economic harm. Moreover, it is often not so much industrial action itself, but the fact that it is threatened, which provides employers with an incentive to respond to workers' claims. It is widely accepted that, without potential recourse to industrial action, collective bargaining would amount merely to "collective begging".[1]

The fundamental entitlement to take such action is recognised in instruments such as the International Covenant on Economic Social and Cultural Rights and the European Social Charter.[2] It has also been recognised in the extensive ILO jurisprudence on freedom of association.[3] In addition, EC instruments have acknowledged the importance of this right.[4]

This chapter examines the essential features of New Labour policy relating to industrial action in the United Kingdom. Our starting point is the historic failure of the UK legislature to introduce a positive right to strike. Instead, participants in industrial action have been given partial protection from dismissal and limited immunities have been granted to unions that organise such action. As we shall see, this state of affairs is not fundamentally changed by the Employment Relations Act 1999, which merely tinkers at the edges of the established legal regime.

The 1999 Act has introduced new individual rights for workers in the context of industrial action. There is a new means by which a striker can claim for unfair

---

[1] A.T.J.M. Jacobs, "The Law of Strikes and Lock-Outs" in R. Blanpain and C. Engels, *Comparative Labour Law and Industrial Relations in Industrialized Market Economies* (5th edn., Deventer: Kluwer, 1993), 423.

[2] International Covenant on Economic, Social and Cultural Rights 1966, Art. 8(1)(d) and European Social Charter 1961, Art. 6(4).

[3] B. Gernignon, A. Odero and H. Guido, *ILO Principles Concerning the Right to Strike* (Geneva: ILO, 1998).

[4] See the Community Charter of the Fundamental Social Rights of Workers 1989, Art. 13; and the "Monti Reg.", EC Reg. 2679/98 on the functioning of the internal market in relation to the free movement of goods among the Member States [1998] OJ L337/8, Art. 2, discussed in N. Bruun and B. Veneziani, "The Right or Freedom to Transnational Industrial Action in the European Union" in ETUI, *A Legal Framework for European Industrial Relations* (Brussels: ETUI, 1999).

dismissal. Also, workers' names need not be provided by the union to the employer when notice of industrial action is given. However, it seems that the trade-off for these new rights will be added responsibilities for trade unions. Unions face new pressures to resolve disputes through discussions with the employer, without recourse to industrial action. They are also expected to give the employer assistance in preparing for any industrial action. No serious attempt has been made to dismantle the legislative constraints on industrial action progressively introduced under Conservative governments between 1979 and 1997. In its efforts to distance itself from "Old Labour" and further its conception of non-conflictual "partnership" this Government refuses to fulfil its international obligations to protect the right to strike.

B. THE FAILURE TO INTRODUCE A POSITIVE RIGHT TO STRIKE

In many European states, the constitution or national legislation proclaims that workers have a positive right to strike.[5] By contrast, UK law on industrial action is peculiar in its failure to provide any such basic entitlement. This is arguably due both to the hostility of the British courts to such a development and the reluctance of the legislature to ensure its introduction. Some anticipated that such a step might be taken when a Labour Government entered office in 1997,[6] but *Fairness at Work* and the Employment Relations Act dashed these hopes.

The common law courts have refused to recognise a "right to strike". They are reluctant to endorse a practice which they regard as disruptive and potentially harmful to the legitimate interests of property owners. They tend to regard workers who take industrial action as being in breach of their contracts of employment, apart from in the most exceptional circumstances. An employer, following such a breach, is usually entitled to terminate the contract and dismiss the worker in question.[7] While this rule has since been modified by legislation which provides partial protection from "selective dismissal",[8] it has further consequences. The courts have found that, where industrial action constitutes a breach of contract, to call a strike can be regarded *inter alia* as a tortious inducement of breach of contract. On this basis, and in reliance on other economic torts, courts have imposed civil liability on organisers of industrial action, whether they be individuals or a union. This task has often been performed with

---

[5] E.g. in France, Greece, Italy and Portugal the right to strike is protected expressly under the constitution. See Jacobs, n.1 above, at 424. See also for two recent detailed surveys of constitutional protection of labour rights within the EU S. Clauwaert, *Fundamental Social Rights in the European Union: Comparative Tables and Documents* (Brussels: ETUI, 1998); and J. Aaltonen, *International Secondary Industrial Action in the EU Member States* (Espoo: Metalli, 1999), 232–44.

[6] J. Moher, "The Future for UK Employment Law Under Labour" [1995] *Employment and Industrial Relations International* 9 at 10.

[7] See K.D. Ewing, *The Right to Strike* (Oxford: Clarendon Press, 1991), Chap. 2; and Lord Wedderburn, "The Right to Strike" in Lord Wedderburn, *Employment Rights in Britain and Europe* (London: Lawrence and Wishart, 1991).

[8] See above Chap. 2 at 40–1.

alacrity, certain members of the judiciary having proved themselves willing to exercise their initiative in extending the range of economic torts applicable to industrial action.[9] Again, legislative intervention has mitigated some of the harsher effects of these common law principles. Trade unions are granted immunity from certain forms of liability in tort, but only under particular conditions.[10]

There has been no grant of a positive entitlement to take industrial action. The Donovan Commission Report considered that, on balance, this was unnecessary:

> The right to strike is, basically, a right to withdraw labour in combination without being subject to the legal consequences which would, in the past, have followed. This situation is now well recognised and we do not think it can be improved by granting the right in express terms.[11]

Subsequently, numerous labour law commentators have questioned this assumption.[12] Immunities do not have the same normative connotations of a positive right, and therefore are arguably more vulnerable to challenge.

During the 1980s, Hayek and others at the Institute of Economic Affairs argued for the abolition of immunities given to trade unions and participants in the context of industrial action. These were presented as indefensible "privileges".[13] Judges also appeared to take this view, being prone to adopt a narrow construction of statutory immunities.[14] Even in the most unusual cases, where the courts did provide a generous interpretation, Conservative governments merely amended the legislation to restrict further the application of these provisions.[15]

---

[9] For a useful outline of developments relating to economic torts see S. Deakin and G. Morris, *Labour Law* (2nd edn., London: Butterworths, 1998) at 872–86; C. Barrow, *Industrial Relations* (London: Cavendish, 1997), 283–302; and H. Carty, "Intentional Violation of Economic Interests: The Limits of Common Law Liability" (1988) 104 *LQR* 250.

[10] TULRCA 1992 s. 219. These conditions were gradually made more stringent under Conservative government from 1980 onwards.

[11] *Royal Commission Report on Trade Union and Employers' Associations 1965–1968 (Donovan Royal Commission Report)* Cmnd 3623 (London: HMSO, 1968) para. 935. It was only in the event that the law relating to trade disputes was codified that the matter needed to receive further consideration.

[12] See on this issue, K.D. Ewing, "The Right to Strike" (1986) 15 *ILJ* 143 and K.D. Ewing, "Rights and Immunities in British Labour Law" (1988) 10 *Comparative Labor Law Journal* 1; L.J. Macfarlane, *The Right to Strike* (Harmondsworth: Penguin Books, 1981) at 14; Lord Wedderburn, *The Worker and the Law* (3rd edn., Harmondsworth: Penguin Books, 1986) 847–56; Lord Wedderburn, "Laws About Strikes" in Lord McCarthy (ed.), *Legal Intervention in Industrial Relations: Gains and Losses* (Oxford: Basil Blackwell, 1992).

[13] F.A. Hayek, *1980s Unemployment and the Unions: Essays on the Impotent Price Structure of Britain and Monopoly in the Labour Market* (2nd edn., London: Institute of Economic Affairs, 1984); A. Shenfield, *What Right to Strike? With Commentaries by Cyril Grunfeld and Sir Leonard Neal* (London: Institute of Economic Affairs, 1986). See also for a contemporary discussion of this rhetoric, K. Syrett, "'Immunity', 'Privilege' and 'Right': British Trade Unions and the Language of Labour Law Reform" (1998) 25 *JLS* 388 especially at 390–3.

[14] See *Express Newspapers* v. *MacShane* [1979] IRLR 210 (CA).

[15] An example is the amendment of TULRA 1974 s. 29 by the Employment Act 1980 which can be regarded as a response to the decision in *NWL* v. *Woods* [1979] IRLR 478 (HL). See S. Auerbach, *Legislating for Conflict* (Oxford: Clarendon Press, 1990) at 81–4 and below this chap. at 138.

The response from the Institute of Employment Rights, on the opposite side of the political spectrum, was to argue for a positive right to strike which would at least "deprive governments, the media and employers of the significant ideological ammunition they have always possessed in being able to distort the nature of the right to strike by condemning it as a privilege to break the law".[16] It was proposed that dismissal of participants in industrial action and civil liability of organisers should become the exception rather than the rule.

Such a change was never likely to happen under the successive Conservative governments which held office from 1979 to 1997. Their express agenda was to continue the "taming of trade unions" and reduce the incidence of industrial action.[17] During this period, the UK was subjected to extensive international criticism relating to its legal treatment of industrial action, within both the International Labour Organisation and the Council of Europe.[18]

As the number of strikes decreased, the Conservatives claimed that their "step by step" legislative strategy had been successful.[19] It is questionable whether these "persistent, simplistic claims" can be verified.[20] The decline in industrial action[21] may well be due to other factors. These may include lower levels of unionisation, depressed economic conditions and changes in the structure of the economy.[22] The more obvious result of Conservative reforms was a growing awareness on the part of employers that legal mechanisms could be used to prevent industrial action from taking place. This awareness gradually led to exploitation of these opportunities.[23]

The question then was how New Labour would position itself between Conservative policies and the legacy of "Old Labour". Pressure from trade unions and internationally meant that the status quo could not simply be preserved. On the other hand, Blair and his Government were wary of being asso-

---

[16] R. Welch, *The Right to Strike: A Trade Union View* (London: Institute of Employment Rights, 1991), 36. See also K.D. Ewing (ed.), *Working Life: A New Perspective on Labour Law* (London: Institute of Employment Rights, 1996), 262–4.

[17] See R. Taylor, *The Trade Union Question in British Politics: Government and Unions since 1945* (Oxford: Blackwell, 1993), Chap. 8. See also above Chap. 1 at 7.

[18] For a brief summary of ILO recommendations see T. Novitz, "Freedom of Association and 'Fairness at Work'—An Assessment of the Impact and Relevance of ILO Convention No. 87 on its Fiftieth Anniversary" (1998) 27 *ILJ* 169. As regards views expressed within the Council of Europe see J. Hendy, "The Human Rights Act, Art. 11 and the Right to Strike" [1998] *European Human Rights Law Review* 582 at 588–92.

[19] See e.g. *Industrial Relations in the 1990s*, Cm 1602 (London: HMSO, 1991), Chap. 1; and *Industrial Action and Trade Unions*, Cm 3470 (London: HMSO, 1996), Chap. 1.

[20] J. Elgar and B. Simpson, "The Impact of the Law on Industrial Disputes in the 1980s" in D. Metcalf and S. Milner (eds.), *New Perspectives on Industrial Disputes* (London and New York: Routledge, 1993), 74.

[21] The WERS Survey of 1998 found that only 2% of workplaces reported industrial action and only 1% strikes. See M. Cully, S. Woodland, A. O'Reilly and G. Dix, *Britain at Work: As Depicted by the 1998 Workplace Employee Relations Survey* (London: Routledge, 1999), 125–6.

[22] See for an analysis of these factors P. Edwards, "Strikes and Industrial Conflict" in P. Edwards (ed.), *Industrial Relations: Theory and Practice in Britain* (Oxford: Blackwell, 1995) at 432 *et seq.*

[23] See B. Simpson, "The Labour Injunction, Unlawful Means and the Right to Strike" (1987) 50 *MLR* 506; and "Employers Step up Legal Challenges" [1994] *Labour Research* 7–9.

ciated with the mythology of the mass strikes and pickets associated with the "Winter of Discontent".[24] New Labour had to find a "third way" accommodation between the two which, though it entailed reform, would not amount to "going back" to the failings of past Labour regimes.[25]

Labour has not responded with a major overhaul of the legislation relating to industrial action. There is to be no positive right to strike written into UK legislation; nor is there to be any reversal of the basic principle that taking such action constitutes a breach of the contract of employment. The system of immunities is retained. There is not even any reform of the law on picketing.[26] As Blair promised even before the election, "the basic elements of the legislation of the 1980s" have been kept.[27] A boon for trade unions was the abolition of the Commissioner for Protection Against Unlawful Industrial Action (CPAUIA), but the rationale for this reform was the saving of public expenditure and the legislative right of members of the public to seek an injunction in respect of unlawful industrial action still stands.[28] Otherwise, the changes made by the Employment Relations Act consist only of improvements to the protection of the individual striker from dismissal and rationalisation of the criteria for trade union immunity from liability in tort. The remainder of this chapter examines the extent of these changes.

C. TRADE UNION RESPONSIBILITY FOR PROTECTION FROM DISMISSAL

The Employment Relations Act 1999 inserted section 238A into TULRCA 1992, providing a new means by which participants in industrial action could seek protection from dismissal.[29] The decision of the Government to give these rights to individual workers can be regarded as a response to recommendations made in the ILO and Council of Europe.[30] However, it is arguable that this carefully drafted provision is deceptive. Section 238A of TULRCA 1992 is not solely concerned with the individual well-being of employees, but also implicitly places significant obligations on trade unions.

---

[24] HC Hansard, 21 May 1998, col. 1101 and HL Hansard, 10 May 1999, col. 985.

[25] See *FAW*, Foreword.

[26] Apparently, the days of "mass picketing" are over. See *FAW*, Foreword. This is despite the fact that this is in breach of ILO standards. See Novitz, n.18 above, at 187.

[27] Speech to the General Municipal & Boilermakers Conference in Brighton, 7 June 1995, cited in Moher, n.6 above, at 11.

[28] See above Chap. 3 at 57.

[29] The content of this provision is outlined in detail above in Chap. 2 at 39–43.

[30] "That is in line with our pre-election commitments, and it is in response to the International Labour Organisation criticism that United Kingdom law provides insufficient protection for workers": HC Standing Committee E, 9 March 1999 at col.288, per Mr McCartney. See HL Hansard, 10 May 1999, col. 1015, per Lord Wedderburn, who observed that the dismissal of a worker for taking lawful strike action "is an affront to international human rights and ILO principles". As regards condemnation of dismissal of strikers within the Council of Europe, see Committee of Ministers Recommendation R ChS(97)3 adopted on 15 Jan. 1997.

Already, the ability to claim unfair dismissal in cases of selective dismissal is dependent upon the industrial action being "official".[31] This was a requirement introduced under Conservative Government by the Employment Act 1990 which placed trade unions in an invidious position.[32] A strike or other industrial action is regarded as "unofficial" in relation to an employee unless he or she is a member of a trade union and the action is authorised or endorsed by that union; or he or she is not a member of the union but there are among those taking part in industrial action members of a trade union by which the action has been authorised or endorsed. Industrial action is not treated as unofficial where none of those taking part in industrial action are members of the union. This means that a union makes employees vulnerable to dismissal if it does not authorise or endorse the action taken by its members.[33] Yet, by providing authorisation or endorsement, the union exposes itself to potential liability in tort.[34] Such liability is likely to arise if the industrial action lies outside the scope of a lawful "trade dispute" or if the necessary procedural requirements have not been satisfied. The latter may well occur where trade union members have taken spontaneous industrial action.[35]

In much the same way, the Employment Relations Act makes the new protection from dismissal dependent on union conduct. Section 238A is headed "participation in official industrial action". However, this provision actually goes further than this, covering only employees who take "protected industrial action".[36] The ability to claim unfair dismissal is therefore dependent upon the ability of the organiser successfully to claim immunity from liability in tort under section 219 of TULRCA 1992:

> Unions must organise the action in accordance with the law, including the detailed provisions concerning notice and ballots. If they do not, the rights will not apply, which means that employers can, without the fear of tribunals against them, dismiss those taking unofficial action.[37]

This arguably places a heavy burden on a trade union to ensure that the employee has access to protection from dismissal. In order to secure these rights and not disappoint its members, the trade union will be placed under additional pressure to ensure that the requirements of section 219 are met. Moreover, the

---

[31]   See TULRCA 1992 ss. 237 and 238.

[32]   Employment Act 1990 s. 9. See also *Unofficial Action and the Law*, Cm 821 (London: HMSO, 1989).

[33]   Moreover, this provision was introduced in conjunction with the requirement that trade unions be regarded as legally responsible for organisation of industrial disputes not only by full-time officials but also shop stewards, unless the trade union unequivocally repudiated the action by notifying all its "relevant" members in writing. See Employment Act 1990 s.6; and now TULRCA 1992 s. 21. See B. Simpson, "The Employment Act 1990 in Context" (1991) 54 *MLR* 418 at 427–9.

[34]   TULRCA 1992 s.20.

[35]   It is estimated that three quarters of strikes in Britain were unofficial at the time the Employment Act 1990 was introduced. See Taylor, n.17 above, at 306.

[36]   And then only if they can establish that this was the reason for the dismissal. See above Chap. 2 at 42.

[37]   HC Standing Committee E, 9 Mar. 1999 at col.289, per Mr McCartney.

limited scope of statutory immunities which, as we shall see below, falls foul of ILO standards,[38] means that it may be difficult for the union to ensure that its members qualify for protection. In this respect, section 238A is less generous than it may at first appear. Indeed, it might be said that New Labour is adopting and perfecting Conservative models of control.

A further responsibility placed on trade unions relates to the eight-week period of protection provided for in section 238A. If the employee's participation in industrial action lasts longer than eight weeks, the employee will not be taken to have been unfairly dismissed, unless the employer failed to take "reasonable" procedural steps to resolve the dispute.[39] This appears to place an important onus on the employer. It seems intended to deter the kinds of deliberately obstructive tactics used by employers during industrial action, for example during the *Timex* dispute.[40]

However, when this provision spells out what conduct one could expect of an employer, it is also the conduct of the *trade union* that is to be taken into account. The tribunal is to consider whether the employer *and the union* complied with procedures established by a collective or other agreement, initiated and participated in negotiations after the start of the protected industrial action and accepted (where reasonable) requests for conciliation and mediation.[41] It is ironic that the presumption that a collective agreement is not intended to be binding is reversed in this context.[42]

The emphasis on co-operative negotiations between employer and union is familiar. For example, it is comparable with the Government's interest in promoting dialogue within the context of the statutory recognition scheme. The emphasis is on encouraging the employer and trade union to meet and seek to resolve their differences:

> We want to set a period that allows reasonable time for parties to resolve their dispute and so avoid dismissals. In our judgment, eight weeks gives enough time for detailed and serious discussions to occur, possibly involving third parties such as the Advisory, Conciliation and Arbitration Service.[43]

This was described by a Government minister as an aspect of "the urgent need for partnership in the workplace, for each side's rights and responsibilities to be recognised, for both sides to understand each other and for employees' worth to be appreciated".[44]

While one might wish to applaud the promotion of co-operative workplace relations, the point is that this provision also places an additional and significant

---

[38] See below this chap. at 137–40.
[39] TULRCA 1992 s. 238A(5)(c).
[40] See K. Miller and C. Woolfson, "Timex: Industrial Relations and the Use of the Law in the 1990s" (1994) 23 *ILJ* 209.
[41] TULRCA 1992 ss. 238A(6) and (7).
[42] See above Chap. 4 at 115–18.
[43] HC Standing Committee E, 9 Mar. 1999 at col. 289, per Mr McCartney.
[44] *Ibid.*

burden on trade unions. It is unlikely that industrial action will often last for longer than eight weeks, but because unions cannot predict how long industrial action will last, they will not want to act in any manner which would forfeit the application of this protection from dismissal. Unions will be aware that their conduct will be subjected to scrutiny, not just in terms of whether they comply with the requirements for statutory immunity when authorising or endorsing industrial action, but also what their officials do subsequently in their dealings with employers. If they act in contravention of an existing collective agreement, even if such an agreement is not stated to be legally binding, this may affect the assessment as to whether the employer has acted "unreasonably". They must also demonstrate their willingness to negotiate and engage in conciliation at all times. Otherwise, they expose their members (and non-union members who take action in association with their members) to dismissal.

There is also arguably a possibility that a trade union could be subject to a civil action by employees who consider that it was the union's conduct which deprived them of the employment protection to which they would otherwise be entitled.[45] For example, a union official's negligence in organising a ballot or unreasonable refusal of a request for mediation could lead to a claim in tort by the employee against the union. Even if such actions are not brought, a union could easily lose the sympathy and support of its members in these or similar circumstances.

D. THE SCOPE OF STATUTORY IMMUNITY FOR TRADE UNIONS

Section 219 of TULRCA 1992 provides statutory immunity for the torts of inducing breach of contract, conspiracy to injure and intimidation.[46] This immunity will not apply unless the industrial action in question has been taken "in contemplation or furtherance of a trade dispute" as defined in section 244 of TULRCA 1992 (the "golden formula") and is not otherwise "excluded from protection".[47] In addition, a trade union must abide by the detailed balloting and notification requirements set out in sections 226–235 of TULRCA 1992.

If the union's call for industrial action does not satisfy all these statutory criteria it will be unlawful. In such circumstances, the employer may seek an injunction. So too may any individual affected or likely to be affected by the impact on the supply of goods or services.[48] A union member can also seek an injunction to prevent industrial action which does not have the support of a

---

[45] See e.g. *Friend* v. *Institution of Professional Managers and Specialists* [1999] IRLR 173 at 174 where it was observed *obiter* that a trade union has a duty in tort to use ordinary care and skill in advising and/or acting for a member in an employment dispute.

[46] This immunity does not cover liability in tort for breach of statutory duty. In particular, this has the effect of leaving some unions which organise strikes in the public sector exposed to liability. See *Meade* v. *Haringey LBC* [1979] ICR 494 (CA).

[47] TULRCA 1992 ss. 222–225.

[48] TULRCA 1992 s. 235A.

lawful ballot.[49] Even if the industrial action goes ahead, the trade union may later be held liable in tort for the loss suffered by the employer.[50] Moreover, no employee will be able to claim protection from unfair dismissal under section 238A of TULRCA 1992 in respect of unlawful or "unprotected" action.

New Labour does little to lift the extensive barriers to immunity in tort set in place by the Conservatives. Nothing is done to alter the narrow range of lawful aims of industrial action. The Government's priorities lie instead with reform of the balloting and notification procedures. Even there, concessions made to protection of individual workers' rights are relatively minor and the *quid pro quo* is an additional obligation placed on trade unions. What is most significant in this context is the decision to retain the bulk of restrictions on industrial action introduced by the Conservatives.

1. The lawful aims of industrial action

No strike, whether it is called by a union or any one else, is covered by the statutory immunity unless it comes within the lawful aims of industrial action set out in TULRCA 1992. At present these are narrowly defined and have been subjected to international criticism. Nevertheless, the Employment Relations Act 1999 does nothing to change the definition of a lawful "trade dispute". No steps have been taken to secure compliance with international labour standards relating to this matter. All that we can be thankful for is that the Government refused to contemplate the reform proposed by the CBI and the Conservative opposition, namely that industrial action called to secure trade union recognition should now be rendered unlawful. Such action continues to be permissible.

a. the subject matter of a "trade dispute" and "political strikes"

Under section 244(1) of TULRCA 1992, a trade dispute is defined as "a dispute between workers and their employer which relates wholly or mainly" to one or more matters listed therein. These cover a broad range of subjects but relate only to matters arising in the course of employment appropriate to collective bargaining. In addition, section 244(2) provides very limited scope for action to be taken relating to a dispute between workers and Ministers of the Crown.[51] Political strikes aimed at challenging Government policy are not envisaged.

---

[49] TULRCA 1992 s. 62.

[50] Under Conservative Government, the Employment Act 1982 s. 15 repealed TULRA 1974 s. 14, thereby exposing trade unions to liability in tort for unlawful industrial action. This was however subject to a limitation on damages available, now found in TULRCA 1992 s. 22.

[51] This is possible only if the dispute relates to matters which have been referred for consideration by a joint body on which he is represented by virtue of any enactment or which cannot be settled without his exercising a power conferred on him by or under any enactment. It seems that its application is confined to circumstances where the employer has to rely on the government to authorise the grant of the workers' demands. See *Sherrard* v. *AUEW* [1973] IRLR 188 (CA) per Lord Denning MR. See also Barrow, n.9 above, at 310.

The lawful aims of industrial action set out in section 244 do not extend as far as the entitlement to strike contemplated by the ILO Committee on Freedom of Association (CFA), which is more broadly stated:

> The right to strike should not be limited solely to industrial disputes that are likely to be resolved through the signing of a collective agreement; workers and their organizations should be able to express in a broader context, if necessary, their dissatisfaction as regards economic and social matters affecting their members' interests.[52]

In other words, trade unions should be able to call industrial action on matters such as "privatisation" or other aspects of government economic policy which have a bearing on their members' interests. "Purely political" strikes are not considered to be legitimate, on the ground that trade unions should try to maintain their independence so as to best represent the concerns of their members.[53] Nevertheless, on various occasions where industrial action has "mixed motives" but there is some connection to workers' economic or social interests, the right to take industrial action has been upheld.[54] The CFA has never required that such economic or social reasons be the predominant motivation for the dispute.

In the UK, prior to 1982, industrial action which related to broader issues was lawful if a connection could be found with the matters listed as the appropriate subject of a "trade dispute". It did not matter whether a strike had more than one object in mind, or that the predominant object was political, as long as the actual demand resisted by the employer had some relationship to a matter on that list.[55] Concerned by the implications of such a test, the Thatcher Government introduced a "wholly or mainly" requirement.[56]

Subsequently, the "predominant motive" test has been used to exclude industrial action from statutory protection. An example is the case of *Mercury Communications* v. *Scott-Garner*,[57] where the Post Office Engineers Union (POEU) called on its members to oppose privatisation in the telecommunications industry and to refuse to connect Mercury, a private company, to the British Telecommunications (BT) network. Mercury sought an injunction on the ground that this was unlawful industrial action. The Court of Appeal found that the main aim of the strike was not to oppose the particular job losses that would follow from privatization, but to express general opposition to this government policy. They considered that, had job security been the union's chief

---

[52] ILO, *Digest of Decisions and Principles of the Freedom of Association Committee of the Governing Body of the ILO ("ILO Digest")* (4th edn., Geneva: International Labour Office, 1996) at para. 484.

[53] *Ibid.*, para. 454 and paras. 481–482.

[54] Case No. 1793 (Nigeria) *295th Report of the ILO Committee on Freedom of Association* (1994) para. 567 at para. 602; Case No. 1884 (Swaziland) *306th Report of the ILO Committee on Freedom of Association* (1997) para. 619 at para. 684.

[55] See the judgments of Lord Diplock in *NWL* v. *Woods* [1979] IRLR 478 (HL) and *Duport Steels Ltd* v. *Sirs* [1980] IRLR 116 (HL).

[56] Discussed in P. Davies and M. Freedland, *Labour Law: Text and Materials* (2nd edn., London: Weidenfeld and Nicolson, 1984) at 802–5.

[57] [1983] IRLR 494 (CA).

concern, the union could have sought to have the matter dealt with under the Job Security Agreement. The union had therefore failed to satisfy the "wholly or mainly" test and could not establish a "trade dispute" under section 244. Ironically, following this action, the privatized British Telecom engaged in employment restructuring, deciding to remove an entire layer of management.[58] So, in fact, the union's fears were borne out.

It is notable that the Employment Relations Act makes no change to the predominant motive test. As the wording of section 244 of TULRCA 1992 continues to contravene ILO standards, the Labour Government remains in breach of its international obligations.

b. *a dispute between workers and their employer:*
the problem of secondary action

During the 1980s, under Thatcher's leadership, the Conservatives began to strip away immunity for industrial action which lay outside the confines of a localised dispute between one employer and a particular group of workers.[59] The final blow was dealt by the Employment Act 1990.[60]

Immunity for secondary action is implicitly excluded by the present wording of section 244(1) of TULRCA 1992 which indicates that a dispute other than that between "workers and their employer" lies outside the scope of a lawful "trade dispute".[61] In addition, immunity in tort for such action is explicitly excluded by section 224 of TULRCA 1992.

This rule has various implications. For example, there is no immunity for industrial action relating to demarcations disputes.[62] It has also recently been demonstrated that this rule can give rise to difficulties where industrial action is taken in relation to the proposed transfer of an undertaking.[63] Moreover, some UK employers have responded to this legislative development by artificially dividing their workforce, creating ostensibly separate "buffer companies". In *Dimbleby & Sons Ltd* v. *NUJ*,[64] the House of Lords refused to pierce an artificial corporate veil, with the result that workers could no longer take action in solidarity with one another, even though they had previously been employed within a single enterprise.

In addition to the problems experienced at a domestic level, the ban on secondary action may have broader repercussions. One potential solution to the

---

[58] P. Davies and M. Freedland, *Labour Legislation and Public Policy* (Oxford: Clarendon, 1993), 621.

[59] Taylor, n.17 above, at 284–7. See Employment Act 1980 s. 17 and Employment Act 1982 ss. 14 and 18.

[60] Employment Act 1990 s.4. See also Simpson, n.33 above, at 432–5.

[61] Subject to the limited exception in TULRCA 1992 s. 244(2) identified above.

[62] See, as regards problems of demarcation arising in the context of union recognition, above Chap. 4 at 67–68 and 85–87.

[63] *University College London Hospital NHS Trust* v. *UNISON* [1999] IRLR 31 (CA).

[64] *Dimbleby* v. *NUJ* [1984] IRLR 161 (HL).

problems posed by the global phenomenon of mobile investment and production is for workers to organise internationally. Increasingly, workers may wish to co-ordinate action across national boundaries so as to counteract the multinational dimensions of the power exercised by certain corporate entities. For example, workers might wish to take action in support of each other where they work in the same or related industries, or where they work for inter-connected companies. In doing so, they could establish transnational standards within an industry or a multinational group of companies.[65] UK legislation on secondary action prevents British workers from engaging in such an endeavour to secure international or European-level collective agreements. This is also a matter for concern.

Again, this rule is in breach of ILO standards. ILO supervisory bodies have established that workers should be able to take industrial action to lend support to others, as long as the primary action they are supporting is lawful. They should also be able to act in solidarity where their bargaining power would otherwise be undermined by the fact that they work in small undertakings.[66] In 1999, the ILO Committee of Experts challenged the UK stance on these issues for the first time since the Labour Government took office. The Committee expressed its concern that employers have tended to restructure their businesses so as to make primary action secondary and also reiterated its recommendations that "workers should be able to participate in sympathy strikes provided the initial strike they are supporting is itself lawful".[67] However, the Government has held to its statement in *Fairness at Work*, refusing to change the law relating to secondary action. Its view is that to do so would be to take the UK "back to the adversarial days of the 1960s and 1970s".[68] On this issue, in its eagerness to distance itself from the manifestations of "old Labour", the New Labour Government seems once again prepared to defy international censure.

c. industrial action over recognition

There was a threat that the lawful aims of industrial action would be narrowed further. Conservative peers proposed that immunity from actions in tort should be withdrawn from a trade union which took industrial action to seek recognition if the procedure in Schedule A1 had not been exhausted or if the procedure had been exhausted and the trade union had not been granted recognition.[69]

Their reasoning would seem to be as follows. Actual or proposed industrial action is usually a key incentive for employers to come to the bargaining table.

---

[65] See K.W. Wedderburn, "Multi-national Enterprise and National Labour Law" (1972) 1 *ILJ* 12.

[66] *ILO Digest*, n.52 above, at para. 283. Also see for a summary of ILO jurisprudence on this point, Novitz, n.18 above, at 186.

[67] (1999) *Report of the ILO Committee of Experts on the Application of Conventions and Recommendations*, ILC, 87th Session, 290–1.

[68] *Ibid*, 290.

[69] HL Hansard, 7 June 1999, cols. 1281–1282.

By contrast, a statutory recognition procedure seems to be designed to reach the same result, only without the cost and conflict associated with strikes. If the statutory scheme is all that the Government say it is, why should there be any need for industrial action in this context? After all, Schedule A1 is described in the Explanatory Notes "as a means of resolving the dispute [as to trade union recognition] without recourse to industrial action".[70]

Nevertheless, the Government rejected the Conservative proposal on the basis that:

> The right of unions to call industrial action is already heavily circumscribed. We do not propose to limit it further. If we did, we would be breaching our International Labour Organisation commitments, which the Government take very seriously.[71]

Given New Labour's highly selective approach to the implementation of ILO commitments, it seems unlikely that breach of ILO standards was viewed with such great distaste. The more obvious answer is that, as observed above, the procedure set in place by Schedule A1 is unlikely to be effective in terms of securing recognition.[72] In the absence of any potential recourse to industrial action, unions would have been deprived of the source of their bargaining power in recognition disputes; something not compensated for as yet by the new statutory recognition scheme. The refusal of New Labour to restrict further the lawful aims of industrial action is therefore a reason for relief, but not necessarily for optimism. UK legislation relating to the definition of a legitimate "trade dispute" remains in breach of ILO standards and no immediate change is foreseeable.

2. Changes to balloting and notification requirements

A trade union cannot claim immunity from actions in tort unless its officials have complied with certain balloting and notice requirements set out in sections 226–234A of TULRCA 1992. Moreover, a union member can seek an order to prevent industrial action which does not have the support of a lawful ballot.[73] These requirements were gradually introduced, becoming progressively more detailed and complex between 1984 and 1993. These statutory provisions were supplemented by an extensive Code of Practice which, while itself imposing no legal obligations, is admissible in evidence as a statement of "good practice".[74] In 1996, John Major's Government produced a White Paper on *Industrial*

---

[70] *Explanatory Notes to Employment Relations Act 1999*, para. 6.

[71] HL Hansard, 7 June 1999, col. 1282, per Lord McIntosh.

[72] See above Chap. 4 at 127–8.

[73] TULRCA 1992 s. 62.

[74] The Code was first issued by the Secretary of State in 1989 and has since been replaced by the 1995 Code of Practice on Industrial Action Ballots and Notice to Employers (Code on Industrial Action). See as to its legal status, TULRCA 1992 s. 207 and the 1995 Code on Industrial Action, para. 7.

Action and Trade Unions, proposing further restrictions relating to balloting and notice requirements,[75] but there was apparently no time to implement these reforms before the General Election of 1997.

According to ILO standards, the requirement of a ballot *per se* is not objectionable if the intention is to promote "respect for democratic rules within the trade union movement".[76] It is only where the cumulative effect of such regulation "by virtue of its detail, complexity and extent" interferes unduly with the ability to call industrial action that there is any need for reform.[77] Within the UK, some have recognised that ballots can strengthen the bargaining position of trade union negotiators and engender trust. Others consider that balloting and notice requirements should be repealed on the ground that they have given employers opportunities to launch legal attacks.[78] The predominant view appears to be that industrial action organised by a trade union should be decided by a ballot, but that the balloting requirements themselves should be simplified and modified to prevent frequent challenges on legal grounds.[79] In addition, the TUC asked that the 1995 Code be amended, as it extended "the already onerous obligations on trade unions by deliberately confusing the legal requirements with what is considered to be 'good practice' ".[80]

Fairness at Work accepted that the law and Code on notice and balloting requirements were "unnecessarily complex and rigid" and needed reform. Yet it was immediately apparent that the Government did not intend to repeal the balloting requirements altogether. The Government merely wished to simplify the law and the Code.[81]

On 26 June 2000, a draft revised Code of Practice on Industrial Action Ballots and Notice to Employers was laid before Parliament. Subject to parliamentary approval, it will take effect from 18 September 2000.[82] The new draft Code is slightly shorter and streamlined, consisting of 53 as opposed to 70 paragraphs, but is not notably different in terms of its format. The TUC's complaints (that the Code makes greater demands on trade unions than is strictly necessary under TULRCA 1992) would still stand under the present draft.[83] Nevertheless,

---

[75] *Industrial Action and Trade Unions*, Cm 3470 (London: HMSO, 1996).

[76] *ILO Digest*, n.52 above, at para. 425; *Report of the ILO Committee of Experts on the Application of Conventions and Recommendations* (1989) ILC, 76th Session, 235–44. See above Chap. 3 at 52.

[77] *Report of the ILO Committee of Experts on the Application of Conventions and Recommendations* (1995) ILC, 82nd Session, 200.

[78] S. McKay, *The Law on Industrial Action Under the Conservatives* (London: Institute of Employment Rights, 1996), 31.

[79] J. Elgar and B. Simpson, *Industrial Action Ballots and the Law* (London: Institute of Employment Rights, 1996), Chap. 4.

[80] TUC, *TUC Response: Fairness at Work White Paper* (London: TUC, 1998) para. 76.

[81] *FAW*, para. 4.26.

[82] In Apr. 2000, there was a public consultation on revisions to the Code and submissions closed in June 2000: DTI, *Revisions to the Code of Practice on Industrial Action Ballots and Notice to Employers: Public Consultation*, URN 00/807 (2000).

[83] E.g., para. 11 of the 1995 Code on Industrial Action states that where more than one union is involved, the ballots should be co-ordinated. In doing so, the 1995 Code exceeds the statutory

the tone of its provisions is subtly but perhaps significantly different. Where in the past, the 1995 Code said what "should" be done, the 2000 Code suggests that "it may be desirable" to take a certain course of action or that the union "may want to consider" a certain procedure.[84]

The principal statutory reforms relate to the relaxation of formal balloting requirements. The alterations made to notice requirements are more problematic. They provide some protection for individual trade union members but few significant benefits for trade unions.

a. limited flexibility in balloting requirements

The first balloting requirements were introduced by the Trade Union Act 1984. Designed to reduce the incidence of strikes organised by unions, even where their aims were lawful, balloting requirements actually succeeded in legitimating such action that had the clear approval of union members. It was this unexpected benefit for trade unions that led the Conservatives to introduce more stringent requirements from 1988 onwards.[85] By 1991, the TUC had observed a sudden change in employer tactics, with "renewed interest in using the law", alongside "a shift in grounds for legal actions with the majority concerned with balloting procedures".[86] A significant number of injunctions were sought to prevent industrial action, which meant that compliance with balloting requirements had to be decided swiftly by the courts, with reference to the balance of convenience. The employer, who was always likely to be inconvenienced by industrial action, was usually able to achieve an injunction where a *prima facie* case could be made that balloting requirements had not been followed.[87] In addition, there remained the potential for employers to threaten such action, leaving unions to decide whether to risk exposure to civil proceedings, given their awareness that there was a poor success rate for unions in the High Court.[88]

Fairness at Work sought to respond to this phenomenon, which it expressly acknowledged, noting that "one study suggests that three quarters of the legal actions brought by employers against trade unions concern the ballot and notice provisions".[89] Neither employers nor unions were blamed for the high incidence of disputes over balloting. The culprit was said to be the complexity of the

---

requirements, as was observed in TUC, n.80 above, para. 77. This provision is nevertheless retained in para. 7 of the draft revised 2000 Code on Industrial Action.

[84] E.g., contrast 2000 Code on Industrial Action, para. 11 with 1995 Code on Industrial Action, para. 16. Also contrast 2000 Code on Industrial Action, para. 28 with 1995 Code on Industrial Action, para. 34.

[85] See Elgar and Simpson, n.79 above, at 83.

[86] "Employers Step Up Legal Challenges" [1994] *Labour Research* 7 at 7. See also Edwards, n.22 above, at 446.

[87] Simpson, n.23 above.

[88] "Employers Step Up Legal Challenges", n.86 above, at 7–9.

[89] *FAW*, para. 4.26.

legislation. "Complexity leads to disputes."[90] Moreover, such disputes were "damaging to business efficacy as well as trade unions".[91] The Government's aim was therefore to rid the balloting requirements of particular uncertainties.

This has been achieved in various ways. For example, what will constitute a strike or action short of a strike has now been settled,[92] even if this was arguably unnecessary, given the decision in *Connex South East* v. *National Union of Rail, Maritime and Transport Workers*.[93] Also clarified are the requirements for aggregate ballots[94] and balloting of merchant seamen.[95] The amendment made to the "health warning" merely follows logically from the new protections from dismissal under section 238A of TULRCA 1992.[96] This warning is not as full as it might be, as it does not completely explain to the employee the complexity of the eight-week rule, a matter which perhaps unduly concerned members of the Conservative opposition.[97] However, there was arguably no way in which a short warning contained on a ballot paper could have explained the rule comprehensively.[98]

A very small degree of flexibility has been introduced, to cater for exceptional circumstances. These reforms are consistent with the sentiments expressed by Millet LJ in *London Underground Ltd* v. *RMT*, where the Court of Appeal allowed a union to call new members of a union out on strike, even though they had not taken part in the initial ballot.[99] A trade union member who has changed jobs after the ballot will be able to participate in industrial action without being involved in the ballot.[100] In addition, there has been a change to the requirements that an employer be notified of the result of the ballot. Previously, a failure to inform some but not all of the employers where workers were balloted of the outcome of a ballot made it unlawful for the union to induce any of its balloted members to take action.[101] Now it is lawful for a union to call on its members to take action where they are employed by an employer who was informed of the result.[102]

---

[90] *FAW*, para. 4.26.

[91] *Ibid.*

[92] TULRCA 1992 new s. 229.

[93] [1999] IRLR 249 (CA). See also HL Hansard, 16 June 1999, cols. 303–306, per Lord Wedderburn; and cols. 307–308 per Lord McIntosh. Note the accompanying consequential amendment, so that the definition of a "strike" in TULRCA 1992 s.246 will no longer apply when it comes to categorisation of overtime and call-out strikes as "action short of a strike" for the purpose of balloting provisions.

[94] TULRCA 1992 ss. 228 and 228A. See HL Hansard, 15 July 1999, cols. 575–577, per Lord McIntosh. Also see the 2000 Code on Industrial Action, paras. 24 and 25.

[95] TULRCA 1992 s. 230. See HL Hansard, 8 July 1999, col. 1077, per Lord McIntosh.

[96] TULRCA 1992 s.229(4). See also 2000 Code on Industrial Action, para. 32.

[97] HL Hansard, 8 July 1999, col. 1075.

[98] See HL Hansard, 8 July 1999, col. 1076, per Lord McIntosh. See also above Chap. 2 at 39–43.

[99] [1995] IRLR 636 at 641 (CA).

[100] TULRCA 1992 s. 232A. See also 2000 Code on Industrial Action, para. 22.

[101] TULRCA 1992 old s. 231A.

[102] TULRCA 1992 new s. 226.

Most important is the new section 232B of TULRCA 1992 which provides that certain "small accidental failures" in balloting requirements can be disregarded in so far as they would not affect the result of the ballot. It should be noted that section 232B does not cover all aspects of the balloting procedure, but only such matters as who is given entitlement to vote, the dispatch of ballot papers, the ability of members to vote conveniently through post and balloting of merchant seamen.[103] These modifications will undoubtedly be welcomed by trade unions, but will not entirely preclude the more petty disputes reaching the courts. For example, if a voting paper for an industrial action ballot does not meet every single requirement listed under section 229 of TULRCA 1992, the industrial action taken by the union will still be unlawful.

More flexibility is provided by section 234(1) of TULRCA 1992 which allows the effectiveness of a ballot to be extended from four weeks up to eight weeks, if both parties agree. This gives the parties potentially more time to negotiate and thereby avoid industrial conflict. It fits neatly within the New Labour view that dialogue has the potential to resolve conflict and restore "partnership" to the workplace.

b. notification which helps employers to "make plans"

The Employment Relations Act 1999 also changes the notice requirements which previously had to be observed by a trade union which called industrial action. Ostensibly, the motivation for this reform is the protection of individual workers, who may be victimised by an employer once their names are known. However, it is accompanied by a new requirement that a union calling industrial action provide the employer with information which will minimise inconvenience to the employer. There is an underlying insistence on co-operation rather than conflict, following from the limited New Labour conception of "partnership".

Under old section 226A of TULRCA 1992, the union contemplating an industrial action ballot was required to provide a notice of the ballot to the employer "describing (so that he can readily ascertain them) the employees of the employer who it is reasonable for the union to believe . . . will be entitled to vote in the ballot".[104] Similarly, under old section 234B of TULRCA 1992, the union had to describe the employees the union intended to induce to take part or continue to take part in industrial action.[105] In *Blackpool and Fylde College* v. *National Association of Teachers in Further and Higher Education*, the Court of Appeal found that these notices required the union actually to name those employees.[106] The Master of the Rolls, Sir Thomas Bingham, giving the leading judgment, considered that, as there was no ambiguity in the section, the court

---

[103] TULRCA 1992 s.232B. See also 2000 Code on Industrial Action, para. 23.
[104] TULRCA 1992 old s. 226A(2)(c).
[105] TULRCA 1992 old s. 234A(3)(a).
[106] [1994] IRLR 227 (CA).

could have no regard to provisions of the European Convention on Human Rights (ECHR) which might support the argument for the right to privacy of a trade union member.

The Employment Relations Act amends sections 226A and 234A, so that there is no longer any express necessity for the disclosure of names. In doing so, the Government seems to have been thinking of the necessity of compliance with the ECHR and the protection of individual employees' rights.[107] However, the new formulation of the notice requirements is not entirely an improvement on the old provisions, for it arguably makes it even more difficult for a trade union to take effective industrial action. It is now necessary to provide "such information in the union's possession as would help the employer to make plans". Wedderburn considered this to be "a most extraordinary provision"[108] as it effectively asks the union to provide the employer with all necessary ammunition to reduce the impact of a strike. One might well wonder what is the point of taking industrial action if it is to have no more than a negligible effect on the employer's business.

At the time the Employment Relations Bill was passed, the Government asserted that no unduly harsh requirement would be placed on the union calling industrial action. Unions would have to provide notice only of matters, such as numbers of the strikers and dates, which were already within their possession. Unions would not be required "to collect additional information which they do not hold; and employers cannot insist on receiving information which the unions do not have".[109]

The 2000 Code of Practice on Industrial Action elaborates on this duty.[110] The union is told that the notice should contain such information in the union's possession, for example, as would be appropriate to enable the employer "to warn his customers of the possibility of disruption so that they can make alternative arrangements or to take steps to ensure the health and safety of his employees or the public or to safeguard equipment which might otherwise suffer from damage from being shut down or left without supervision".[111] It seems that, as under the 1995 Code,[112] "factors such as the size and turnover rate of the employer's workforce; the variety of work done for the employer; the number of locations at which it is carried out; and any experience of ballot notifications concerning the same employer may be relevant to a decision about how much detail needs to be included".[113] It is said that it will reduce the risk of litigation if the union checks that the employer accepts that the information provided complies with the union's statutory duties and that, if the employer believes that

---

[107] See above Chap. 4 at 91.
[108] HL Hansard, 16 June 1999, col. 297, per Lord Wedderburn.
[109] HL Hansard, 16 June 1999, col. 300, per Lord McIntosh.
[110] 2000 Code on Industrial Action, paras. 15–18 and para. 51.
[111] *Ibid.* para. 14.
[112] See 1995 Code on Industrial Action, para. 21.
[113] 2000 Code on Industrial Action, para. 17.

the notice contains insufficient information, the employer informs the union of this.[114]

During Parliamentary debates, the Government Minister did accept that such a notice requirement might limit the impact of industrial action, but appeared unconcerned by this:

> I hope that all unions have moved beyond trying to make industrial action as damaging as possible, regardless of the effect on the long-term survival of the business. We are trying to promote a long-term partnership approach. During a short-term dispute, it is important not to lose sight of the overriding common interest of workers and employers in the success of the business.[115]

Yet when asked whether employers were under the same obligation to provide unions with all relevant information,[116] it became apparent that the Minister did not envisage this parity.[117] In the context of industrial action, the rhetoric of "partnership" takes on a unitary aspect. The employer's needs appear to be paramount.

E. CONCLUSION

The law on industrial action has not been greatly altered by the Employment Relations Act 1999. There will still be no positive right to strike in the UK. Moreover, the bulk of legislation introduced by the Conservatives to restrain industrial action is left unchanged. The statutory and regulatory devices used throughout the 1980s and 1990s have been modified but not substantially altered. Trade unions continue to be discouraged from contemplating industrial action. This chapter has reviewed the few reforms relating to industrial action introduced by New Labour, considering how they draw on this heritage and reflect the new rhetoric of rights, responsibilities and "partnership".

As promised in *Fairness at Work*, new rights are bestowed on individual participants in industrial action. They are provided with a further means by which to seek protection from unfair dismissal. In addition, their names are not to be given to their employer when they are balloted for industrial action or when notice is given of industrial action. Some limited flexibility has also been introduced in respect of balloting requirements. While we welcome these changes, they are overshadowed by other developments.

The first is the extent to which the new protection from dismissal is dependent upon the conduct of trade unions. Trade unions will be reluctant to jeopardise the employment of their members by calling "unprotected" industrial action. It is submitted that the likely impact of these provisions is that unions will be hesitant to call such action, will ensure that their aims fit squarely within the

---

[114] *Ibid.* para. 16.
[115] HL Hansard, 16 June 1999, col. 300, per Lord McIntosh.
[116] HL Hansard, 16 June 1999, col. 301, per Lord Monkswell.
[117] HL Hansard, 16 June 1999, col. 301, per Lord McIntosh.

confines of a lawful trade dispute, will be careful to take all procedural and other appropriate steps and will be conciliatory in dealings with the employer. Given that the lawful aims of industrial action still do not meet ILO standards, this is disappointing. It is also a matter of concern that unions, in their eagerness to protect the individual jobs of their members, may be more passive and less ready to protect the common interests of their membership in improved terms and conditions of employment.

The second important point is that, even though a trade union will not be obliged to disclose the names of members, this is paired with a new requirement that notice be given which will "help the employer make plans". The latter goes beyond the ambit of past statutory notice requirements, imposing a one-sided obligation on the part of unions to assist the very employer which industrial action is intended to inconvenience. Even though balloting requirements have been relaxed slightly, this additional obligation is likely to reduce the incidence of industrial action.

In this context, it seems that the Government has chosen to be deliberately obstructive, perhaps because industrial conflict does not fit neatly within the paradigm of a co-operative "partnership" between workers and their employer. New Labour does not acknowledge that, without potential recourse to industrial action, it is not "partnership" but managerial prerogative that is maintained. New Labour claimed that these legislative reforms relating to industrial action would restore "balance" to UK industrial relations,[118] but it seems that the scales are still tipped in favour of the employer.

---

[118] HL Hansard, 16 June 1999, col. 294, per Lord McIntosh.

6

A Revised Role for Trade Unions: Information, Consultation, Representation and Partnership

THE ACTIVITIES TRADITIONALLY associated with trade unions consist of collective bargaining and industrial action. As we have seen, New Labour does not appear overly eager to promote such activities. The mechanisms for union recognition and collective bargaining introduced by the Employment Relations Act 1999 seem remarkably ineffective. Moreover, the bulk of Conservative legislation which sought to restrict industrial action has been retained.

However, the Blair Government is not hostile to unions *per se*. It is envisaged that they can play a potentially useful function within the "partnership" which New Labour wishes to foster in the workplace. In particular, it is acknowledged that they have the capacity to perform a valuable consultative and communicative role which is non-conflictual and supportive.

We can identify three means by which the Government encourages trade unions to perform this role. First, recognised independent trade unions are specifically designated as suitable recipients of information and participants in consultation procedures. Secondly, special provision is made for trade union representatives to accompany individual workers in grievance and disciplinary proceedings. Finally, trade unions are eligible to apply for a grant from a "Partnership Fund" which will assist the establishment of co-operative workplace relations.

None of these activities is entirely new to trade unions. Many unions have already been engaged in consultation, representation of workers and strategic management planning. What is significant is the legislative effort to emphasise the part that trade unions can play in each. Our interest lies in the potential repercussions of these developments for collective representation of workers through trade unions.

To some extent, these initiatives will be welcomed. For example, there have been fears that EC requirements that worker representatives be informed and consulted could constitute a "challenge to the long-established practice that unions provide the single channel for promoting workers' interests".[1] The decision to make specific provision for recognised trade unions in the implementation of EC obligations is therefore likely to assuage such fears.

It is also possible that the trade union movement will view this as an opportunity to establish a broader base of support, appreciation of their value and greater access to collective bargaining. In 1990 Ewing advocated:

> a step-by-step procedure whereby the concept of recognition is defined as having three different elements: the right to represent members in grievance and disciplinary procedures; the right to be consulted on a range of issues on behalf of members; and the right to negotiate on behalf of members. As a union builds up different levels of support in an enterprise so the extent of its recognition rights would enlarge: each step is a rung on the ladder to the next.[2]

He considered that different thresholds of membership or workplace support should give rise to different forms of recognition, such that a lower threshold would be set for consultation than negotiation rights. This proposal was adopted and developed by the TUC in subsequent consultation and policy documents. For example, *Your Voice at Work*[3] argued for consultation rights where a union had 10 per cent membership or more within the appropriate work group. In the absence of any significant trade union membership, workers would be able to seek consultation rights through elected representatives, which might include trade union representatives. By such means, trade unions could gradually establish their relevance in the workplace, incrementally acquiring enhanced status, the goal being broad-based recognition in respect of collective bargaining.[4] An even bolder ambition has been stated by Hendy, who points to the right of each individual to be represented by a union on any matter arising at work, as a matter of choice.[5] The implementation of this entitlement would be even more likely to provide unions with a central role in the British workplace.

In *Fairness at Work*, the Government indicated that "trade union growth" should be possible where trade unions were able to convince employers and workers of their "value". This would depend on how much help unions could bring to "the success of an enterprise for employers, and how much active support they can offer employees".[6] We shall consider the extent to which the string of New Labour reforms relating to information, consultation, representation and "partnership" are likely to lead towards the fulfilment of this objective.

---

[1] M. Cully, S. Woodland, A. O'Reilly and G. Dix, *Britain at Work: As Depicted by the 1998 Workplace Employee Relations Survey* (London and New York: Routledge, 1999) at 85. See also P. Davies, "A Challenge to Single Channel" (1994) 23 *ILJ* 272.

[2] K.D. Ewing, "Trade Union Recognition—A Framework for Discussion" (1990) 19 *ILJ* 209 at 212.

[3] TUC, *Your Voice at Work* (London: TUC, 1995), 11.

[4] See also TUC, *Representation at Work* (London: TUC, 1994) paras. 50 and 53.

[5] See J. Hendy, *Every Worker Shall Have the Right to be Represented at Work* (London: Institute of Employment Rights, 1998); also mentioned above Chap. 4 at 89 and below this chap. at 167.

[6] *FAW*, para. 4.11.

B. INFORMATION AND CONSULTATION OF RECOGNISED TRADE UNIONS

Statutory rights to consultation are not novel. A home-grown British example is the Coal Industry Nationalisation Act 1946, which placed a duty to consult on the then National Coal Board as part of statutory recognition procedures.[7] Today, entitlements to information and consultation are most commonly associated with EC directives such as those relating to health and safety, collective redundancies and transfers of undertakings.[8] The most recent of these consultative obligations arises under the European Works Councils Directive,[9] which was implemented by New Labour in 1999.[10] However, the Government has not displayed enthusiasm for the expansion of EC initiatives of this type, rejecting Commission proposals for an EC directive on information and consultation of workers in companies operating only at a national level,[11] on the basis that this was beyond the legitimate scope of EC powers.[12]

No EC Directive requires that the worker representatives who are to be informed or consulted need be trade union representatives.[13] Indeed, "developments in European legislation constitute the single most important reason for believing that non-union forms of employee representation may come to assume increasing significance".[14] This is bound to be of concern to trade unions. Moreover, non-union representative systems are often criticised by the workers they claim to represent.[15] The basis for such criticism is easy to comprehend. Workers tend to appreciate the independence of union representatives as opposed to representation by management appointees or employees elected through management structures. Unions also have greater access to resources which can aid communication. They usually have more experience and expertise in accessing external information and providing administrative support. In addition, unions are more likely to be able to co-ordinate appropriate strategies across individual workplaces within an industry. Furthermore, the potential to

---

[7] Ewing, n.2 above, at 216.

[8] See EC Framework Dir. on Health and Safety 89/391 [1989] OJ L183/1; EC Dir. on Collective Redundancies 98/59 [1998] OJ L225/16 (CRD) and EC Dir. on Acquired Rights 77/187 [1977] OJ L61/26 (ARD) as amended by EC Dir. 98/50 [1998] OJ L201/88.

[9] EC Dir. 94/45/EC [1994] OJ L254/64; extended to the UK under EC Dir. 97/74 [1998] OJ L10/22.

[10] See below this chap. at 159–66.

[11] COM(98)612.

[12] *FAW*, para. 4.5. Such a measure was described as "difficult to reconcile with subsidiarity and would cut across existing practices in member states to no benefit". See also M. Walker, "Blair blocks union rights" *Guardian*, 17 Mar. 1998.

[13] W. Brown, S. Deakin and M. Hudson, *The Individualisation of Employment Contracts in Britain* (London: DTI, 1998), 75.

[14] M. Terry, "Systems of Collective Employee Representation in Non-Union Firms in the UK" (1999) 30 *IRJ* 16 at 19.

[15] P. Findlay, "Union Recognition and Non-Unionism: Shifting Fortunes in the Electronics Industry in Scotland" (1993) 24 *IRJ* 28 at 37. See also P. Kidger, "Employee Participation in Occupational Health and Safety: Should Union-Appointed or Elected Representatives be the Model for the UK?" (1992) 2 *Human Resource Management* 21.

have recourse to industrial action means that consultation becomes more than a nominal exercise because employers are given an incentive to consider seriously the views of the workforce.

Employers' responses to trade union representation in information and consultation procedures seem to be mixed. Employers tend to value the ability of trade unions to provide a cheap and effective mechanism for passing messages to the workforce and gauging their responses. Unions can help in talking workers through both the need for and the manner of adjustment.[16] This may, in part, explain why the incidence of consultative arrangements remains greater in unionised workplaces and why where there are worker representatives in the workplace these are most commonly union representatives.[17] As one senior manager observed in a recent survey, "the central challenge of derecognising the trade union is that you have to replace the communication system provided by the union with good communications of your own".[18] What is inconvenient for an employer is the capacity of independent union representatives to be obstructive and challenge management decisions. It has been observed in *Britain at Work*, based on the findings of the WERS Survey, that:

> Joint consultative committees function most effectively from *management's* viewpoint where they have more control over the appointment of worker representatives to sit on them. Where unions have been able to put forward worker representatives, meetings are held less frequently and managers regard the committee as being less effective.[19]

To this extent, the interests of employers and workers are unlikely to coincide.

What the Government has done is to promote trade union involvement in workplace information and consultation. These Government initiatives do not constitute a substantial departure from *de facto* trends, but mark the legislative endorsement of these practices. In doing so, it could be argued that the Government has acted to counteract the possible threat posed by non-union representative arrangements. While previously Conservative governments caricatured unions as "the enemy within", New Labour has sought to grant unions the status of "social partners", which have a potentially legitimate role in consultative structures.[20]

The difficulty is that the opportunities presented to trade unions in this context are not straightforward or consistent. Only a trade union which has acquired statutory recognition under the procedure set out in Schedule A1 can claim information and consultation rights as regards training, but any recognised trade union (whether recognition be acquired by a voluntary or statutory process) can claim the entitlement to information and consultation as regards

---

[16] Brown *et al.*, n.13 above, at 70.
[17] Cully *et al.*, n.1 above, at 95.
[18] Brown *et al.*, n.13 above, at 35–6.
[19] Cully *et al.*, n.1 above, at 102.
[20] "That is, of course, what they were always called in the countries of the EU": HL Hansard, 10 May 1999, col. 1008, per Baroness Turner.

collective redundancies or transfers of undertakings. Also, the representatives of a recognised independent trade union can seek information and initiate the creation of a European Works Council (EWC), but are not necessarily entitled to sit on the Special Negotiating Body (SNB) which determines the constitution of an EWC. It is only if the employer refuses to negotiate or the SNB and central management can reach no agreement that default provisions apply which allow the recognised independent trade union to elect or appoint members to the EWC. These discrepancies seem to indicate that New Labour has not taken any basic principled stance on the essential substance of the entitlement to trade union involvement in information and consultation procedures.

An additional difficulty is that access to information and consultation is restricted to *recognised* trade unions, indicating that the Government has disregarded the TUC proposal that there be a lower threshold of membership for a union to qualify for information and consultation rights. Moreover, there is the problem that entitlements to information and consultation are not consistently regarded as collective labour rights held by trade unions but only as individual employment rights held by the workers concerned. Although the union that should have been informed or consulted can make an application for breach; usually only the individual worker can claim compensation.[21] The fundamental link between the two is overlooked.

1. Training

In *Fairness at Work* the Government asserted that information and consultation were "a primary objective of collective arrangements".[22] This is perhaps curious, for the only actual initiative taken by New Labour in this regard concerns training. Even then, this measure seems to have been taken as a compromise, after substantial lobbying from employers had resulted in "training" being excluded from the core subject matter of collective bargaining under Schedule A1. Instead, an independent trade union which has received statutory recognition, where a method of collective bargaining has been specified by the CAC, is to be consulted over the employer's policy on training.[23]

It is important to note the limited application of these consultation requirements, which do not apply to recipients of recognition outside the scope of Schedule A1. This is not a legislative measure which will have a tremendous impact in terms of forcing employers to consult over training. At best, these provisions will establish a model of "good practice". Whether this practice is so very "good" is questionable, given that it sends the implicit message that

---

[21] The exception arising in the context of complaints relating to the establishment or operation of an EWC, where the potential financial penalty is enforceable only by the Secretary of State and not the union or the individual employee. See below this chap. at 165.

[22] *FAW*, para. 4.4.

[23] ERelA 1999 s. 5; inserting TULRCA 1992 s. 70B–C.

collective bargaining over training is unnecessary.[24] Moreover, the efficacy of the procedure set out in sections 70B and 70C of TULRCA 1992 is also doubtful.

a. the procedure for consultation over training

In many respects, the procedure for consultation over training has all the hallmarks of New Labour's determination to promote "partnership". The parties are required to meet and discuss training policy and plans. Emphasis is placed on non-conflictual dialogue.

Every six months, the employer must invite the trade union to send representatives to a meeting for the purpose of:

(a) consulting about the employer's policy on training for workers within the bargaining unit,

(b) consulting about his plans for training those workers during the period of six months starting with the day of the meeting,

(c) reporting about training provided for those workers since the previous meeting.[25]

Trade union representatives have the potential to provide the employer with written representations about matters raised at the meeting within four weeks of the date of the meeting. The employer must take such representations "into account"[26]; although it is uncertain what precisely the latter means and to what extent such an obligation will be enforceable.

Dialogue is meaningful only where both parties have the necessary information. It is here that the flaws in this procedure become apparent. Two weeks before the meeting takes place, the employer must provide the trade union with any information:

(a) without which the union's representatives would be to a material extent impeded in participating in the meeting, and (b) which it would be in accordance with good industrial relations practice to disclose for the purposes of the meeting.[27]

Yet, these obligations to disclose information do not exceed those which apply generally in the context of collective bargaining and, as such, are considerably limited. The list of restrictions set out in section 182 of TULRCA 1992 continues to apply in this context, which is a matter for concern, given the very strong case which can be made for reform of these provisions.[28] In the absence of broader rights to disclosure of information, it is questionable whether the exer-

---

[24] See above Chap. 4 at 113–15.

[25] TULRCA 1992 s. 70B(2) and (3).

[26] TULRCA 1992 s. 70B(6).

[27] TULRCA 1992 s. 70B(4).

[28] TULRCA 1992 s. 70B(5). See SI 2000/1300, Sched., para. 15, Step 3 and TULRCA 1992 ss. 181 and 182, discussed above Chap. 4 at 105–6. Also see H. Gospel, "Disclosure of Information to Trade Unions" (1976) 5 *ILJ* 223 and H. Gospel and G. Lockwood, "Disclosure of Information for Collective Bargaining: The CAC Approach Revisited" (1999) 28 *ILJ* 233.

cise envisaged in section 70B of TULRCA 1992 will achieve genuine improvements in consultation over training.

b. enforcement of the procedure

If the employer does not comply with these obligations, the trade union may bring a complaint before an employment tribunal.[29] If the employer is found to be in breach, the tribunal shall make a declaration to that effect and has the discretion to make "an award of compensation to be paid by the employer to each person who was, at the time when the failure occurred, a member of the bargaining unit".[30] This award is not to exceed two weeks' pay per person.[31] This is a relatively small sum in comparison with that available in respect of a failure to inform or consult over collective redundancies and transfers of undertakings.[32]

What is most significant is that proceedings for enforcement of an award of compensation may not be commenced by the trade union, but can be brought only by persons to whom compensation is payable.[33] This strategy was borrowed from the procedures for enforcement of information and consultation in respect of transfers and collective redundancies.[34] This limited provision for remedies means that recognised trade unions can act for their members in collective bargaining negotiations and in consultation, but cannot seek compensation on their behalf. There is no right of consultation for the union, only for each individual worker which it represents. We consider that this is an unrealistic and artificial constraint on the remedies available.

Workers may well struggle to bring individual claims for their maximum compensation of two weeks' pay. They are likely to be reluctant to do so as individuals in isolation, for fear of identification and the impact this may have on their future job and career prospects. It is also less efficient and effective for them to bring their claims individually. If this monetary payment is to be an effective sanction against the employer, the claimants would do well to coordinate their actions. For this they may want to utilise the resources and co-ordinative capacity of their trade union. The legal fracturing of the symbiotic relationship between trade unions and their members seems undesirable.

2. Transfers of undertakings and collective redundancies

New Labour has made significant changes to the information and consultation requirements arising in the context of collective redundancies and transfers of

---

[29] TULRCA 1992 s. 70C(1) and (2).
[30] TULRCA 1992 s. 70C(3).
[31] TULRCA 1992 s. 70C(4).
[32] TULRCA 1992 ss. 189 and 190; and TUPE reg. 11(11).
[33] TULRCA 1992 s. 70C(6).
[34] See below this chap. at 158–9.

undertakings. These are best understood in contrast with the legacy of Conservative legislation which made the involvement of trade unions dependent upon the desire of the employer. The present Government has undoubtedly done more than its Conservative predecessors to ensure that, in such circumstances, recognised independent trade unions will be the recipients of information and participants in consultation. Nevertheless, the dearth of adequate sanctions for employer breach of these consultative requirements and the individualistic aspect of enforcement procedures are likely to continue to undermine the efficacy of these provisions in the UK.

a. the legislative history

Both the Collective Redundancies Directive (CRD) and the Acquired Rights Directive (ARD) make special provision for information and consultation of "worker" and "employee" representatives.[35] Such representatives are to be "provided for by the laws and practices of the Member States". There is no requirement under the CRD or ARD that these representatives consist of trade union officials. However, from 1975 to 1994, this was how the requirements imposed by these instruments were applied under UK legislation. The problem with this interpretation was that, from 1980 onwards, there was no legal requirement that an employer recognise a trade union and an employer could use this as an excuse to provide no information or consultation whatsoever.

A crucial turning point was the decision of the European Court of Justice in *Commission* v. *UK*,[36] which found that, in this respect alongside others, British law had not satisfactorily implemented the CRD and ARD. The Court did not impose criteria for recognition of trade unions as representatives, but merely required that the UK provide for the designation of representatives where the employers did not agree to recognise a trade union.[37] This judgment unwittingly provided the then Conservative Government with the ammunition to introduce new regulations[38] which, focussing on the notion of employer choice, allowed employers the option to evade consultation even with recognised trade unions,[39] as long as employers offered their workers the opportunity to elect representatives.[40]

Recent empirical research suggests that, despite this option, very few employers chose to consult elected or appointed representatives over a recognised trade

---

[35] CRD, Art. 2 and ARD, Art. 6.

[36] Cases C–382/92 and 383/92 *Commission* v. *UK* [1994] ECR I–2435 and 2479.

[37] On the limitations of this decision, see Lord Wedderburn, "British Labour Law at the Court of Justice: A Fragment" (1994) 10 *IJCLLIR* 339.

[38] The Collective Redundancies and Transfer of Undertakings (Protection of Employment) (Amendment) Regs. 1995, SI 1995/2587, which amended TULRCA 1992 and the Transfer of Undertakings (Protection of Employment) Regs. 1981, SI 1981/1794 (TUPE).

[39] TULRCA 1992 s. 188(1B) and TUPE reg. 10(2A).

[40] TULRCA 1992 s. 188(7A) and TUPE reg. 10(8).

union.[41] Where there is a recognised trade union, it makes sense to utilise established channels of communication rather than jeopardise and destabilise an existing relationship by choosing another route.[42] The lack of employer opposition to informing and consulting recognised trade unions may well have been one factor which prompted the incoming Labour Government to change the law.

Early in 1998, a DTI Consultation Paper stated that the Government would review the legislation requiring information and consultation with "employee representatives" under the CRD and ARD, on the basis that the existing provisions still did not "provide a clear and satisfactory framework for the necessary information and consultation".[43] In particular, it was proposed that the employer be obliged to inform and consult the representatives of any recognised trade union covering the affected workplace. It was "not in the interests of orderly industrial relations to open up an *alternative channel* of consultation".[44] Only in cases where there were affected workers not covered by a recognised union would there be consultation with other representatives.[45] More detailed provisions would be introduced relating to the "suitable arrangements" which should be made to elections of trade union representatives.[46] In this Consultation Paper, reference was made to the forthcoming White Paper on *Fairness at Work*. Later that year, the promised White Paper reiterated that the Government planned to make amendments to the information and consultation requirements relating to redundancies and transfers.[47]

b. the 1999 Regulations

These information and consultation requirements were not altered by the Employment Relations Act 1999 but by statutory instrument, as is common for implementation of EC directives in the UK.[48] It is now the case that, where the obligation to inform and/or consult arises, if all the workers affected are of a description in respect of which an independent trade union has been recognised, then the employer must inform and consult the representatives of that union. There is no requirement that recognition be granted under the statutory

---

[41] Only four out of 2,048 cases appeared to fall within this category. See M. Hall and P. Edwards, "Reforming the Statutory Redundancy Consultation Procedure" (1999) 28 *ILJ* 299 at 306, based on research carried out for the DTI set out in J. Smith, P. Edwards and M. Hall, *Redundancy Consultation: A Study of Current Practice and the Effects of the 1995 Regulations* (London: DTI Employment Relations Research Series No. 5, 1999) URN 99/512.

[42] Hall and Edwards, n.41 above, at 307.

[43] DTI, *Employees' Information and Consultation Rights on Transfers of Undertakings and Collective Redundancies* (London: DTI, 1998) URN 97/988, para. 1.

[44] *Ibid.*, at para. 19.

[45] *Ibid.*, at para. 22.

[46] *Ibid.*, at paras. 25–26.

[47] *FAW*, para. 4.32.

[48] Collective Redundancies and Transfer of Undertakings (Protection of Employment) (Amendment) Regs. 1999, SI 1999/1925.

procedure; it may also be voluntarily granted by the employer. It is only where these conditions are not met that the employer can choose between either (i) representatives already appointed or elected who have authority to receive information and to be consulted on behalf of the workforce; or (ii) new representatives elected in accordance with the statutory procedure.[49]

For the first time since 1995, recognised trade unions are the first "port of call" in respect of information and consultation requirements. They may no longer be bypassed in favour of other representatives, unless some of the workforce affected falls outside the scope of recognised union representation.[50] This formulation does, to some extent, fall short of the TUC claim that unions should be informed and/or consulted where they meet the 10 per cent membership threshold. The decision to restrict union involvement in information and consultation to recognised trade unions may therefore be problematic, given the ongoing difficulty in achieving recognition, even under Schedule A1. Nevertheless, even where there is no recognised trade union, there still may be opportunities for union representatives to be among the employee representatives informed or consulted. They should be able to stand as candidates for election under the new statutory procedure, as long as they are affected employees on the date of the election.[51] This is because no affected employee can be unreasonably excluded from standing for election.[52] Trade union membership or activities cannot be a reasonable ground for exclusion, given the protection from discrimination on these grounds already guaranteed under TULRCA 1992.[53] Moreover, all affected employees on the date of the election are entitled to vote.[54] Trade union members cannot be excluded from participating in the ballot. This means that, while union officials may not be amongst those consulted, lay union representatives may play some role in the process. To this extent, unions may be able to assist employees facing a collective redundancy or transfer situation and thereby establish their "value" and build their membership base.

c. sanctions available for failure to inform or consult

The 1999 Regulations have also introduced amendments which broaden the pool of potential complainants where an employer has failed to comply with information or consultation obligations. In the case of a failure relating to the election of employee representatives, a complaint may be presented to an employment tribunal by any of the affected employees or by any of the employ-

---

[49] TULRCA 1992 s. 188(1B) and TUPE reg. 10(2A).

[50] DTI, *Employees' Information and Consultation Rights on Collective Redundancies and Transfers of Undertakings* (London: DTI, 1999) URN 99/1036.

[51] TULRCA 1992 s. 188A(1)(e) and TUPE reg. 10A(1)(e).

[52] TULRCA 1992 s. 188A(1)(f) and TUPE reg. 10A(1)(f).

[53] See TULRCA 1992, Part III.

[54] TULRCA 1992 s. 188A(1)(g) and TUPE reg. 10A(1)(g).

ees who have been dismissed as redundant.[55] This is in addition to the existing rights of affected employees, employee representatives and the relevant trade union. Also, where a question arises whether or not any employee representative was an appropriate representative, the onus is placed on the employer to show that the employee representative had the authority to represent the affected employees.[56]

Where a complaint is found by the tribunal to be well-founded, the tribunal may make an award for compensation to be paid by the employer to each affected employee.[57] This is the only penalty imposed on the employer for violation of these information and consultation requirements. There is no right under TULRCA 1992 or TUPE to an order which would prevent redundancies or a transfer taking place in the absence of such information and/or consultation.[58]

Neither the union nor the relevant employee representatives can take any action where the employer fails to pay the required compensation. From that point onwards, it is the individual employee who must seek enforcement of the payment to which he or she is entitled.[59] This separation of collective and individual aspects of enforcement is derived from the provisions of the EPA 1975, but it was arguably open to New Labour to take a different approach. This form of enforcement places the individual employee in an awkward position, for many employees will be loathe to challenge an employer in a tribunal while remaining in their employ. It is only where the employee has been made redundant or been dismissed prior to a transfer that he or she is likely actively to seek compensation. The lack of adequate legislative sanctions for non-compliance therefore has the potential to undermine the efficacy of the reforms made by New Labour.

3. European Works Councils

A "works council" is a standing body of worker representatives who are to be informed and/or consulted by the employer on various matters concerning that workplace. Ideally, this would be a forum where management offers "meaningful consultation" which will "build trust, co-operation and commitment from

---

[55] TULRCA 1992 s. 189(1)(a) and TUPE reg.11(1)(a).

[56] TULRCA 1992 s. 189(1A) and TUPE reg. 11(2A).

[57] TULRCA 1992 s.190 and TUPE reg. 11(4).

[58] See S. Deakin and G. Morris, *Labour Law* (2nd edn., London: Butterworths, 1998) at 793. See however *King* v. *Eaton* [1998] IRLR 686, the unusual decision of the Scottish Court of Session where an interdict was issued to prevent redundancies taking place where there had been inadequate consultation over the proper method of selection. If this principle were applied across to the statutory entitlement to consultation, a more effective remedy might be available, but its extension seems unlikely.

[59] TULRCA 1992 s. 192 and TUPE reg. 11(5).

the workforce".[60] Where reorganisation of working arrangements or other changes is proposed, the works council can provide a vehicle for dialogue, through which an accommodation can be reached that responds to the needs of workers as well as employers. It fits neatly within a "partnership" model whereby the worker can be viewed as a stakeholder in the undertaking.[61]

This is an institution which operates in various European states, notably Germany. The role of the German works council is distinct from and designed to supplement that of trade unions. While trade union members may sit on the German works council, that body is required to act in the best interests of the plant and is not permitted to organise industrial action. The latter is left to the trade union itself.[62] While some have recommended the importation of works councils into the UK, others have been more sceptical of their merits. In particular, Däubler has observed that works councils tend to generate an unrealistic identification of workers' interests with those of their employer, such that workers fail to demand the wage rises they would in other circumstances.[63] Participation in management decision-making can become an "exercise in futility" where worker representatives are choosing, at best, between "various forms and procedures for maximising profits".[64] He has argued that it is the interests of the workers which worker representatives should be permitted to represent. It has also been observed by Lord Wedderburn that works councils or other information and consultation arrangements are likely to achieve little in the absence of strong trade union representation, collective bargaining and a right to strike.[65]

The works council is not a concept which is entirely foreign to UK employers who do often establish workplace-level consultative committees.[66] What is new to the UK is a legal obligation to do so. This obligation has arisen by virtue of the European Works Councils Directive (EWCD),[67] which has now been implemented by the Transnational Information and Consultation of Employees Regulations 1999 (TICER).[68] This has been regarded as a "further landmark in

[60] H. Collins, "Flexibility and Empowerment" in T. Wilthagen (ed.), *Advancing Theory in Labour Law and Industrial Relations in a Global Context* (Amsterdam: North-Holland, 1998) at 127. See also C. McGlynn, "European Works Councils: Towards Industrial Democracy?" (1995) 24 *ILJ* 78 at 83–4.

[61] S. Wheeler, "Works Councils: Towards Stakeholding?" (1997) 24 *JLS* 44 at 51–2.

[62] See S. Simitis, "Worker Participation in the Enterprise—Transcending Company Law?" (1975) 38 *MLR* 1 at 12. See also W. Däubler, "Co-determination: The German Experience" (1975) 4 *ILJ* 218 at 225.

[63] W. Däubler, "The Employee Participation Directive—A Realistic Utopia?" (1977) 14 *CMLRev.* 457 at 479 in his discussion of positive and negative aspects of employee representation on decision-making bodies.

[64] *Ibid.* at 473. See also the observations made in A. Fox, *Man Mismanagement* (2nd edn., London: Hutchinson, 1995) at 116–9.

[65] Lord Wedderburn, "Labour Standards, Global Markets and Labour Laws in Europe" in W. Sengenberger and D. Campbell, *International Labour Standards and Economic Interdependence* (Geneva: International Institute for Labour Studies, 1994).

[66] See "Partnership at Work: A Survey" (1997) 645 *IRS Employment Trends* 3.

[67] EC Dir. 94/95/EC [1994] OJ L254/64.

[68] SI 1999/3323, which entered into force on 15 Jan. 2000.

the 'Europeanisation' of UK labour law by extending statutory rights to information and consultation".[69]

In those workplaces which currently have consultative committees, the worker representatives who sit on the committees tend to be lay union representatives, especially where there is a recognised trade union.[70] The question facing New Labour, when implementing the EWCD, was whether and to what extent the Regulations should provide for the involvement of trade union representatives in European Works Councils (EWCs). The trade union movement was eager to secure such involvement.[71] It was opposed by a powerful lobby from various multinational companies which tried to evade negotiation of EWC agreements with unions.[72] We shall examine the extent to which TICER makes provision for trade union representation within EWCs and its potential implications.

a. The European Works Councils Directive (EWCD)

The European Works Councils Directive (EWCD) was adopted under the Maastricht Agreement on Social Policy in 1994 and was extended to the UK in December 1997.[73] It affects only "Community-scale" undertakings or groups of undertakings with at least 1,000 employees within the Member States and at least 150 employees in at least two Member States. Its objective is to provide the opportunity to establish either a "European Works Council" (EWC) or a procedure for informing or consulting workers in respect of each such undertaking or group of undertakings. The EWC is to "work in a spirit of cooperation with due regard to their reciprocal rights and obligations". The same is to apply to "cooperation between central management and employees' representatives in the framework of an information and consultation procedure".[74]

The EWCD emphasises the importance of voluntary negotiation and agreement between the employer and worker parties. Article 13 of the original EWCD allowed multinationals to pre-empt the Directive by entering into an agreement, covering the entire workforce, and providing for transnational information and consultation.[75] Article 3 of the "Extension" Directive made

---

[69] M. Carley and M. Hall, "The Implementation of the European Works Councils Directive" (2000) 29 *ILJ* 103 at 123.

[70] Cully *et al.*, n.1 above, at 101.

[71] K. Ewing (ed.), *Working Life* (London: Institute of Employment Rights, 1996). See also TUC, *A Trade Unionist's Guide to European Works Councils* (London: TUC, 1995) and ETUI, *European Works Councils: Inventory of Affected Companies* (Brussels: ETUI, 1996).

[72] See Lord Wedderburn, "Consultation and Collective Bargaining in Europe: Success and Ideology" (1997) 26 *ILJ* 1 at 24.

[73] See EC Dir. 97/74 [1998] OJ L10/22. This reflected the decision of the Labour Government to "opt in" to the Social Agreement, consolidated by signature of the Amsterdam Treaty. See "Extending the EWCs Dir. to the UK" (1997) 286 *EIRR* 21.

[74] EWCD, Art. 9.

[75] See S. Laulom, "The Uncertain Future of 'Pre-Directive' Agreements: An Analysis of Art. 13 of the European Works Council Directive" (1995) 24 *ILJ* 382.

similar provision for pre-emptive agreements which could be concluded until 15 December 1999.

Otherwise, negotiations for the establishment of a EWC or an information or consultation procedure can be initiated by central management or at the written request of either 100 employees (or their representatives) in at least two undertakings or establishments in at least two different Member States. "Employees' representatives" are broadly defined in the EWCD as those "provided for by national law and/or practice".[76] This formulation provides scope for the process to be initiated by trade unions, depending on the legal norms and practice of the Member State in question, but this is not essential.

A "Special Negotiating Body" (SNB) is to have "the task of determining, with central management, the scope, composition, functions and term of office of the European Works Council(s) or the arrangements for implementing a procedure for the information and consultation of employees".[77] In carrying out these functions, the SNB is entitled to "be assisted by experts of its choice".[78] The identity of these experts is not specified, but it is arguable that these could include trade union representatives with expertise in the matters in question. If the SNB decides by a two-third majority not to enter into an agreement that is the end of the matter. However, if the SNB does wish to reach an agreement but central management refuses to negotiate for six months, or if no agreement can be concluded after three years, the subsidiary provisions governing the creation of an EWC (set out in the Annex to the Directive) are to be applied.[79]

The membership of the SNB is therefore of considerable importance. The EWCD does not prescribe how this is to be determined. It is for the Member States to decide the method to be used for the election or appointment of the members of the SNB in their territories.[80] They also have considerable freedom to determine the default provisions governing election or appointment of members to the EWC. There is no requirement that the SNB or EWC must consist of representatives of a recognised trade union or otherwise.

Most Member States, in implementing the EWCD, have required that members of the SNB be workers from the undertaking, but in Austria, Ireland and Portugal, provision is made for full-time union officials to be nominated.[81] Trade unions play a central role in appointing members to the SNB in Italy,

---

[76] EWCD, Art. 2(1)(d).

[77] EWCD, Art. 5(3).

[78] EWCD, Art. 5(4).

[79] EWCD, Art. 7.

[80] Subject to the requirements set out in EWCD, Art. 5(c), which require that one member be appointed to represent each Member State within which a Community-scale undertaking has an establishment or group of undertakings has an undertaking; and that there are supplementary members in proportion to the number of employees working in the establishments or undertakings as laid down by the legislation of the Member State within the territory of which the central management is situated.

[81] See http://www.etuc.org/Policy/EWC/NegBody/

Greece, Portugal and Spain.[82] "All Member States have adopted rules governing appointment to the EWC which are identical to those used for the SNB."[83] In addition, all countries have introduced provisions authorising the SNB and EWC to consult experts, which the Commission understands to mean that "SNBs and EWCs can draw on the assistance of trade union representatives belonging to national or European confederations".[84] It was open to the Labour Government to make special provision for trade union representatives to initiate the EWC negotiation process, to sit on the SNB and to appoint members to the EWC. Moreover, provision was expected to be made such that an SNB and EWC could have access to consult trade union representatives as experts. Bercusson welcomed the potential of European Works Councils (EWCs) to "extend the trade union role";[85] the extent to which this would be achieved was determined by TICER.

b. Transnational Information and Consultation of Employees Regulations 1999 (TICER)

Even before 1997, Community-level undertakings or groups of undertakings with bases in the UK were starting to take voluntary steps to include UK workers in EWCs.[86] Some of these agreements involved representation through trade unions. For example, at GKN the trade unions recognised by the company nominated representatives to a number of UK seats on the EWC.[87] However, other British companies, such as Marks and Spencer, apparently sought to avoid any form of union representation, opting instead for Article 13 agreements "with unspecified, shadowy 'employee representatives'".[88] The Labour Government was faced with a broad array of precedents from which to choose. Ultimately, a decision was made to provide explicitly for recognised and independent trade unions to play a potential role in this process.

i. designation of "employees' representatives"

The Transnational Information and Consultation of Employees Regulations 1999 (TICER) define "employees' representatives" as meaning both representatives of the recognised independent trade union who normally participate as negotiators in the collective bargaining process and certain other elected

---

[82] Commission Report to the European Parliament and the Council on the Application of Council Dir. 94/45/EC of 22 Sept. 1994, COM(2000)188 at 12.

[83] *Ibid.* at 14.

[84] *Ibid.* at 17.

[85] B. Bercusson, *European Works Councils—Extending the Trade Union Role* (London: Institute of Employment Rights, 1997).

[86] C. Barrie and S. Milne, "Firms Opt In Despite the Opt Out", *Guardian*, 28 Sept. 1996; "Works Councils More Prevalent than Expected" (1998) 664 *IRS Employment Trends* 3.

[87] *European Works Councils: A Guide to Effective Consultation and Representation* (London: Involvement and Participation Association, 1996) at 11–12.

[88] Wedderburn, n.72 above, at 24.

employee representatives.[89] Trade union officials cannot claim priority over other employees' representatives, in their entitlement to be involved in establishing an EWC. It is merely that their potential role in the process is expressly acknowledged.

As employees' representatives, trade union representatives may request information which will enable them to determine whether it is feasible to make a request that an EWC be created.[90] They also have the capacity to request negotiations for establishment of an EWC.[91]

ii. trade union representation on SNBs

Unions argued that UK representation on SNBs should follow existing union structures, and that provision should be made for the election of employees' representatives only in the absence of recognised trade unions. Employers objected, arguing that full-time union officials should not even be eligible for election to the SNB.[92] The Government opted for a compromise. SNBs are not to replicate existing collective bargaining structures, but the representatives of a recognised independent trade union are entitled to stand in the ballot of UK employees as candidates for election as UK members and they have the capacity to bring a complaint if the appropriate procedures are not followed.[93]

It is only where a consultative committee exists, which is already responsible for information and consultation in relation to all UK employees, that there is potential for a recognised independent trade union to be excluded from participation in a SNB. Even then, the representatives of the recognised trade unions may make a complaint where the committee in question does not meet the requirements set out in TICER.[94]

iii. default provision for trade union representation on EWCs

The provisions most beneficial to trade union representation are to be found in the Schedule to TICER which provides the statutory default composition of an EWC where the SNB and management can come to no agreement within three years. Where there is an independent trade union, recognised by the employer for the purpose of collective bargaining, it may elect or appoint the UK membership of the EWC.[95] This complements and is consistent with the requirement that a recognised independent trade union be informed and/or consulted in case of collective redundancies or transfers of undertaking.[96]

---

[89] SI 1999/3323, reg. 2.

[90] SI 1999/3323, reg. 7. Moreover, they may bring a complaint if the employer fails to provide such information. See reg. 8.

[91] SI 1999/3323, reg. 9.

[92] Carley and Hall, n.69 above, at 115.

[93] SI 1999/3323, reg. 13(3) and (4).

[94] SI 1999/3323, reg. 15.

[95] SI 1999/3323, Sched., para. 3(1) and (2)(a).

[96] See above this chap. at 155–9.

There is however no obligation to include trade union representation where a union cannot achieve recognition. This makes the failings of the statutory procedure for recognition under Schedule A1 again a matter for concern. Moreover, it remains possible for the SNB to agree a mode of election or appointment to the EWC which does not provide for automatic representation of the recognised independent trade union.

iv. trade union representatives as "experts"

TICER follows the requirements of the EWCD and allows the SNB and EWC to consult experts.[97] It does not state that trade union officials or other representatives can fulfil this expert function, giving no indication as to who will qualify as an expert. It was probably unnecessary to do so, given how this requirement has been interpreted in other European Member States.[98]

v. enforcement procedures

TICER also provides for disputes over the failure to establish an EWC or a procedure for information and consultation. Complaints to the Employment Appeal Tribunal (EAT)[99] can be brought by the SNB or, in the absence of an SNB, by an employee, employees' representative or a person who was a member of the SNB. Where an EAT finds a complaint to be well-founded it may issue an order setting out the steps the defaulter is required to take and may also issue a penalty notice requiring central management to pay a certain sum to the Secretary of State. Similar provisions apply where disputes arise over the operation of an EWC or the information or consultation procedure, but in such circumstances the potential complainants constitute only central management and the EWC (or information and consultation representatives) in question.[100]

It will be interesting to see how frequently such orders are issued and whether the Secretary of State chooses to enforce the penalty notices. It is curious that, whereas in other contexts information and consultation are treated as *individual rights* to be claimed by each individual employee, in the setting of an EWC no financial compensation is payable to affected employees.

c. evaluation

In the context of European Works Councils, New Labour has done much to secure a potential role for the recognised independent trade union. The union which has this status can seek information, initiate negotiations, participate in the SNB and, if the default Schedule has to be applied, may also elect or appoint members to the EWC. In addition, although this is not absolutely settled, there is also potential for unions to act as experts who assist the SNB and EWC. These

---

[97] See SI 1999/3323, reg. 16(5) and Sched., para. 9(4).
[98] See above this chap. at 163.
[99] In this context, recourse to the Employment Tribunal (ET) is bypassed.
[100] SI 1999/3323, regs. 20–22.

provisions may well be advantageous for workers, given the practical benefits that union representation can offer in the context of consultation.[101] Nevertheless, a number of difficulties may also arise by virtue of these provisions.

The first problem we detect is that, in the absence of recognition, there is no necessary role for trade unions. A worker or group of workers cannot simply nominate that their union is to be informed or consulted on its behalf. There is no lower threshold (such as 10 per cent membership) which will spark union rights to consultation. This same criticism is applicable to other steps taken by New Labour in respect of information and consultation over training, collective redundancies and transfers of undertakings. The paucity of the provisions made by the Employment Relations Act 1999 for statutory recognition makes this a difficult target for many unions to reach. The result is that many are unlikely to be able to claim the information and consultation entitlements set out above.

The second is the residual fear that the co-operative involvement of recognised trade unions within EWCs may not be as beneficial as it might seem. As Däubler observed, within a works council, employee representatives are required to look first to the welfare of their employer.[102] Both the EWCD and TICER require the trade union representative who becomes an "employees' representative" to work with management "in a spirit of cooperation".[103] It is an internationally established principle that the primary concern of a trade union should be to represent the social and economic interests of its members and other workers.[104] To ask trade union representatives to work with management or subscribe to managerial goals has the potential to undermine their essential function. This may account for the early disappointment in the EWC mechanism expressed by many employee and union representatives.[105] The potential for trade unions to play a role within EWCs (or indeed information and consultation mechanisms generally) might not be so worrying were it complemented with genuine access of recognised trade unions to collective bargaining. However, our close analysis of the provision made for collective bargaining and industrial action by the Employment Relations Act 1999 makes us doubtful that this will be the case in Britain.

---

[101] See above this chap. at 151–2. Also see *European Works Councils: A Guide to Effective Consultation and Representation* (London: Involvement and Participation Association, 1996) at 10–13.

[102] See above this chap. at 160.

[103] SI 1999/3323, reg. 17(1) and 19. It should be noted that such an obligation is not expressly included in the texts implementing the Dir. in Denmark, France, Finland and the Netherlands. See COM(2000)188 at 13.

[104] See ILO, *Digest of Decisions and Principles of the Freedom Association Committee of the Governing Body of the ILO (ILO Digest)* (4th edn., Geneva: International Labour Office, 1996) paras. 447 and 448.

[105] "Managers and Unions are Sceptical about European Works Councils" (1998) 664 *IRS Employment Trends* 5.

C.   TRADE UNIONS TO "ACCOMPANY" INDIVIDUALS

At present, the norm is that most employers allow workers to be accompanied in grievance and disciplinary proceedings. Where there is a recognised trade union in the workplace, it is more likely that the employer will specify that union representatives and full time officials should play this role.[106] However, it remains lawful for an employer to refuse a union representative the right to accompany the worker concerned. The TUC has pointed out that this legal position is anomalous. "While people are given the right to join a trade union, they have no right to call on the services of their union when they have a problem at work."[107] It has also been argued by Hendy that this is in violation of international law which confers "a right vesting in every worker to be represented at work by his or her union on any matter arising from or in the course of work".[108] As was observed in Chapter 2, the Employment Relations Act has made limited provision for a worker to be "accompanied" at meetings with the employer concerning grievance or disciplinary proceedings.[109] A worker may opt for assistance from a fellow workmate not associated with a trade union, a trade union representative in the workplace or a trade union official.

What is perhaps peculiar about these provisions is that they do not make union assistance contingent on recognition. This therefore comes closer to the objective of the TUC, which wished to involve non-recognised trade unions in such forms of representation so as gradually to improve their profile. It is not surprising that the Conservative opposition members were fiercely opposed to this development, fearing that this was trade union recognition through the back door.[110] Nevertheless, while this procedure allows unions which have not received recognition to meet employers and establish their "value" to workers, this is a far cry from fully fledged access to recognition for the purposes of collective bargaining.

Moreover, the choice of companion is left to the worker. There is no requirement that there automatically be trade union representation where the worker is a member or where there is a recognised trade union in the workplace. All that is provided is the potential for a union to provide this service should it be called on to do so. This is not a trade union right but that of the worker. The collective dimension to this scenario is overlooked; a union's rights to represent its members is not acknowledged.[111]

Even where the worker requests trade union representation, such representation is not treated by the Employment Relations Act 1999 as essential. The

---

[106] Cully *et al.*, n.1 above, at 98.
[107] TUC, *Fairness at Work—TUC Response* (London: TUC, 1998), para. 86.
[108] Hendy, n.5 above, at p. iv. See also J. Hendy and M. Walton, "An Individual Right to Union Representation in International Law" (1997) 26 *ILJ* 205.
[109] ERelA 1999 ss. 10–13. See above Chap. 2 at 24–9.
[110] See e.g. HL Hansard, 16 June 1999, cols. 333–334.
[111] Ewing, n.2 above, at 215.

failure of the employer to allow a union representative to be present will not overturn the employer's decision on the grievance or reverse any disciplinary measures taken.[112] Furthermore, as this is the worker's right, as opposed to that of the union, compensation for failure to respect this right is to be claimed by and paid to the worker.[113] This is an essentially individualistic model of choice within the employment relationship, which takes little account of the counter-balance in bargaining power provided by trade unions within this sphere. The new legislation does not acknowledge the difficulty a worker may experience speaking for herself in such a scenario; nor is there evidence of any appreciation of a worker's potential reluctance to make a complaint where she continues in her present employment.

D. THE PARTNERSHIP FUND

In *Fairness at Work*, the Government stated its intention to "make funds available . . . in order to assist and develop partnerships at work". This was an aspect of New Labour's commitment to spread good practice from the best organisations to the rest, so as to effect "a change in the culture of employment relations".[114] Section 30 of the ERelA 1999 now provides that the Secretary of State may spend money "for the purpose of encouraging and helping employers (or their representatives) and employees (or their representatives) to improve the way they work together".[115]

It seems that this was more a rhetorical gesture than a legislative necessity. The Partnership Fund could just as well have been established as an administrative act. Nor was the Government providing any extra money; it was to come from the DTI's existing provision. Lord McIntosh admitted that the point of this provision's inclusion was "to make it clear on the face of the Bill that we were prepared to support projects at the workplace based on employers and employee representatives working together to support innovative projects to develop the partnership approach in the workplace".[116]

The Conservatives feared that this clause was "nothing less than a licence for the Government to hand out taxpayer's money to trade unions, on the pretext that they are encouraging improvements in industrial relations".[117] It was said to be "pay-day for the unions and pay-up day for the employers".[118] However,

---

[112] ERelA 1999 s. 11.

[113] As above this chap. at 155 and 159. Compare with the proposals made for enforcement of a right to representation by a trade union in Ewing, n.2 above, at 215.

[114] *FAW*, para. 2.7.

[115] This is a broad power, as is evident from ERelA 1999 s. 30(2), which states that "money may be provided as the Secretary of State thinks fit (whether as grants or otherwise) and on such terms and he thinks fit (whether as to repayment or otherwise)".

[116] HL Hansard, 10 May 1999, col. 1047, per Lord McIntosh.

[117] HL Hansard, 10 May 1999, col. 972, per Baroness Miller.

[118] HL Hansard, 10 May 1999, col. 1027, per Lord Cavendish.

they should be reassured by the limited resources which New Labour has decided to devote to the Partnership Fund. The Government is making only £5 million available over four years. The Fund will pay for up to 50 per cent of the costs of individual projects up to a maximum of £50,000 per project. This is more an attempt to publicise examples of "good practice" than a serious attempt to fund large-scale workplace reorganisation.

In the first round of applications for grants from the Partnership Fund, 35 bidders were successful. The closing date for applications in the second round was 21 July 2000. The criteria for a successful bid appear to be broad. Applicants have ranged from employers, employer federations, trade unions and other employee representatives, to training councils, public sector bodies and charities. There is no set number or combination of partners.[119] Funding has been given to certain trade union applicants in conjunction with employers; even the TUC has been a successful applicant.[120] Nevertheless, there is no apparent preference for union representation, as is evident from the case studies presented on the Department of Trade and Industry (DTI) website. For example, Pizza Express used monies from the Partnership Fund to establish an "Employee Forum", rather than build relations with any trade union. Another recipient of DTI funding, Scott Bader, provided for representation of employees through a Community Council rather than a trade union.[121] It seems that, in the Government's conception of "good practice", trade unions are not essential to partnership but are a potentially useful optional add-on.

E. CONCLUSION

Through a variety of means, the Blair Government has sought to revise the role of trade unions within the workplace. The focus of these reforms is on the capacity of unions to act outside the scope of collective bargaining. There are new legal requirements that recognised independent trade unions are not to be bypassed but are to be informed and consulted, in the spheres of training, collective redundancies, transfers and European Works Councils (EWCs). Employers must respect the entitlement of workers to be accompanied by a trade union representative in grievance and disciplinary proceedings. In addition, trade unions may seek a grant from the Partnership Fund to improve workplace relations.

None of these measures is objectionable *per se*. The TUC's determination to launch a "Partnership Institute" and its current series of regional "partnership" events indicates that it perceives that these developments present the trade union

---

[119] See http://www.dti.gov.uk/partnershipfund/index.htm.

[120] Both as a sole applicant and jointly on another project with the CBI. See http://www.dti.gov.uk/partnershipfund/success.htm.

[121] See http://www.dti.gov.uk/partnershipfund/success.htm.

movement with valuable opportunities.[122] Trade unions will have potentially greater access to communication with management than was available hitherto. Moreover, they may be able to attract a broader base of membership through the diversification of their functions. The TUC regards as promising the new boost in trade union membership which, although relatively minor, still marks a halt to the trend of membership decline.[123]

Yet, while these developments provide some scope for optimism, it is arguable that the individualistic orientation of these developments, alongside their emphasis on consultation as opposed to co-determination, ultimately fails to serve the interests of unions and their members. In this respect, we have a number of concerns.

The first difficulty lies with the emphasis placed by the Government on information and consultation as an individual right of the worker, as opposed to a collective entitlement which can be claimed through a trade union. A similar stance is taken on the right to be accompanied. In this manner, trade unions are artificially differentiated from their members.

Secondly, there is a possibility that these reforms may detract from the essential function of a trade union, which is to protect workers' interests. The notion that collective bargaining is "perpetually aggressive" or inherently conflictual is a fallacy.[124] Nevertheless, the potential divergence between the wishes of management and the needs of workers can lead to conflict. In the latter scenario, unions must be free to act for the workers whom they represent. The danger is that the rhetoric of "partnership" and the investment of unions in the maintenance of co-operative information and consultation procedures may prevent a union from doing so. This danger is arguably exacerbated by the failure of New Labour to make legislative changes which genuinely improve access to recognition, engagement in collective bargaining and participation in industrial action. This suggests that New Labour is not anxious to provide genuine protection for collective rights.

Finally, we have observed that the Government does not appear to regard the involvement of unions as essential to the processes of information, consultation, representation and "partnership". Information and consultation of employee representatives will also take place in the absence of a recognised trade union, the worker can choose to be accompanied by someone other than a trade union representative and a wide variety of persons and organisations have potential access to monies from the "Partnership Fund". This reminds us that unions are not necessary to the New Labour project. The onus is placed on unions either to opt into these new roles or to bear the consequences of exclusion. While unions

---

[122] See TUC Press Releases: "A Perfect Partnership for Unions and Employers in Yorkshire", 29 June 2000, and "A Perfect Partnership for Unions and Employers in the North West", 23 June 2000, available on http://www.tuc.org.uk/vbuilding/tuc/.

[123] TUC, "Official Survey shows 100,000 union membership boost", TUC press release, 22 June 2000.

[124] Wedderburn, n.72 above, at 7.

may not like the terms on which they are required to participate, they must do so if they are to demonstrate their relevance. This is a clever strategic move by the Government, likely to promote co-operative behaviour amongst Britain's beleaguered trade unions and develop a new "culture of relations in and at work".[125] What is more questionable is whether this culture will benefit British workers.

[125] *FAW*, Foreword.

7

Conclusion

I N THE CONTEXT of labour law, legal entitlements which support the collective organisation of workers have come to be labelled "collective rights". Such rights recognise the role which trade unions play in defending workers' collective interests through collective bargaining and, in certain circumstances, industrial action. International organisations, such as the ILO and Council of Europe, have sought to promote their incorporation into domestic legal systems.

New Labour presented itself as willing to engage with the protection of "collective rights", devoting a chapter of *Fairness at Work* to this subject. Moreover, extensive parts of the Employment Relations Act 1999 draw on these White Paper proposals, an example being Schedule A1 on union recognition, which runs to 172 paragraphs in its own right. However, we have been forced to conclude that, beneath this froth of legislative activity, the reality is rather different. "Collective rights", as they are conventionally understood, were not on this Government's agenda.

This may be explained in terms of New Labour's desire not to be seen to return to the policies and practices associated with British industrial relations of the 1970s. As was stressed, both before and after the 1997 election, there was to be "no going back". This political imperative seems to have taken precedence over compliance with international labour standards. Accordingly, there was no change to the key elements of Conservative legislation relating to industrial action and internal trade union affairs. This does not mean that New Labour adopted wholesale the general hostility to trade unions expressed by Conservative governments. In contrast to its immediate antecedents, the Blair Government sought to reassure the TUC lobby, indicating that it believed trade unions could play a potentially positive part in the negotiation and achievement of a flexible labour market. Nevertheless, this involvement of unions was not to be allowed to pose a significant challenge to business interests. This complex amalgam of policies resulted in an elaborate compromise, which can be linked by the theme of "partnership".

A. NEW LABOUR'S "PARTNERSHIP": THE ROLE ENVISAGED FOR TRADE UNIONS

We have sought to identify some of the key features of this "partnership". We have observed that it is a relationship presumed to be between an individual employer and an individual worker. Individual "choice" is therefore considered central to its maintenance. Indeed, the "individual" choice of employers (not seen as a collective entity of capital) is respected, such that it is to be limited only under the most stringent of conditions. Collective rights, which have the capacity to undermine individual choices (both of employers and workers) have therefore been viewed with suspicion. Mechanisms for managing the workplace are to be achieved, in so far as this is possible, by "voluntary" agreement in a non-conflictual environment. Underlying this partnership are certain basic "rights" for the individual worker, but these are matched with "responsibilities", especially for trade unions.

In the name of "partnership", New Labour has provided an alternative vision of the role that trade unions should play in the workplace. Trade unions are to be viewed as secondary to the primary relationship between employer and worker. They are seen not so much as having a legitimate interest in the defence of their members' collective interests, but as a tool which management or (on occasion) a worker may harness in the course of workplace relations. Unions are there to assist their individual members and may act as a useful conduit for information and consultation. Their chief functions are to facilitate good workplace relations and flexibility; not to act as a constraint on managerial prerogative or a counter-balance to the employer's bargaining power. Nor is their inclusion, even in these limited spheres, to be taken for granted. It will depend on their ability to demonstrate "value" to workers and, more importantly, employers.

B.   THE LIMITED SCOPE OF NEW LABOUR'S "COLLECTIVE RIGHTS" REFORMS

In this book, we have investigated how this conception of "partnership" has been translated into the actual legislative reforms made by New Labour. We have examined measures taken relating to individual rights to freedom of association, rights to trade union autonomy, rights to trade union representation, recognition and collective bargaining, as well as the right to take industrial action. As regards each of these "collective rights", we have found the Employment Relations Act 1999 to be limited in the scope and effect of the reforms made. Individual choice is consistently prioritised over collective welfare. Existing obligations which encumber trade union administration and activities are retained, while more extensive responsibilities are added to their burden. It seems that New Labour has little interest in the promotion of collective bargaining.

We began by considering the new individual rights conferred by the Employment Relations Act, which were described deceptively by the White Paper as "collective". While we welcome these reforms, such as they are, we believe that they are likely to provide only the most limited support for trade unions, the key problem being that freedom of association is treated solely as a matter of individual choice of a worker to associate or dissociate. Collective bargaining and coverage by a collective agreement are not regarded as fundamental aspects of trade union membership, despite the principles established within the ILO. Indeed, the expected benefits of membership are so narrowly construed as to make it remarkable that workers ever choose to associate in a trade union at all. We are concerned by the maintenance of artificial distinctions drawn between the trade union, its activities and those of its members.

This individualised conception of rights is also evident in the minimal changes made to legislation regulating the internal governance of trade unions. New Labour has failed to acknowledge the limitations of the Conservative conceptions of "democracy" and "choice", which underlie the present statutory regime and currently hinder the effective management of trade union affairs. The law relating to disciplinary action by trade unions against their members remains unaltered. Unions are not even permitted to choose their own members. In this respect, the Government is again in breach of its international obligations. Compliance with detailed and excessive statutory rules will continue to absorb valuable union time, to the detriment of their other activities. The abolition of the Commissioner for the Rights of Trade Union Members (CRTUM) does mean that the state will no longer provide financial or institutional support for complaints against trade unions, but the Certification Officer will now provide an alternative avenue for the exercise of the individual trade union member's statutory rights. The reason for the abolition of the Commissioner appears to have been the rationalisation of costs, rather than any scruple relating to the principle of trade union autonomy.

The elaborate procedure for recognition which has been created may appear at first glance to satisfy union demands. On closer inspection, as we have demonstrated, it becomes apparent that it is structured in such a way as to make it near impossible for all but the most determined trade unions, with a significant degree of support in the workplace, to capture the prize of recognition. The lengthy multi-tiered procedure is conducive not so much to "voluntary agreement" as extensive delays which may well discourage workers seeking recognition. The threshold requirements for balloting and the balloting requirements themselves also operate as a deterrent. The union which eventually achieves statutory recognition will be entitled to enter into collective bargaining with the employer over the limited subject matter of pay, hours and holidays. Most will have to settle for something less. Where the union has received statutory recognition, but the employer has refused to bargain, a procedure agreement will be imposed. This procedure is likely in most circumstances to follow the method of bargaining prescribed by the Secretary of State, which continues to preserve the superior bargaining position of employers. It will be extremely difficult to enforce employer compliance with the procedure agreement and almost as hard to enforce any eventual collective agreement on terms and conditions of employment.

The few concessions that appear to have been made with regard to industrial action are also characterised by their obverse side, whereby unions are in fact further discouraged from calling industrial action. This overshadows the minor relaxation of balloting requirements. The new unfair dismissal protection, for participants in "protected" industrial action, increases the pressure on the trade union calling a strike. The union will have to ensure that it does not do so in a manner which would jeopardise its members' rights. Similarly, while the trade union is no longer required to give employers the names of workers who are to be called out on strike, the union is placed under a new obligation to provide any information in its possession which will enable the employer to "make plans" to minimise the effect of the strike. The protection of individual rights has thereby led to a potentially significant additional burden of responsibility on trade unions. These measures are also likely to reduce the efficacy of industrial action.

The revised roles envisaged for trade unions by New Labour are also limited. Trade unions in general have not been given any rights to information or consultation. Only where a trade union is recognised does it have priority over other possible channels of information or consultation. The departure from this rule is that workers will be able to call upon a trade union official, even where the employer has not granted recognition, to accompany them in grievance or disciplinary proceedings. However, unions are by no means essential to the New Labour project for "partnership" in industrial relations. Grants from the "Partnership Fund" are awarded to projects which do not involve trade unions as well as those which do. Information and consultation rights can be exercised in the absence of a trade union. Also, a worker can choose to be accompanied by someone other than a trade union official. Unions may seek to utilise the opportunities presented by New Labour, proving their "value" to employers by playing a facilitative role within the workplace. Already, we have seen various "partnership" seminars held by the TUC, encouraging affiliates to do so. The difficulty is that if unions become too wedded to a collaborative role, they may find it difficult to represent workers' interests where they diverge from those of management.

Despite the rhetoric of the White Paper which acknowledged the role of collective rights, placing them alongside individual rights and family-friendly policies, the legislative outcome is one which demonstrates a distinct lack of interest in trade union representation, collective bargaining and industrial action. Trade unions are offered an option to participate in workplace relations, but only in a limited secondary role which is primarily co-operative. The capacity for legitimate conflict in industrial relations is airbrushed away. The new culture of consensual workplace relations does not seem to entail so much "partnership" as continued concessions to a management agenda.

C. THE CASE FOR FURTHER REFORM

Given the shortcomings of the Employment Relations Act 1999 and New Labour's other industrial relations measures, we suggest that there remains considerable scope for further reform of collective rights in British labour law. Moreover, it is arguable that such reforms can be made without wholly abandoning other facets of New Labour's industrial relations policies.

For example, it is possible to formulate a legislative framework for industrial action which complies with international labour standards, but which in no way implies a return to the industrial relations of the 1970s. Constraints can be placed on the abuse of power by trade unions which are not as extreme as those presently contained in British legislation. Furthermore, it should not be so very difficult for a Labour Government to appreciate that unions themselves can place an important constraint on the abuse of power by *employers* in the employment relationship. Arguably, a productive "partnership" requires a balance rather than an imbalance of bargaining power. It is this which is most likely to foster a truly co-operative working relationship, which generates respect. While we concede that this is not an easy balance to achieve, it might be sensibly done by reference to the minimum rights established in the ILO and Council of Europe.

Similarly, flexibility and employability within the labour market can be developed *with* the involvement of trade unions both at national and enterprise level, if the right institutional conditions are put in place. Even New Labour has, to a limited extent, acknowledged this in the White Paper and elsewhere. The relationship between flexibility and collective rights is not a zero-sum game with an increase in one necessarily leading to a decrease in the other. This has been recognised in other countries where improved employability and economic success have been achieved through social dialogue.[1] This could also be possible in Britain.

Moreover, we see potential for New Labour to be badly embarrassed by introducing legislation which is simply unworkable. If New Labour's aim is to use law to foster a "change in the culture of relations in and at work", which nurtures "voluntary understanding and co-operation", it will not want to see extensive litigation arising as a result of its reforms. This is likely to incite frustration and conflict. For purely pragmatic reasons, there is reason to amend the Employment Relations Act 1999, especially as regards the complex statutory recognition procedure.

As a minimum the reforms which we would propose are as follows. They are derived from our observations in previous chapters.

1. Improvement of individual rights to freedom of association

The existing legislative provisions relating to individual rights to freedom of association require reform in various respects. Most importantly, the vital link

[1] For a recent study, see P. Auer, *Social Dialogue and Employment Success: Europe's Employment Revival: Four Small European Countries Compared* (Geneva: ILO, 1999). See also OECD, *Trade, Employment and Labour Standards: A Study of Core Workers' Rights and International Trade* (Paris: OECD, 1996).

between individual trade union membership and the right to enjoy the fruits of collective bargaining should be established in British labour law. This would mean, in concrete terms, that employers would not be permitted to subvert collective bargaining by encouraging individuals to opt out and that individual derogations from the collective norm would be permitted only to the extent that they were for the worker's benefit. The position of striking workers also needs to be brought into line with international law. The limited new right offered to employees taking part in "protected" industrial action, is a very small step in the right direction. This must be taken further by providing, for example, that the dismissal of any worker engaged in lawful industrial action is treated as a nullity. Other areas in which New Labour's measures could be developed include an expansion of the right to be accompanied in disciplinary and grievance proceedings. The trade union official should be permitted to act in a representative function, as an advocate for the worker, should she desire this. Encouraging procedural fairness within the enterprise is in the interest both of employers and workers.

2. Further reform of the law on trade union governance

Reform of the law on trade union governance could be achieved by retaining the principle of democratic voting in elections and ballots, but removing the overzealous anti-trade union measures introduced by the Conservatives. Respect for the principle of freedom of association should mean that trade unions are allowed to discipline and choose their own members according to their own rules, provided that the requirements of natural justice are satisfied.

3. The need for review of the statutory scheme for trade union recognition

If a statutory route to union recognition is to be retained, then it must be converted from the present sham. The process of obtaining recognition must be made easier, such that it is a realistic proposition for workers and trade unions. This requires removing the employer bias in the criteria for defining the bargaining unit, lowering the thresholds of support which must be demonstrated to the CAC before a ballot can be held and preventing employers from blocking recognition of more representative unions by concluding recognition deals with non-representative ones. When a recognition ballot takes place the thresholds for success also need to be brought in line with standard democratic principles, which require a simple majority of those voting. More must be done to ensure that employers do not unfairly seek to influence workers to vote against trade union recognition. Greater sanctions should be introduced for employers who deliberately obstruct the balloting process, for at present the only "sanction" is a declaration of recognition.

Reform is also necessary with regard to the consequences of recognition. The Default Procedure Agreement (DPA) imposed by the CAC should not be procedurally biased in favour of the employer, nor should the subject matter of bargaining be restricted to pay, hours and holidays. There should be some realistic sanction on employers who fail to observe the terms of the procedure agreement. The present remedy of specific performance is entirely unsuitable. Possibilities for its replacement could include binding arbitration, the award of terms and conditions to workers and administrative sanctions.

We consider that these reforms are imperative if the statutory recognition procedure is to acquire any credibility at all. While we note that provision has been made for the Government to move certain numerical thresholds up or down and to intervene in the treatment of certain applications, we consider that this kind of *ad hoc* tinkering will not suffice. Indeed, it even has the potential to jeopardise the independence and thereby the efficacy of the CAC. More substantive legislative change is required.

4. Removal of certain restrictions on industrial action

Without the threat of recourse to industrial action, collective bargaining would amount to little more than "collective begging". Given this, there is a strong case for reform of the current extensive restrictions on industrial action. We support the continued requirement of balloting before industrial action which serves to bolster its legitimacy. However, many of the present technical and detailed balloting and notice requirements are unnecessarily obstructive. In particular, the new requirement that the union supply all information available to allow the employer "to make plans" is likely to undermine the efficacy of the action taken. Any element of surprise is denied to workers. There is also a strong case for substantive reform which, in line with international law requirements, expands the scope of lawful industrial action. In particular, the definition of "trade dispute" needs to be widened and some forms of secondary action, especially against associated corporate entities, should be made lawful. Such amendments should improve the deterrent effect of threatening a strike.

5. Expansion of trade union participation in information and consultation procedures

Finally, we agree with New Labour that the scope for trade unions to fulfil additional functions outside standard collective bargaining procedures could usefully be expanded. Indeed, we believe that even more should be done. Rights to regular information and consultation should be widened both in terms of material content, going beyond training, and in terms of the parties to such arrangements, so that all trade unions, not only recognised ones, can take part.

The funding of "partnership" projects could also be directed to favour trade unions, because of their internal institutional structures which could enable best practice to be spread effectively. Nevertheless, this should be regarded as an additional facet to trade unions' existing role in collective bargaining. It should in no way be permitted to undermine the more traditional methods by which trade unions seek to protect workers' collective interests.

Whether New Labour will be willing to make any of these further reforms remains to be seen. The Employment Relations Act 1999 was promised to be "an industrial relations settlement", but only for *this* Parliament.[2] This leaves open the possibility that a future Labour Government will revisit collective labour law in its endeavours to promote "partnership". We hope that they will do so, for this is what "fairness at work" truly demands.

[2] *FAW*, Foreword (emphasis added).

Annex:
Commencement Orders made under
the Employment Relations Act 1999

Title	Statutory Instrument No.	Sections and Schedules Brought into Force	Date Came into Force
The Employment Relations Act (ERA) 1999 (Commencement No. 1 and Transitional Provisions) Order 1999	SI 1999/2509 (c.63)	Sections 18(6), 38, 42.	9 September 1999
ERA 1999 (Commencement No. 2 and Transitional and Saving Provisions) Order 1999	SI 1999/2830 (c.72)	Sections 2, 3, 7, 8, 9, 13(1) to (3), 18(1) to (5), 19–23, 26–33, 34(4), 35, 36(1) (partially), 37, 39, 40, 43, and Schedules 2, 4, 6, 7 (partially) and 9 partially).	25 October 1999 (Sections 2, 3, 13(1) to (3), 18(1) to (5), 19–23, 26–33, 34(4), 35, 36(1) (partially), 37, 39, 40, 43 and Schedules 2, 6, 7 (partially) and 9 (partially). 15 December 1999 (Sections 7, 8, 9 and Schedule 4).
ERA 1999 (Commencement No. 3 and Transitional Provision) Order 1999	SI 1999/3374 (c.90)	Section 34(1), (2), (3), (5) and (6), Section 36(1), (2) and (3) (together with the corresponding repeals in section 44 and Schedule 9).	17 December 1999

Title	Statutory Instrument No.	Sections and Schedules Brought into Force	Date Came into Force
ERA 1999 (Commencement No. 4 and Transitional Provision) Order 1999	SI 2000/420 (c.11)	Section 24	22 February 2000
ERA 1999 (Commencement No. 5 and Transitional Provision) Order 1999	SI 2000/875 (c.20)	Section 16 and Schedule 5	24 April 2000
ERA 1999 (Commencement No. 6 and Transitional Provisions) Order 2000	SI 2000/1338 (c.39)	Sections 1, 5, 6 and 25, and Schedule 1	6 June 2000

Remaining Provisions of the Act:
Right to be Accompanied in Disciplinary and Grievance Hearings
(sections 10 to 15):
The revised ACAS Code of Practice was laid before Parliament on 7 June
2000. Subject to approval for the revised Code, it and the new rights will come
into force on 4 September 2000.

Industrial Action Ballots and Notice (Section 4 and Schedule 3):
The draft revised Code of Practice was laid before Parliament on 26 June 2000.
Subject to Parliamentary approval, it and the new rules will take effect on
18 September 2000.

Bibliography

AALTONEN, J., *International Secondary Industrial Action in the EU Member States* (Espoo: Metalli, 1999).

ACKERS, P., and PAYNE, J., "British Trade Unions and Social Partnership: Rhetoric, Reality and Strategy" [1998] *International Journal of Human Resource Management* 529.

ADAMS, R.J., "Why Statutory Union Recognition is Bad Labour Policy: the North American Experience" (1999) 30 *Industrial Relations Journal (IRJ)* 96.

ARMSTRONG, E., and LUCAS, R., *Improving Industrial Relations: The Advisory Role of ACAS* (London: Croom Helm, 1985).

ATKINSON, J., "Flexibility: Planning for an Uncertain Future" [1985] *Manpower Policy and Practice* 26.

AUER, P., *Social Dialogue and Employment Success: Europe's Employment Revival: Four Small European Countries Compared* (Geneva: ILO, 1999).

AUERBACH, S., *Legislating for Conflict* (Oxford: Clarendon Press, 1990).

BARNARD, C., and DEAKIN, S., "A Year of Living Dangerously? EC Social Rights, Employment Policy and EMU" (1999) 30 *IRJ* 355.

BARROW, C., *Industrial Relations Law* (London: Cavendish Press, 1997).

BEARDWELL, I. (ed.), *Contemporary Industrial Relations: A Critical Analysis* (Oxford: OUP, 1996).

BEAUMONT, P.B., "Time Delays, Employer Opposition and White Collar Recognition Claims: The Section 12 Results" (1981) 19 *British Journal of Industrial Relations (BJIR)* 238.

BENEDICTUS, R., "Employment Protection: New Institutions and Trade Union Rights" (1976) 5 *Industrial Law Journal (ILJ)* 12.

BERCUSSON, A., *European Works Councils—Extending the Trade Union Role* (London: Institute of Employment Rights, 1997).

BLAIR, T., *The Third Way: New Politics for the New Century* (London: Fabian Society, 1998).

BLANPAIN, R., and ENGELS, C. (eds.), *Comparative Labour Law and Industrial Relations in Industrialized Market Economies* (5th edn., Deventer: Kluwer, 1993).

—— and WEISS, M. (eds.), *The Changing Face of Labour Law and Industrial Relations: Liber Amicorum for Clyde W. Summers* (Baden-Baden: Nomos Verlagsgesellschaft, 1993).

BRODIE, D., "Beyond Exchange: the New Contract of Employment" (1998) 27 *ILJ* 79.

BROWN, D., and McCOLGAN, A., "UK Employment Law and the International Labour Organisation: The Spirit of Co-Operation" (1992) 21 *ILJ* 265.

BROWN, W., "The Contraction of Collective Bargaining in Britain" (1993) 31 *BJIR* 189.

—— DEAKIN, S., HUDSON, M., PRATTEN, C., and RYAN, P., *The Individualisation of Employment Contracts in Britain* (London: DTI, 1998).

BURCHELL, B., DAY, D., HUDSON, M., LADIPO, D., MANKELOW, R., NOLAN, J., REED, H., WICHERT, I., and WILKINSON, F., *Job Insecurity and Work Intensification* (York: Joseph Rowntree Foundation, 1999).

BURCHELL, B., DEAKIN, S., and HONEY, S., *The Employment Status of Individuals in Non-standard Employment*, Employment Relations Research Series No.6 URN 99/770 (London: DTI, 1999).

BURKITT, B., "Excessive Trade Union Power or Contemporary Myth?" (1981) 12 *IRJ* 65.

CARLEY, M., and HALL, M., "The Implementation of the European Works Councils Directive" (2000) 29 *ILJ* 103.

CARTY, H., "Intentional Violation of Economic Interests: The Limits of Common Law Liability" (1988) 104 *LQR* 250.

CASEY, N.A., *The Right to Organise and to Bargain Collectively: Protection within the European Social Charter* (Strasbourg: Council of Europe, 1996).

CLAUWAERT, S., *Fundamental Social Rights in the European Union: Comparative Tables and Documents* (Brussels: ETUI, 1998).

CLEGG, H.A., *The Changing System of Industrial Relations in Great Britain* (Oxford: Basil Blackwell, 1979).

COLLINS, H., "Market Power, Bureaucratic Power and the Contract of Employment" (1986) 15 *ILJ* 1.

—— *Justice in Dismissal* (Oxford: Clarendon, 1992).

CROW, B., and HENDY, J., *Reclaim Our Rights: Repeal the Anti-Union Laws* (London: Reclaim Our Rights Campaign, 1999).

CULLY, M., O'REILLY, A., MILLWARD, N., FORTH, J., WOODLAND, S., DIX, G., and BRYSON, A., *The 1998 Workplace Employee Relations Survey: First Findings* (London: DTI, 1999).

—— WOODLAND, S., O'REILLY, A., and DIX, G., *Britain at Work: As Depicted by the 1998 Workplace Employee Relations Survey* (London and New York: Routledge, 1999).

DANIEL, W., and STILGOE, E., *The Impact of Employment Protection Laws* (London: Policy Studies Institute, 1978).

DÄUBLER, W., "Co-determination: The German Experience" (1975) 4 *ILJ* 218.

—— "The Employee Participation Directive—A Realistic Utopia?" (1977) 14 *CMLRev.* 457.

—— *Das Arbeitsrecht* (5th edn., Reinbeck: Rowohlt, 1995).

DAVIES, P.L., "A Challenge to Single Channel" (1994) 23 *ILJ* 272.

—— and Freedland, M. *Labour Law: Text and Materials* (2nd edn., London: Weidenfeld and Nicolson, 1984).

—— —— *Labour Legislation and Public Policy* (Oxford: Clarendon Press, 1993).

—— LYON-CAEN, A., SCIARRA, S., and SIMITIS, S., (eds.), *European Community Labour Law: Principles and Perspectives: Liber Amicorum Lord Wedderburn* (Oxford: Clarendon Press, 1996).

—— "Failure to Comply with Recognition Recommendation" (1979) 8 *ILJ* 55.

DEAKIN, S., and MORRIS, G., *Labour Law* (2nd edn., London: Butterworths, 1998).

DICKENS, L., "ACAS and the Union Recognition Procedure" (1978) 7 *ILJ* 160.

—— *Whose Flexibility?* (London: Institute of Employment Rights, 1992).

—— JONES, M., WEEKES, B., and HART, M., *Dismissed* (Oxford: Blackwell, 1985).

DOYLE, B., "A Substitute for Collective Bargaining? The Central Arbitration Committee"s Approach to Section 16 of the Employment Protection Act 1975" (1980) 9 *ILJ* 154.

DUBINSKY, L., *Resisting Union-Busting Techniques: Lessons from Quebec* (London: Institute of Employment Rights, 2000).

EARNSHAW, J., GOODMAN, J., HARRISON, R., and MARCHINGTON, M., *Industrial Tribunals,*

Workplace Disciplinary Procedures and Employment Practice Employment Relations Research Series No.2 (London: DTI, 1998).

EDWARDS, P. (ed.), *Industrial Relations: Theory and Practice in Britain* (Oxford: Blackwell, 1995).

ELGAR, J., and SIMPSON, B., *Industrial Action Ballots and the Law* (London: Institute of Employment Rights, 1996).

ELIAS, P., and EWING, K., *Trade Union Democracy, Members' Rights and the Law* (London: Mansell, 1987).

EUROPEAN TRADE UNION INSTITUTE (ETUI), *A Legal Framework for European Industrial Relations* (Brussels: ETUI, 1999).

EWING, K.D., "The Strike, Courts and Rule Books" (1985) 14 *ILJ* 160.

—— "The Right to Strike" (1986) 15 *ILJ* 143.

—— "Rights and Immunities in British Labour Law" (1988) 10 *Comparative Labour Law Journal* 1.

—— "Trade Union Recognition—A Framework for Discussion" (1990) 19 *ILJ* 209.

—— *The Right to Strike* (Oxford: Clarendon Press, 1991).

—— "Trade Union Derecognition and Personal Contracts" (1993) 22 *ILJ* 297.

—— *Britain and the ILO* (2nd edn., London: Institute of Employment Rights, 1994).

—— (ed.), *Working Life: A New Perspective on Labour Law* (London: Lawrence and Wishart, 1996).

—— "Freedom of Association and the Employment Relations Act 1999" (1999) 28 *ILJ* 283.

—— "Dancing with the Daffodils?" (2000) 50(1) *Federation News* 1.

—— GEARTY, C., and HEPPLE, B. (eds.), *Human Rights and Labour Law* (London: Mansell, 1994).

—— and NAPIER, B. "The Wapping Dispute and Labour Law" (1986) 45 *CLJ* 285.

FINDLAY, P., "Union Recognition and Non-unionism: Shifting Fortunes in the Electronics Industry in Scotland" (1993) 24 *IRJ* 28.

FLANDERS, A., and CLEGG, H. (eds.), *The System of Industrial Relations in Britain* (Oxford: Basil Blackwell, 1954).

FORDE, M., "Citizenship and Democracy in Industrial Relations: An Agenda for the 1990s?" (1992) 55 *MLR* 241.

—— *Surveillance and Privacy at Work* (London: Institute of Employment Rights, 1998).

FOSH, P., MORRIS, H., MARTIN, R., SMITH, P., and UNDY, R., "Politics, Pragmatism and Ideology: the "Wellsprings" of Conservative Union Legislation (1979–1992)" (1993) 22 *ILJ* 1.

FOX, A., *Man Mismanagement* (2nd edn., London: Hutchinson, 1995).

FREDMAN, S., "The New Rights: Labour Law and Ideology in the Thatcher Years" (1992) 12 *OJLS* 24.

GERNIGON, B., ODERO, A., and GUIDO, H., *ILO Principles Concerning the Right to Strike* (Geneva: International Labour Office, 1998).

—— *Collective Bargaining: ILO Standards and the Principles of the Supervisory Bodies* (Geneva: International Labour Office, 2000).

GOSPEL, H., "Disclosure of Information to Trade Unions" (1976) 5 *ILJ* 223.

—— and LOCKWOOD, G., "Disclosure of Information for Collective Bargaining: The CAC Approach Revisited" (1999) 28 *ILJ* 233.

GOULD, W.B., *Agenda for Reform: The Future of Employment Relationships and the Law* (Cambridge, Mass.: The MIT Press, 1996).

GREGG, P., and YATES, A., "Changes in Wage-Setting Arrangements and Union Presence in the 1980s" (1991) 29 *BJIR* 361.

HALL, M., "Beyond Representation and EU Law" (1996) 25 *ILJ* 15.

—— and EDWARDS, P., "Reforming the Statutory Redundancy Consultation Procedure" (1999) 28 *ILJ* 299.

HART, M., "Union Recognition in America—the Legislative Snare" (1978) 7 *ILJ* 201.

HAYEK, F.A., *1980s Unemployment and the Unions: Essays on the Impotent Price Structure of Britain and Monopoly in the Labour Market* (2nd edn., London: Institute of Economic Affairs, 1984).

HENDY, J., *Every Worker Shall Have the Right to be Represented at Work by a Trade Union* (London: Institute of Employment Rights, 1998).

—— "The Human Rights Act, Article 11 and the Right to Strike" [1998] *European Human Rights Law Review* 582.

—— and WALTON, M., "An Individual Right to Union Representation in International Law" (1997) 26 *ILJ* 205.

HEPPLE, B., "The Role of Trade Unions in a Democratic Society" [1990] *ILJ (South Africa)* 645.

—— "The Future of Labour Law" (1995) 24 *ILJ* 303.

—— and FREDMAN, S., *Labour Law and Industrial Relations in Great Britain* (Deventer: Kluwer, 1992).

HILLAGE, J., and POLLARD, E., *Employability: Developing a Framework for Policy Analysis* Research Report RR85 (London: Department for Education and Employment, 1998).

HUMPHREYS, N., *Trade Union Law* (London: Blackstone, 1999).

HUTTON, W., *The State We're In* (London: Jonathan Cape, 1995).

—— "New Keynesianism and New Labour" (1999) 70 *Political Quarterly* 97.

HYMAN, R., *Strikes* (4th edn., London: Macmillan,1989).

JACOBI, O. (ed.), *Economic Crisis, Trade Unions and the State* (London: Croom Helm, 1986).

JAMES, B., and SIMPSON, R., "*Grunwick* v. *ACAS*" (1978) 41 *MLR* 573.

JAMES, P., and WALTERS, D., "Non-Union Rights of Involvement: The Case of Health and Safety at Work" (1997) 26 *ILJ* 35.

KAHN-FREUND, O., *Labour and the Law* (2nd edn., London: Stevens & Sons, 1977).

—— *Labour Relations: Heritage and Adjustment* (Oxford: OUP, 1979).

KIDGER, P., "Employee Participation in Occupational Health and Safety: Should Union-Appointed or Elected Representatives be the Model for the UK?" (1992) 2 *Human Resource Management* 21.

KIDNER, R., "The Individual and the Collective Interest in Trade Union Law" (1976) 5 *ILJ* 90.

KILPATRICK, C., NOVITZ, T., and SKIDMORE, P. (eds.), *The Future of Remedies in Europe* (Oxford: Hart, 2000).

KING, D., and WICKHAM-JONES, M., "Training Without the State? New Labour and Labour Markets" (1998) 26 *Policy and Politics* 439.

KNELL, J., *Partnership at Work*, Employment Relations Research Series No. 7 (London: DTI, 1999).

LAULOM, S., "The Uncertain Future of "Pre-Directive" Agreements: An Analysis of Article 13 of the European Works Council Directive" (1995) 24 *ILJ* 382.

LEVITAS, R., *The Inclusive Society* (London: Macmillan, 1998).

LEWIS, D., "The Public Interest Disclosure Act 1998"(1998) 27 *ILJ* 325.

LEWIS, R. (ed.), *Labour Law in Britain* (Oxford: Basil Blackwell, 1986).

—— and SIMPSON, B., *Striking a Balance? Employment Law After the 1980 Act* (Oxford: Martin Robinson, 1981).

LOCKWOOD, G., "Disclosure of Information for Collective Bargaining: The CAC Approach Revisited" (1999) 28 *ILJ* 233.

LOURIE, J., *Fainess at Work Cm 3968*, House of Commons Research Paper 98/99 (London: House of Commons, 1998).

—— *Employment Relations Bill 1998/99 Bill 36*, House of Commons Research Paper 99/11 (London: House of Commons, 1999).

MCCARTHY, LORD (ed.), *Legal Intervention in Industrial Relations: Gains and Losses* (Oxford: Basil Blackwell, 1992).

—— *Fairness at Work and Trade Union Recognition: Past Comparisons and Future Problems* (London: Institute of Employment Rights, 1999).

MACFARLANE, L.J., *The Right to Strike* (Harmondsworth: Penguin Books, 1981).

MCGLYNN, C., "European Works Councils: Towards Industrial Democracy?" (1995) 24 *ILJ* 78.

MCILROY, J., "The Enduring Alliance? Trade Unions and the Making of New Labour 1994–1997" (1998) 34 *BJIR* 537.

MCKAY, S., *The Law on Industrial Action Under the Conservatives* (London: Institute of Employment Rights, 1996).

MCPHILLIPS, D.C., "Employer Free Speech and the Right of Trade-Union Organization" (1982) 20 *Osgoode Hall Law Review* 138.

MELLISH, M., and DICKENS, L., "Recognition Problems under the Industrial Relations Act" (1972) 1 *ILJ* 229.

METCALF, D., and MILNER, S. (eds.), *New Perspectives on Industrial Disputes* (London and New York: Routledge, 1993).

MILLER, K., and WOOLFSON, C., "Timex: Industrial Relations and the Use of the Law in the 1990s" (1994) 23 *ILJ* 209.

MILLWARD, N., STEVENS, M., SMART, D., and HAWES, W., *Workplace Industrial Relations in Transition: The ED/ESRC/PSI/ACAS Survey* (Aldershot: Dartmouth, 1992).

MOHER, J., "The Future for UK Employment Law Under Labour" [1995] *Employment and Industrial Relations International* 9.

MONAGHAN, K., *Challenging Race Discrimination at Work* (London: Institute of Employment Rights, 2000).

MORRIS, A., and O'DONNELL, T. (eds.), *Feminist Perspectives on Employment Law* (London: Cavendish, 1999).

MORRIS, D., "The Commissioner for the Rights of Trade Union Members—A Framework for the Future?" (1993) 22 *ILJ* 104.

NOVITZ, T., "Freedom of Association and "Fairness at Work"—An Assessment of the Impact and Relevance of ILO Convention No. 87 on its Fiftieth Anniversary" (1998) 27 *ILJ* 169.

—— "International Promises and Domestic Pragmatism: To What Extent will the Employment Relations Act 1999 Implement International Labour Standards Relating to Freedom of Association" (2000) 63 *MLR* 379.

O'FARRELL, J., *Things Can Only Get Better* (London: Doubleday, 1998).

PITT, G., *Employment Law* (3rd edn., London: Sweet & Maxwell, 1997).

PRICE, R.J., "Union Recognition: General Accident Fire and Life Assurance Corporation Ltd (Second Report)" (1973) 3 *ILJ* 58.

RYAN, B., "Unfinished Business? The Failure of Deregulation in Employment Law" (1996) 23 *JLS* 506.

SAMUEL, L., *Fundamental Social Rights: Case Law of the European Social Charter* (Strasbourg: Council of Europe Publishing, 1997).

SENGENBERGER, W., and CAMPBELL, D., *International Labour Standards and Economic Interdependence* (Geneva: International Institute for Labour Studies, 1994).

SHENFIELD, A., *What Right to Strike?*, With Commentaries by Cyril Grunfeld and Sir Leonard Neal (London: Institute of Economic Affairs, 1986).

SIMITIS, S., "Worker Participation in the Enterprise—Transcending Company Law?" (1975) 38 *MLR* 1.

SIMPSON, B., "The Labour Injunction, Unlawful Means and the Right to Strike" (1987) 50 *MLR* 506.

—— "The Summer of Discontent and the Law" (1989) 18 *ILJ* 234.

—— "The Employment Act 1990 in Context" (1991) 54 *MLR* 418.

—— "Individualism versus Collectivism: An Evaluation of Section 14 of the Trade Union Reform and Employment Rights Act 1993" (1993) 22 *ILJ* 181.

—— "Freedom of Association and the Right to Organise: The Failure of an Individual Rights Strategy" (1995) 24 *ILJ* 235.

—— "Fairness at Work" (1998) 27 *ILJ* 245.

SKIDMORE, P., "Workers" Rights—A Euro-Litigation Strategy" (1996) 25 *ILJ* 225.

SMITH, J., EDWARDS, P., and HALL, M., *Redundancy Consultation: A Study of Current Practice and the Effects of the 1995 Regulations* (London: DTI Employment Relations Research Series No. 5, 1999) URN 99/512.

SMITH, P., and MORTON, G., "Union Exclusion and the Decollectivisation of Industrial Relations in Contemporary Britain" (1993) 31 *BJIR* 97.

—— "Union Exclusion in Britain: Next Steps" (1994) 25 *IRJ* 3.

SYRETT, K., " 'Immunity', 'Privilege' and 'Right': British Trade Unions and the Language of Labour Law Reform" (1998) 25 *JLS* 388.

TAYLOR, R., *The Trade Union Question in British Politics: Government and Unions since 1945* (Oxford: Blackwell, 1993).

TERRY, M., "Systems of Collective Employee Representation in Non-Union Firms in the UK" (1999) 30 *IRJ* 16.

THOMPSON, N., "Supply-side Socialism: The Political Economy of New Labour" (1996) 216 *New Left Review* 38.

TOWERS, B., *Developing Recognition and Representation in the UK: How Useful is the US Model?* (London: Institute of Employment Rights, 1999).

—— " '. . . the most lightly regulated labour market . . .' The UK's Third Statutory Recognition Procedure" (1999) 30 *IRJ* 82.

TOWNSHEND-SMITH, R., "Trade Union Recognition Legislation—Britain and America Compared" (1981) 1 *Legal Studies* 190.

—— "Refusal of Employment on Grounds of Trade Union Membership or Non-membership: the Employment Act 1990" (1992) 21 *ILJ* 102.

TREMLETT, N., and BANERJI, N., *The 1992 Survey of Industrial Tribunal Applications*, Employment Department research series no.22 (London: Department of Employment, 1994).

UNDY, R., "Annual Review Article: New Labour's "Industrial Relations Settlement": The Third Way?" (1999) 37 *BJIR* 315.

—— Fosh, P., Morris, H., Smith, P., and Martin, R., *Managing Trade Unions: The Impact of Legislation on Trade Union Behaviour* (Oxford: Clarendon Press, 1996).

Waddington, J., and Whitson, C., "Why Do People Join Unions in a Period of Membership Decline?" (1997) 35 *BJIR* 515.

Wedderburn, Lord, "Multi-national Enterprise and National Labour Law" (1972) 1 *ILJ* 12.

—— "The Employment Protection Act 1975: Collective Aspects" (1976) 39 *MLR* 169.

—— *The Worker and the Law* (3rd edn., Harmondsworth: Penguin, 1986).

—— *Employment Rights in Britain and Europe: Selected Papers in Labour Law* (London: Lawrence and Wishart, 1991).

—— "British Labour Law at the Court of Justice: A Fragment" (1994) 10 *IJCLLIR* 339.

—— *Labour Law and Freedom: Further Essays in Labour Law* (London: Lawrence & Wishart, 1995).

—— "Consultation and Collective Bargaining in Europe: Success and Ideology" (1997) 26 *ILJ* 1.

—— "A British Duty to Bargain—A Footnote on the End-Game" (1998) 27 *ILJ* 253

—— "Collective Bargaining or Legal Enactment: the 1999 Act and Union Recognition" (2000) 29 *ILJ* 1.

—— Lewis, R., and Clark, J. (eds.), *Labour Law and Industrial Relations: Building on Kahn-Freund* (Oxford: Clarendon Press, 1983).

—— Rood, M., Lyon-Caen, A., Däubler, W., and van der Heijen, P. (eds.), *Labour Law in the Post-Industrial Era* (Dartmouth: Aldershot, 1994).

Weekes, B., Mellish, M., Dickens, L., and Lloyd, J., *Industrial Relations and the Limits of Law* (Oxford: Blackwell, 1975).

Welch, R., *The Right to Strike: A Trade Union View* (London: Institute of Employment Rights, 1991).

—— "The Behavioural Impact on Trade Unionists of the Trade Union Legislation of the 1980s: A Research Note" (1993) 24 *IRJ* 236.

Wheeler, S., "Works Councils: Towards Stakeholding?" (1997) 24 *JLS* 44.

White, S., "Rights and Responsibilities: A Social Democratic Perspective" (1999) 70 *Political Quarterly* 166.

Whiteside, N., and Salais, R. (eds.), *Governance, Industry and Labour Markets in Britain and France* (London: Routledge, 1998).

Wilthagen, T. (ed.), *Advancing Theory in Labour Law and Industrial Relations in a Global Context* (Amsterdam: North-Holland, 1998).

Wood, J., "The Central Arbitration Committee: A Consideration of its Role and Approach" (1979) 89 *DE Gazette* 9.

Wood, S., and Godard, J., "The Statutory Recognition Procedure in the Employment Relations Bill: A Comparative Analysis" (1999) 37 *BJIL* 203.

Wynn-Evans, C., *Employment Relations Bill: A Practical Summary* (London: Tolley, 1999).

Index